THE LOWERING OF HIGHER
EDUCATION IN AMERICA

THE LOWERING OF HIGHER EDUCATION IN AMERICA

WHY FINANCIAL AID SHOULD BE BASED ON STUDENT PERFORMANCE

Jackson Toby

PRAEGER

An Imprint of ABC-CLIO, LLC

A B C ⬟ C L I O

Santa Barbara, California • Denver, Colorado • Oxford, England

Cataloging-in-Publication Data is on file with the Library of Congress

ISBN: 978-0-313-37898-0
EISBN: 978-0-313-37899-7

14 13 12 11 10   1 2 3 4 5

This book is also available on the World Wide Web as an eBook.
Visit www.abc-clio.com for details.

Praeger
An Imprint of ABC-CLIO, LLC

ABC-CLIO, LLC
130 Cremona Drive, P.O. Box 1911
Santa Barbara, California 93116-1911

This book is printed on acid-free paper ∞

Manufactured in the United States of America

In memory of my late wife, Marcia L. Toby

"We mean well and do ill and justify our ill-doing
by our well-meaning."
—Reinhold Niebuhr

"It is not going to college that matters, but studying
when one gets there, wanting to study and liking it."
—Jacques Barzun, Letter to the Editor,
New York Times, March 5, 1985.

CONTENTS

ACKNOWLEDGMENTS

In the course of fifteen years of working sporadically on this book, I have accumulated material and intellectual debts to so many people that I probably will fail to mention at least a few. One of my excuses for taking so long to complete the book is that I chose an extremely complicated subject, the complexity of which I underestimated. A friend calls me a great underestimator.

A generous grant from the John M. Olin Foundation provided the initial resources for my research; James Piereson, Executive Director of that Foundation, has my everlasting gratitude. In 2003 Kimberly Dennis, then the Director of the National Research Initiative of the American Enterprise Institute, further supported my research by nominating me to be a Visiting Scholar at AEI and supplying funds to finish the book. Kim also read and commented on draft chapters and gave unflagging encouragement. Ryan Stowers, then also with the National Research Initiative, and Veronique Rodman were also very helpful. Along the way I learned much from conversations and e-mail exchanges with scholars at AEI, including Marvin Kosters, Frederick Hess, Charles Murray, Samuel Thernstrom, Henry Olsen, and others. I got research assistance from several young assistants and interns, most of whom are no longer at AEI: Lauren Campbell, Lindsay Shore, Jordan Chapman, Jon Flugstad, Benjamin Schwab, and Courtney Myers.

I also benefited enormously from discussions with colleagues at other places: Professor James Rosenbaum of Northwestern University, Professor Joseph J. Seneca of Rutgers University, Professor David Mustard of the University of Georgia, Professor Richard Vedder of Ohio University,

Professor Stuart Rojstaczer, then of Duke University, Professor Valen Johnson of the University of Michigan, Jean Rash of the Rutgers University Office of Financial Aid, Nancy Winterbauer, also at Rutgers University, Erin Dillon of the Education Sector, Dr. Andrew Gillen, Professor Nathan Glazer, who made helpful suggestions about policy recommendations for student loans as well as editorial suggestions, Mark Kantrowitz of FinAid.org, Dr. Patrick Ford, Civic Literacy Program of the Intercollegiate Studies Institute, and Robert Tomsho of *The Wall Street Journal.* Aurora D'Amico and Thomas Snyder of the National Center for Education Statistics of the U.S. Department of Education were invaluable guides to the forests of federal education statistics.

Richard Tedesco collaborated with me on the research reported in Chapter 4: designing instruments, carrying out interviews, and analyzing the data. He also graciously found material on the Internet that I am too ignorant about computers to find myself. Daina Harvey, a Rutgers graduate student in sociology, also helped me to locate data on the Internet. Shan Harwood helped me gain access to Rutgers computers.

Mark L. Goldhammer, then a graduate student in economics at Rutgers University, did exemplary work in 1995 analyzing for Chapter 5 the original complex data files of the Recent College Graduate Survey gathered by the National Center for Education Statistics of the United States Department of Education.

While all of these people helped me to understand various aspects of the American system of higher education as well as how to handle the empirical data, many of them emphatically disagree with the educational policies that I recommend in the book.

Finally I must express my gratitude to Robert Hutchinson, the senior acquisitions editor at Praeger Publishers, who found merit in an early version of the manuscript and has since made many, many useful suggestions that helped me to improve it. Stan Wakefield put me in touch with Robert Hutchinson, thereby performing the role of intellectual matchmaker.

INTRODUCTION

Professor Reinhold Niebuhr, the Protestant theologian, remarked that we mean well and do ill and justify our ill-doing by our well-meaning. This observation applies to the American approach to education generally and to higher education specifically. We rightly want young people to receive enough education to enable them to function well in an information-drenched society where better-paid and more interesting occupations increasingly require a high level of verbal and computer literacy. So we pressure children to go to school, to study, to resist the temptation to drop out before graduating from high school, and to go on to college. Excellent advice though this may be for the majority of American youngsters, insisting that every high school graduate should go to college is unrealistic.

Not everyone possessing a high school diploma or a G.E.D. Equivalency certificate is ready for college. Many lack receptivity for reading and studying, perhaps because of interests that colleges do not ordinarily foster, such as playing rock music, perhaps because of unpleasant previous experiences in the educational system, perhaps because of personal disabilities or family circumstances that prevented developing necessary academic skills, or perhaps because they were disengaged in high school, unresponsive in class when they came at all, half-asleep, and unwilling to do assigned homework.

Prepared or not, youngsters hear that they ought to go to college for their own good, and, persuaded by adults, a majority of high school graduates apply, regardless of enthusiasm for further education. (At the present time nearly three-quarters of high school graduates enroll in two-year or four-year colleges, although only about half of those who start as freshmen graduate within six years for four-year colleges and within four years for two-year colleges.)

In order to accommodate them, colleges expanded enormously their enrollment capacity in the second half of the twentieth century. Moreover, colleges upgraded living arrangements for students, including recreation centers, fitness centers, tennis and basketball courts, and air-conditioned dormitories, some with private baths. They reduced academic demands for students so that regular class attendance is no longer necessary in most classes. Mandatory courses are few or nonexistent, and grade inflation has made studiousness optional. Federal and state governments provide grants and loans to pay for college expenses, thereby making economic barriers to college enrollment low-despite high tuition. Although scholarships based on superior academic performance still exist, "financial aid" subsidizes more students than academic scholarships do. "Financial aid," originally justified as providing access to college for bright youngsters from disadvantaged families, now works toward universalizing higher education.

In short, we refuse to take "no" for an answer. Having convinced high school graduates to enroll in college, we make it easy for almost any high school graduate to get accepted at some college and pleasant for them when they get there.

This book attempts to make the case that the educational and economic costs of the public policy of making college education a universal entitlement outweigh the benefits of exposing most of the age cohort to what, in a verbal stretch, people still call *higher* education.

Chapter 1

HOW COLLEGES UNDERMINE HIGH SCHOOL EDUCATION

Even in an earlier era, college administrators were aware that what is taught in primary and secondary schools and how effectively it is taught affects the intellectual atmosphere of colleges. What they did not realize is that what is taught in *colleges* and how it is taught has a feedback effect on the educational processes at lower educational levels. They assumed that boards of education alone controlled secondary education by, for example, setting graduation requirements for college prep courses. Then the colleges admitted or did not admit the high school graduates. College professors and administrators often complained that primary and secondary schools did not do a good enough job. For example, in the 1930s, the president of the University of Chicago, Robert Hutchins, commented that too many students wanted to get college degrees but did not seem very interested in learning what professors wanted to teach them. His satirical solution to the problem: give everyone a bachelor's degree at birth along with a birth certificate, and let those truly interested in learning go to college.[1] He was joking, of course, although he showed his disdain for the high school preparation of most students by arranging for excellent students to enter the University of Chicago after two years of high school.

The late Albert Shanker, when he was president of the American Federation of Teachers, came much closer to explaining why high school teachers produced poor educational results. He pointed out the unfairness of blaming primary and secondary schools for the poor preparation of college freshmen in reading, writing, arithmetic, history, and geography because the colleges fail to provide *incentives* for students to learn them in the pre-college years. Here is what he said:

Whatever colleges pretend, their influence over high school standards
and student achievement is decisive. Kids are just like adults: they will
work to get what they want. If they know they have to work hard, listen in class, and come to school every day with their homework done
in order to get into college, they'll do that. If they know they can get
by with less and still get into college, that is what they'll do.[2]

Students passionately eager to be accepted by highly selective colleges
like Harvard, Yale, Princeton, Swarthmore, Brown, Wesleyan, and MIT, or
even to one of the 205 colleges that are moderately selective, that is, reject-
ing sixty percent or more of their applicants for freshman admission, show
that Shanker was right.[3] Students aiming at such institutions keep their eye
on their prized goal, admission to a selective college; most of them study
diligently in high school and compete to produce an outstanding résumé.
Students who seek admission to these colleges work to improve their
chances for admission in other ways; they engage in extracurricular activities that they and their parents believe are likely to impress admissions
officers; they spend summers on internships; they plot their strategy and
they worry, perhaps too much.[4] But they were a tiny segment of the
17,660,000 students enrolled in American colleges in the 2006–2007 academic year, enough however to enable the selective colleges to set high
admissions standards. The highly selective colleges have many more applicants for every place in the freshman class than they can accommodate.
Raising admission standards, which Shanker recommended, is possible for
these selective colleges, but it is not a practical way to mobilize incentives
for diligent academic work in high schools where most students lack this
aspiration. The obstacle to having colleges raise admissions standards is
that 3,700 colleges and universities in the United States compete with one
another for students. Some very popular selective colleges can impose any
admissions standards they wish, but most cannot because, as Shanker
pointed out, students need not learn very much in order to get into some
college.

In a later section of this chapter, I will present the evidence showing how
little time and effort most American high school students actually spend
on what we expect them to be doing: learning and studying. Although the
majority of American high school students want to attend college, they are
either not aware of what they are expected to do once they get there or they
have not learned enough in primary and secondary school to function
academically as college students should. They have poor reading comprehension and poor quantitative skills. Reading comprehension depends not
only on knowing the meaning of individual words in assignments that
they receive (obtained partly from practice in reading books and newspa-

pers) but also on understanding the cultural context of those words. Professor E. D. Hirsch Jr. coined the term, "cultural literacy," to explain why context is so important in reading comprehension; the meaning of individual words is not enough.[5]

Those who aspire to become professional baseball players are more realistic; they know that they have to practice throwing the ball, catching it, hitting it with a bat, and running around the bases. Even if they think they have innate baseball potentialities, they know that they have to practice, practice, practice from an early age in order to develop the trained capabilities that they will need to be a professional player. For some reason, which is not immediately obvious, most American youngsters do not seem aware of the analogous connection between learning academic skills thoroughly at an early age and doing well in college. Why not? The problem for many children is lack of parental guidance. Young children do not have a long time horizon. Without the encouragement of parents, they find it much more pleasant to watch television or play with friends than to do boring homework assigned by the classroom teacher. The younger the child, the harder it is to learn what psychologists call the ability to "defer gratification." The parent has to insist that homework is important and must be completed before watching television or going out to play with friends; in short, the parent has to impose discipline by nagging and supervising until the child is mature enough to engage in self-discipline. This process of encouragement and supervision at home has to go on for years in order for the child to lay down the academic basis for doing well in college courses. If it is easy to get into college for 80 or 90 percent of the students who wish to attend college, even conscientious parents have difficulty persuading primary and secondary school students to put in a great deal of effort learning material that may not interest them as much as play or television. If it were difficult to get into any college and parents succeeded in convincing their children that college is very important, fear of not being admitted would be an incentive to study in the earlier grades.

Unfortunately, some children do not have parents capable of performing this crucial parental role. In single-parent families, which the high divorce rate has made more common, the parent living with the child or children may be out working and consequently not physically available to supervise. Other parents have incapacitating physical or mental illness or substance abuse problems. A child can rarely impose on himself or herself the discipline that a parent can mobilize. Even when children have internalized the goal of mastering academic material and reach adolescence, this value often requires reinforcement. A New York Times story about SAT coaching reports the case of a junior at Niskayuna High in suburban Albany who willingly enrolled in an SAT online coaching class but was not doing all of the required homework; he had learned that only on the sixth day of failing to turn in his homework would his delinquency be noticed.[6] So he turned in his assignments only on the sixth day. To his surprise, a vigilant staff member of the tutorial service detected his ploy, telephoned his mother, who scolded him, and he resumed doing the work he had agreed to do.

Economically marginal, poorly educated parents are, on the average, less likely to understand *how* to use the educational escalator to middle-class status than affluent well-educated parents. Nevertheless, affluent well-educated parents may not have their children's education at the centers of their agendas. They may be preoccupied with interesting and important careers and leave the supervision of their children to nannies or household workers. Sometimes affluent families with two loving and highly successful working parents do a poor job of educational socialization of their children. In short, preparing children to do well in college starts long before the application process begins, and parental failure to discharge these difficult responsibilities occurs at all economic, educational, ethnic, and racial levels. I turn now to a superb empirical study of what American high school students actually do.

THE BEHAVIOR OF AMERICAN HIGH SCHOOL STUDENTS

Discussions of primary and secondary education frequently contrast the excellent education available in suburban schools with the miserable education available in inner-city schools. Sometimes this is attributed to the greater financial resources available in suburban schools, but this is an unlikely explanation because it is contrary to empirical evidence. To nearly universal surprise, James Coleman's landmark study published in 1966 showed that variability in the financial resources of school districts did not account for differential student achievement.[7] Furthermore, a careful study of ordinary American high schools demonstrated that poor academic achievement is *not* concentrated in inner-city high schools; poor academic achievement is far more widespread. The high schools in a study on which I am about to report seem reasonably representative of American public secondary schools; unfortunately, a large portion of students in them received mediocre educations. That does not mean that all American secondary school students receive a poor education. What it does mean is that a youngster has either to attend an unusually good school or to swim against the cultural tide in the average high school in order to obtain an outstanding secondary school education. I turn now to the study that led me to this gloomy conclusion.

In the fall of 2005, 28,219 secondary or combined secondary and primary schools enrolled 16,258,000 students in grades 9–12 (14,908,000 in public and 1,350,000 in private schools).[8] The majority of American college students come from public high schools. In the 1980s three distinguished social scientists—sociologist and professor Sanford Dornbusch of Stanford University, educational psychologist and professor Bradford Brown of the University of Wisconsin–Madison, and developmental psychologist and professor Laurence Steinberg of Temple University—launched a ten-year study to attempt to explain why the academic accomplishments of American high school students compared unfavorably with those of students in other countries.[9] Nine public high schools were selected for intensive study over several years. The researchers studied the same students by means of questionnaires and interviews as they proceeded from ninth to twelfth grade during the 1987–1988, 1988–1989, and 1989–1990 school years. The nine high schools were in two states, California and Wisconsin, but they were carefully "selected to yield a sample of students from different socioeconomic brackets, a variety of ethnic backgrounds (African-, Asian-, European- and Hispanic-American), different family structures (e.g., intact, divorced, and remarried), and different types of communities (urban, suburban, and rural)."[10] More than 20,000 teenagers and their families were interviewed over the course of the research—approximately 12,000 in each academic year.[11]

All students who attended school on the day arranged for administering carefully designed questionnaires filled them out except for about 5 percent of the total student population who either chose not to participate or whose parents refused permission for participation. Also missing from the sample were those students absent from school on that day (approximately 15 percent of enrolled students). Questionnaire respondents were evenly divided between males and females and between ninth, tenth, eleventh, and twelfth graders. Focused interviews with groups of students at each school, one-on-one interviews with 600 low-achieving, medium-achieving, and high-achieving students at six of the nine schools, and one-on-one interviews with 500 hundred parents of students supplemented these yearly questionnaire surveys in the nine schools.

What did the researchers conclude? About 40 percent of American high school students just go through the motions of secondary education. They do not learn much because they are "disengaged" in school. Here is how Professor Steinberg described his observations of "disengaged" students in the classroom:

> many students . . . are not part of the action. Some are daydreaming, staring off into space, their minds far away from the business at hand. Some are sleeping, heads resting atop their desks. Others are busy but not at the business of school; they are writing letters to

friends, drawing sketches in their notebooks, talking with classmates, making plans for the evening or weekend.[12]

It took the research team four years to analyze the mountains of data that they collected. The overall portrait Professors Dornbusch, Brown, and Steinberg painted of American public high schools suggested that the bad showing our students make in international comparisons was no accident. Here are some of the specifics:

- More than one-third of the students surveyed said that they got through the school day mainly "goofing off with their friends."
- Half of the students in the survey reported not doing the homework they were assigned. On average, these American high school students reported four hours a week doing homework. Nearly 90 percent of the students reported copying someone else's homework at least once during the past year. Two-thirds of students participated in at least one extracurricular activity; half participated in interscholastic or intramural sports.
- Fewer than 15 percent read for pleasure as much as five hours a week. One-fourth said they never read at all. However, they spent on average twenty to twenty-five hours a week socializing with friends—with one-third spending five or more hours a week "partying." They also spent about fifteen hours watching television.
- Students worked hard, although not on their studies. Two-thirds of high school students had part-time jobs; half worked more than fifteen hours a week. They worked not to contribute to the family budget or to save for college, but mostly to buy clothing, records, cars, and other personal expenses.

No research study is perfect. The conclusions drawn depend of course on the validity of the research procedures, including the degree to which the sample faithfully represented the universe of American public high school students. One can argue that the students of nine public high schools in Northern California and Wisconsin may differ in significant ways from students in public high schools in Utah, Delaware, or Maine— or that the 20 percent of students who did not fill out questionnaires may be worse or better than the majority who cooperated. Unlike ball bearings that have no choice about being in a designated sample, human beings have the option of refusing to participate. It is less easy to criticize the research strategy or the specifics of the questionnaires and interviews. Guiding the research teams were superbly qualified social investigators with years of experience studying school-age adolescents. Furthermore, in order to gain the financial support that they obtained, their strategies and methods had to be vetted by four different granting agencies, each of which had professional consultants to help them sit in judgment. These vetting procedures make it likely that what Professors Dornbusch, Brown, and Steinberg concluded about the behavior of public high school students in the contemporary United States is reasonably accurate for students coming to college from the 27,000 American *public* secondary schools. Moreover, a recent report by the Pacific Research Institute on 300 suburban high schools in affluent California communities found similar results: "less than half of the students in at least one grade level performed at proficiency in state math and English tests."[13]

According to research conducted by Professor James Coleman and his colleagues, educational results—and consequently preparation for college—is somewhat better in *private* and *parochial* schools.[14] Professors Dornbusch, Brown, and Steinberg mentioned the ease with which high school students can get admitted to college as part of the reason for so much student disengagement at high school. But they also placed a good deal of the blame on disengaged parents who didn't care much what grades their children received at school and a peer group culture that emphasizes recreation and socializing rather than taking school seriously. Like Albert Shanker, I place greater emphasis than they do on easy access to college. It seems likely that both parents and peers would take a more positive attitude toward high school achievement if they knew that admission to college and financial aid when admitted depended on it. Low admissions standards at colleges affect all high school students planning to attend college except those aiming for the most selective colleges and universities.

WHY INADEQUATELY PREPARED STUDENTS WANT TO ATTEND COLLEGE AND WHY COLLEGES ADMIT THEM

There are two mysteries: (1) Why are students who show by their behavior in high school that they lack even a mild interest in education nevertheless eager to attend college? (2) Why do colleges, aware of these students' lack of aptitude for college-level education, nevertheless admit them?

Solving the first mystery requires an understanding of the American Dream. Ambitious and poverty-stricken people throughout the world have long considered the United States a land of unlimited opportunity. Socioeconomic opportunities attract more than a million immigrants a year legally and perhaps another half-million illegally.[15] The attraction of these economic opportunities explains why illegal would-be immigrants run enormous risks to get here.[16] Great opportunities still exist in the

United States—Ronald Reagan spoke famously about it being "morning in America"—but opportunities are different now from the socioeconomic opportunities of the nineteenth and early twentieth centuries. At one time the American dream was pursued through learning the English language, finding unskilled laboring jobs in factories or farms, and possibly starting small businesses. Increasingly, however, as growing crops and manufacturing products like automobiles and washing machines have become less important to the American economy than knowledge skills used in professional services, the main economic escalator has become education; getting ahead now requires skills and information learned at school. Primary and secondary education used to be enough; now, as lawyers, accountants, and managers have become more necessary to business organizations, higher education is usually needed.

Unlike social ascent through labor and entrepreneurship, knowledge skills are difficult to obtain without the encouragement of parents, peers, and teachers because children need to build a foundation in primary and secondary schools for subsequent education at colleges and universities. Encouragement is crucial because, as I have mentioned before, children must not merely enroll in primary and secondary schools; they must attend regularly, pay attention in class, and do homework.[17] Otherwise, they will not be ready for higher education. Parents, even parents not themselves well educated, usually encourage their children in the early grades to go to school and to regard school as an opportunity rather than as an obligation. But some parents do not lay the groundwork for higher education in their children because they do not realize that mere attendance is not enough; classroom teachers need parents to collaborate with them by encouraging educational effort by sustained monitoring, not merely occasional lectures or sporadic punishment for bad marks. Children do not choose their parents. But without the right parents—not perfect parents but parents attentive to the educational prerequisites for higher education—even children possessing the intellectual potential to succeed in college are unlikely to do so.

What happens is predictable. Some children learn enough through attending primary and secondary schools to be qualified to do well in college-level courses. Of course, variations exist; some students are well enough prepared for relatively undemanding colleges; others learn enough to aspire realistically to attend highly selective colleges. Other children attend school because they are compelled by law and by their parents but learn so little that they are unqualified academically to pass college-level courses. Prepared or not, youngsters hear that they ought to go to college, because after attending college they can obtain better paid and more interesting jobs than would be possible for a mere high school graduate. Persuaded by this adult message, a majority of high school graduates apply for college. (At the present time, nearly three-quarters of high school graduates enroll in two-year or four-year colleges, although many of those who start as freshmen fail to graduate within six years for four-year colleges and within four years for two-year colleges. (Later in this chapter, Tables 1.1 and 1.2 show the graduation rates in four years for students at four-year colleges and in two years for students at two-year colleges.) The message that persuaded them is not wrong, but it is misleading. Merely attending college is not enough to obtain a college education any more than merely attending high school prepared a student for college-level work. As a result, many high school graduates apply for college enrollment thinking that college life means freedom from parental restrictions and four fun-filled years with the same perfunctory effort necessary that they expended in high school. The reputation of many colleges as "party schools" is compatible with this belief.

A misleading notion of what a college education entails is coupled with the correct information that college graduates earn over a lifetime much more money from their jobs than high school graduates. Together these two beliefs help to explain the otherwise mysterious desire of large proportions of high school graduates to attend college. They want to have a good time and to get a good job afterward. Low on the priority list for perhaps half of college freshmen is serious education. However, college academic work is not as easy as some students believe; it is more intellectually demanding for inadequately prepared students than they anticipated. About half the number of students who enroll as freshmen fail to graduate in six years, many because they quit for good. The dropout rate worries college administrators and professors. Exactly why students fail to graduate is not clear; obviously there are many reasons in addition to inadequate academic preparation in secondary school and misleading notions about what a college education entails. But evidence indicates that the better the academic preparation of entering freshmen, the greater the likelihood of college completion. Professor Peter Salins, who was provost and vice-chancellor for academic affairs of the State University of New York from 1997 to 2006 and is currently a faculty member at SUNY's Stony Brook campus, compared the college completion rates at different campuses of the SUNY system.[18] This comparison enabled him to conduct what was in effect a controlled experiment of the impact of increasing selectivity on college completion rates. Nine campuses (Buffalo, Stony Brook, Brockport, Cortland, New Paltz, Old Westbury, Oneonta, Potsdam, and Purchase) raised the minimum SAT admissions score after 1997. At all nine campuses, the six-year graduation rate rose, in some cases dramatically; the graduation rate rose 10 percent at Stony Brook and 95 percent at Old Westbury. At the seven campuses that did not raise their SAT cutoffs, graduation rates declined. This study suggests that a great many students want to attend college but lack commitment to education or the ability to profit intellectually from the college experience. National data collected by American College Testing (ACT) makes the same point. For many years ACT has been tracking with national data the persistence to graduation of students in about 2,500 colleges and universities, some public, some private, some four-year and some two-year; these data show that the more selective colleges have lower dropout rates. As shown in Table 1.1, seventy-three percent of students at the highly selective four-year private colleges graduated in four years as compared with 26.8 percent of students from the open-enrollment, four-year public colleges.

But, as shown in Table 1.2, too few two-year colleges are highly selective or moderately selective for statistics on the persistence of students to graduation to be meaningful.

Table 1.1
College Persistence Rates to Graduation in Four Years in Four-Year Colleges by Selectivity of College

College Type	Persistence to Graduation for 205 Public Colleges*	Persistence to Graduation for 159 Private Colleges*
Highly Selective (majority of students admitted from top 10% of graduating class)	58.9%	73.0%
Selective (majority of students admitted from top 25% of graduating class)	31.7%	54.2%
Traditional (majority of students admitted from top 50% of graduating class)	20.8%	38.2%
Liberal (some students admitted from below 50% of graduating class)	18.0%	35.2%
Open (all high school graduates accepted)	26.8%	46.7%
All colleges, selective or unselective	29.4%	52.9%

Source: Adapted from ACT Educational Services, *National Collegiate Retention and Persistence to Degree Rates*, 2008.
ACT Institutional data File, 2008. www.act.org/research/policymakers/reports/retain.htm.
* The ACT database includes 2,582 two- and four-year colleges, but the present table was constructed using only data from colleges that are part of institutions offering bachelor's, master's, and doctor's degrees. These data show the graduation rate in four years. Data for six-year graduation rates show considerably higher persistence rates, but the robust positive correlation between selectivity and persistence continues.

Table 1.2
College Persistence Rates to Graduation in Two Years in Two-Year Colleges by Selectivity of College

College Type	Persistence to Graduation for 178 Public Colleges	Persistence to Graduation for 29 Private Colleges
Highly Selective (majority of students admitted from top 10% of graduating class)	*	*
Selective (majority of students admitted from top 25% of graduating class)	*	*
Traditional (majority of students admitted from top 50% of graduating class)	*	*
Liberal (some students admitted from below 50% of graduating class)	*	17.6%
Open (all high school graduates accepted)	26.7%	14.6%
All colleges, selective or unselective	36.0%	14.7%

Source: Adapted from ACT Educational Services, *National Collegiate Retention and Persistence to Degree Rates 2008*. ACT Institutional data File, 2008. www.act.org/research/policymakers/reports/retain.htm.
Note: The ACT database includes 2,582 two- and four-year colleges. The present table was constructed using data from two-year colleges. These data show the graduation rate in two years. Persistence for four years to graduation are higher, but, unlike the data from four-year colleges, the number of cases of selective two-year colleges is too small for the computation of valid correlations between selectivity and persistence to graduation in either two or four years.

What about the second mystery: why do colleges not have more demanding admissions criteria, as Shanker recommended and as the selective colleges already have? Simply put, admissions standards are low at most of the 3,700 American colleges and universities because without low admissions standards, they would not attract enough applicants for admission to remain financially solvent. The history of the last half century explains how colleges painted themselves into this corner. The widespread faith in the economic value of higher education increased applications for admission to most institutions. Youngsters and their parents wanted to improve their chances for high-paying jobs. College officials could not fail to notice this increased interest in higher education in the 1950s and 1960s; they grew afraid that their college might be left behind in the competitive rush to grow bigger and better. They expanded their facilities and their faculties in the face of robust student demand. The result was massive building programs, the recruitment of additional faculty, and an enormous expansion of enrollments over the past half-century, especially in the public institutions. In the 1960s, 1970s, and 1980s, existing colleges greatly expanded their faculties, dormitories, and academic resources, and new colleges, especially community colleges, were established. In the fall of 1947, 2,338,226 students were enrolled in an institution of higher education. By the fall of 2004, enrollments had skyrocketed, with colleges and universities enrolling an astounding 17,272,044 students. The growth was more dramatic in *public* institutions of higher education, where in 1947 only 1,152,377 students were enrolled. Public college and university enrollment grew to 12,980,112 students by 2004. Private enrollment was also on the rise, albeit not as steeply. In 1947, 1,185,849 students were enrolled in a private college or university. By 2004, that number stood at 4,291,932 students—doubtless an increase, but a much smaller one than the increase for public college enrollments.[19] Table 1.3 shows the enormous growth in college enrollment over the hundred years from 1900 to 2000 as a percent of the population aged 18–24; it rose from 22.77 per thousand in 1900 to 544.92 per thousand in 2000.

The increase in college enrollment over the past half-century occurred to a much greater extent in public rather than private colleges and was greater for female students than for male students.[20] This enrollment explosion significantly exceeded the increase in the size of the college-age (15–24 years) population, which increased approximately 77 percent

Table 1.3
Higher Education Enrollment per 1,000 Population

Year	Ages 18–24
1900	22.77
1910	29.99
1920	46.03
1930	75.54
1940	96.07
1950	170.05
1960	225.68
1970	323.93
1980	388.38
1990	506.38
2000	544.92

Source: Richard Vedder, *Going Broke by Degree: Why College Costs Too Much.* Washington, D.C.: AEI Press, 2004, p. 94.

between 1950 and 2000.[21] Enrollment growth in private institutions was not quite so dramatic. In the fall of 1947, 1,127,000 students were enrolled in 4-year private colleges and universities and 59,000 were enrolled in 2-year private colleges. By 1990, 2,726,000 students were enrolled in 4-year private colleges and universities and 243,000 in 2-year private colleges. Thus, enrollments more than doubled in four-year private institutions and quadrupled in two-year private colleges.

For the last decade of the twentieth century, enrollments continued to grow but not so rapidly. In 1990, 11,959,000 undergraduates were enrolled in American colleges and universities, and in 2001 13,715,000 undergraduates were enrolled. This expansion was at least partly in response to pressure from the public to increase *access* to higher education. American educational administrators probably did not realize the consequences for academic standards of expanding access so much. They perceived students clamoring to be admitted and did not consider that if hundreds of colleges increased freshman capacity simultaneously, the system of higher education as a whole would have excess capacity. But even if they had been fully aware that excess capacity would tend to lower admission standards for the next generation of students, they had no mechanism for restricting expansion of the entire system of American higher education. Intellectually they dimly realized that expansion entailed risks, but emotionally most of them believed that the demand for more and more education was both rational and insatiable. The overexpansion of colleges and universities in the twentieth century resembled the underestimation of risk by mortgage lenders in the first decade of the twenty-first century that led to a destructive credit crisis.

Corporations that expand beyond the demand for their product must ultimately downsize or go bankrupt, but colleges are shielded from market pressures by governmental support, endowments, and philanthropic gifts. Nevertheless, a few colleges have closed in the past twenty years in response to competitive pressures, but not many; the American Council of Education reported that four colleges closed in 2007.[22] Some colleges struggle to fill their classes and dorms at the same time that others are overcrowded. It is a competitive system. An important factor driving success or failure in the competition for students among all but the top-tier colleges is academic standards—low academic standards. If colleges are perceived as too difficult—or incompatible with having a good time—they will have trouble recruiting students. As a later chapter will show in detail, colleges compete relentlessly for freshman applicants; they recruit students more vigorously than they have in the past; and they admit students with weaker academic qualifications than they might have taken fifty years ago.

In short, Shanker's method for encouraging American high school students to work harder in their courses in preparation for tougher college admissions standards is unrealistic. Most American colleges cannot toughen admissions standards without losing enrollments. Unselective colleges that raise admission requirements would probably experience difficulty filling openings in their freshman classes. Once college expansion occurred in the 1960s and 1970s, the leverage that colleges could exert over the preparation of students in the high schools decreased. Many colleges have to admit students unable or unwilling to perform at high academic levels in order to survive. With high school students aware of low admissions standards at many colleges, American high schools contain students who spend more time at malls than doing homework even though they intend increasingly to want to go to college. Verbal aptitude test scores fell since the late 1960s at the same time that college enrollments were rising; mathematical aptitude test scores also fell but recovered by 2008 to their 1968 level.[23]

Not all high school students want to attend college. When American high school students are asked on surveys whether they plan to attend college, a large majority say that they do. In a recent Horatio Alger Association survey of high school students, 82 percent indicated that they would attend either a four-year or two-year college or university.[24] The number of high school students with college aspirations has been relatively stable since the survey was first taken. More than half of all students between ages 18 and 19 actually enroll in a college or university, demonstrating that many of these high school students actually follow through with their intentions to pursue a postsecondary education and enroll.

The tuition at public colleges and universities is generally much less than at private colleges and universities, thus giving them a competitive edge. Consequently the list of the most selective *public* colleges and universities—shown in Table 1.4—contains in the top ranks extremely selective institutions; but the selectivity falls off toward the end of the list. The number in the left column is the percent of applicants admitted in 2007 and the number in the right column is the average composite ACT scores for admitted students in the seventy-fifth percentile of applicants. For example, the average composite ACT score of students in the seventy-fifth percentile of those admitted to Harvard was 35 in 2007. Among the *least* selective private and public institutions, both private and public institutions are clearly in trouble; the majority accept more than 90 percent of applicants. This means that the less selective the institution, public or private, the lower the academic qualifications students need for admission.

According to the 2004 report of the National Association of College Admission Counseling mentioned earlier in the chapter, 2.6 percent of

Table 1.4

Percentage of Applicants Admitted to the Twenty-Five Most Selective Private and Public Four-Year Colleges, and the Percentage of Applicants Admitted to the Twenty-Five Least Selective Private and Public Four-Year Colleges, 2007–2008 School Year.

Most Selective Private Non-Profit Schools		
	Percentage Admitted	ACT Scores*
Yale University	9%	34
Harvard University	9%	35
Princeton University	10%	34
Stanford University	10%	33
Massachusetts Institute of Technology	12%	34
Columbia University in the City of New York	12%	33
Brown University	14%	33
Dartmouth College	16%	34
University of Pennsylvania	16%	33
Washington University in St. Louis	17%	33
Cornell University	21%	32
Long Island University–C.W. Post Campus	22%	23
University of Southern California	25%	32
Rice University	25%	34
Johns Hopkins University	26%	33
Inter-American University of Puerto Rico–Metro	26%	
Tufts University	27%	33
Carnegie Mellon University	28%	32
Northwestern University	30%	33
Lehigh University	32%	
Vanderbilt University	33%	33
Brandeis University	36%	32
New York University	37%	31
Western Governors University	37%	
George Washington University	38%	

continued

American colleges and universities selected for admission less than a quarter of those high school graduates who applied to them, whereas 82.5 percent accepted more than half. While about two hundred of the 3,700 U.S. colleges and universities have medium to high standards for admission,

Table 1.4 (*continued*)

Most Selective Public Schools		
	Percentage Admitted	ACT Scores*
California State University–Dominguez Hills	14%	18
Salisbury University	17%	24
University of Mary Washington	23%	27
University of California–Berkeley	24%	30
University of California–Los Angeles	26%	30
Southern Connecticut State University	29%	
Grambling State University	30%	18
CUNY Bernard M. Baruch College	31%	
Alabama A&M University	32%	19
University of Baltimore	34%	
CUNY Hunter College	34%	
University of North Carolina at Chapel Hill	34%	30
College of William and Mary	34%	32
CUNY Lehman College	35%	
University of Virginia–Main Campus	35%	
Jackson State University	36%	20
SUNY College at New Paltz	36%	26
Florida International University	37%	25
SUNY at Geneseo	37%	30
University of Puerto Rico–Rio Piedras Campus	38%	
Middle Tennessee State University	39%	24
Bowie State University	40%	
West Virginia University	40%	26
Alabama State University	42%	18
University of Florida	42%	29

the rest are unselective to varying degrees. Most of the two thousand four-year colleges and universities are closer to the unselective pole as are nearly all of the junior colleges. Although they cannot brag about their selectivity, they can and do brag about other features in an effort to compete for freshman applicants.

ENTITLEMENT TO HIGHER EDUCATION: AN INTERNATIONAL PERSPECTIVE

My hypothesis is that easy admission to college in the United States is a disincentive to conscientious studying in the earlier grades. American high

Table 1.4 (*continued*)

Least Selective Private Non-Profit Schools

	Percentage Admitted	ACT Scores*
Inter American University of Puerto Rico–San German	99%	
Universidad Politecnica de Puerto Rico	97%	
National–Louis University	93%	23
Davenport University	91%	
Florida Institute of Technology	81%	28
Hawaii Pacific University	80%	24
Suffolk University	80%	24
Embry Riddle Aeronautical University–Worldwide	79%	
Drake University	78%	29
Dowling College	76%	
New York Institute of Technology–Old Westbury	76%	24
Robert Morris University	76%	24
Rider University	75%	24
Pace University–New York	75%	
Case Western Reserve University	75%	31
University of Denver	74%	28
Park University	73%	28
Wilkes University	73%	
Drexel University	72%	28
Johnson & Wales University	72%	
Adelphi University	69%	24
Yeshiva University	69%	28
Inter American University of Puerto Rico–Ponce	68%	
Bradley University	67%	27
Ithaca College	67%	28

school students who want to go to college primarily to enjoy themselves and to obtain interesting, well paying jobs when they graduate but who do not plan to attend a selective college are tempted to be "disengaged," as professors Dornbusch, Brown, and Steinberg called it on the basis of their research. If this is true of American students, is it also true of high school students in other countries?

Although this seems like a straightforward question, it is not easy to obtain a straightforward answer to it. What is known is that some societies impose extremely tough academic obstacles for students wishing to attend

Table 1.4 *continued*

Least Selective Public Schools		
	Percentage Admitted	**ACT Scores***
Washburn University	100%	25
Missouri Southern State University	99%	25
CUNY College of Staten Island	99%	
Angelo State University	99%	23
University of Wisconsin–Milwaukee	98%	24
Indiana University/Purdue University–Fort Wayne	97%	23
The University of Texas at El Paso	97%	21
Utah State University	97%	26
Utah State University–Continuing Education	97%	22
Colorado State University–Pueblo	96%	23
Western Kentucky University	96%	24
University of Wyoming	96%	26
The University of Montana	95%	25
University of Wisconsin–Parkside	95%	22
South Dakota State University	94%	25
University of Wisconsin–Platteville	94%	24
Auburn University–Montgomery	92%	22
Arizona State University at the Tempe Campus	92%	26
Oregon State University	92%	26
Arkansas Tech University	91%	26
University of Northern Colorado	91%	24
The University of Texas at San Antonio	91%	23
University of Utah	91%	27
University of Wisconsin–River Falls	91%	24
University of Southern Indiana	90%	23

Source: U.S. Department of Education, National Center for Education Statistics, Integrated Postsecondary Education Data System. http://nces.ed.gov/IPEDS/. Data are for colleges enrolling 5,000 or more students.
* The ACT figure is the composite score of students in the 75th percentile of applicants admitted to that school. Cells without ACT data are for colleges that did not supply such data. ACT scores range from very low (1) to very high (36).

the college of their choice. South Korea raises perhaps the highest academic hurdles for high school seniors hoping to be admitted to what applicants perceive as a "good" college.[25] On one day, Thursday, November 13, 2008, 590,000 high school seniors went to one of about 1,000 exam centers throughout Korea to take a *nine-hour* test consisting mainly of multiple-choice questions. These questions were constructed by 400 carefully selected professors and teachers isolated for a number of weeks during the preparation of the test at a resort surrounded by police. Students submit eagerly to this ordeal because the grades they receive determine whether the best universities will admit them, leading in turn to better opportunities for careers with top companies and with the government. Examination day is taken very, very seriously by Korean society. The Korean stock market and many businesses opened an hour later than usually that day in order to keep the roads clear for students traveling to the testing centers. Planes are forbidden to land or take off at Korean airports during certain hours of the day lest the noise interfere with the listening portion of the test. Buddhist temples and Christian churches were filled with parents praying for their children's success on the test. The Korea Electric Power Corporation placed about 4,000 technicians on duty to monitor power lines feeding the test centers. At the end of the day, the evening newspapers publish the questions and the correct answers. More than 80 percent of high school graduates go on to college but not always immediately. Those who do poorly on the test may wait a year and retake the test. Although most Korean high school graduates can be admitted to some college, unlike American high school graduates most Korean high school graduates believe that admission to the most selective colleges is necessary for a good career. Mainland China screens high school seniors for college admission with a National Higher Education Entrance Examination similar to the Korean system.[26] During the Cultural Revolution from 1966 to 1976, Mao Tse-tung closed Chinese universities and exiled intellectuals and professionals to the peasant hinterland; but in 1977 Chinese universities reopened and entrance exams were reestablished.[27] However, the reopening of universities and the rebuilding of faculties took time, and meanwhile enrollments were small and consequently highly selective.[28] Unlike the United States, Japan did not expand its system of higher education to the same extent that the United States did; consequently most Japanese colleges can demand considerable academic achievement from applicants.[29] As in Korea, Japanese high school students are tested by long and difficult examinations. Unlike Korea and China, in Japan each university has its own examination, thus compelling students to take several different examinations if they wish to apply to more than one university.

The United States is not unique in convincing students and their parents (1) that higher education is crucial for occupational success and (2) that financing higher education is a governmental obligation. Many countries have gone as far as or further than the United States in institutionalizing a right to a college education and even to a professional education. Table 1.5

Table 1.5
Bachelor's Degree Recipients per 100 Persons of College Age by Sex in Selected Countries, 2005

	Total	Male	Female
Australia	59.9	47.9	72.5
Brazil	17.5	13.3	21.6
Chile	11.5	9.7	13.4
Denmark	52.9	37.2	69.2
Finland	53.8	38.8	69.7
Germany	20.5	20.0	21.1
Ireland	40.7	33.3	48.0
Italy	44.8	37.3	52.7
Japan	36.9	41.3	32.2
Korea, Republic of	35.5	34.8	36.2
Mexico	15.2	14.5	15.9
Netherlands	47.2	36.6	54.3
New Zealand	49.0	29.1	62.0
Poland	45.0	32.8	57.6
Slovakia	21.6	14.3	29.4
Spain	35.0	27.1	43.9
Sweden	44.0	30.8	57.6
Switzerland	25.0	26.1	23.9
United States	34.2	28.1	40.7

Source: T. D. Snyder, S. A. Dillow, and C. M. Hoffman, *Digest of Education Statistics 2008,* "International Comparisons of Education, Postsecondary Degrees," National Center for Education Statistics, Institute of Education Sciences, U.S. Department of Education, Washington, D.C. Chapter 6, Table 415, p. 604. http://nces.ed.gov/pubs2009/2009020_6.pdf.
N.B.: I have simplified the original table in the Digest of Education Statistics for presentation here.

shows bachelor's degrees by country for males and females separately. As in the United States, more females than males receive bachelor's degrees in the countries included in the table except in Japan and Switzerland, although the difference in Germany was small.

An obvious problem arises when appreciable portions of the 18–24 age cohort pursues higher education. Higher education is expensive. The poorer the country, the more burdensome it is for the economy to remove these young adults from the workforce so that they can attend college. Furthermore, in the welfare states of Europe—and even in Third World countries that adopt the European tradition of treating higher education as a governmental service—journalistic accounts suggest that institutionalizing an unconditional right to higher education is incompatible with educational excellence. Great Britain, like the United States, greatly expanded its system of higher education after World War II. Whereas before that war Oxford, Cambridge, and London Universities essentially monopolized higher education, after the war the British government financed many "red-brick" colleges and universities as part of an expansion of what came to be called "the welfare state." The colleges of the Universities of Oxford and Cambridge had endowments, so they were not completely dependent on government funding as the new colleges and universities were. But even the Universities of Oxford and Cambridge were more dependent on financial support from the British government than are Harvard, Yale, Princeton, and a number of private colleges like Oberlin, Williams, and Swarthmore in the United States that have substantial endowments from generous alumni. *The Financial Times* estimates that Oxford's endowment is only about one-fourth the size of Harvard's, and that one-third of Cambridge's total funding is provided by the government.[30] In short, the American system of higher education relies less on direct government funding of schools, so private colleges and universities are able to compete for students with taxpayer-subsidized state universities and colleges and with community colleges.

The prominence of private colleges and universities may help to explain the different attitudes of American and British students toward tuition and other expenses. In the United States, students attending private colleges and universities (and their parents) expect to pay a considerable portion of the charges for tuition and room and board. American students are accustomed to working at low-level summer jobs or even at part-time jobs during the academic year to contribute to these charges. However, until the 1960s such charges were low for two reasons. One was that the operating costs of colleges and universities were low; professors received small salaries and administrations had not become highly bureaucratized and expensive. Another reason was that income from endowments subsidized substantially the per capita cost of educating students. However, when the costs of higher education escalated in the 1980s and 1990s and American students were asked to pay higher tuition, not only in private colleges and universities but even in public colleges and universities where tuition had been free or nominal, American students accepted the additional burden.[31]

The greater role of government in the British higher educational systems helps to explain why Tony Blair, Labor Prime Minister, survived a vote of confidence in the House of Commons in January 2004 only by a narrow margin: 316 to 311.[32] This vote was not about the ongoing controversy over whether or not Blair was justified in sending British troops to Iraq to help the United States oust Saddam Hussein; it was about tripling the tuition charges to students attending British colleges and universities, beginning in 2006, two years after the vote. (These charges would be means-tested as they are at present; less than half of British students pay anything at all.)[33] But students were outraged that they were being asked to pay for what they regarded as a welfare benefit to which they were entitled, not as a service that they had to buy from educational providers. The National Union of Students staged massive protests, including organizing a student strike on February 25, 2004.[34]

> "The drive to privatize public services, including universities, is very much a European issue," said Mandy Telford, president of the National Union of Students, a British group that has organized dozens of demonstrations against tuition fees, including a national march on London in October that is thought to have been the biggest student demonstration in Britain in decades . . . .
>
> "There's going to be a shutdown of all higher education," said Ms. Telford, a recent graduate of the University of Strathclyde in Scotland. "Obviously there is a university funding crisis, but we think the government should go back to the drawing board and figure out how to get the money through more progressive taxation. Students shouldn't contribute in any way."[35]

The funding crisis that Ms. Telford alludes to afflicts not only British universities but universities in Germany, France, Belgium, The Netherlands, Sweden, and the other welfare states of Europe. When only 10 or 15 percent of the age cohort went on to postsecondary education, the national budgets could finance higher education through general taxation. But when 40 percent or more of the age cohort began to attend colleges and universities, governments had to choose between raising some of the expense by charging students tuition and room and board or permitting universities to become so overcrowded that their educational mission was in danger. In short, the tradeoff was between access and excellence.

Although Germany is one of the richest countries in Europe, its universities have become seriously overcrowded; their students cannot get much attention from professors. This happened primarily because higher education became an entitlement. Peter Hommelhof, the rector of fabled Heidelberg University [founded in 1386], explained to a *New York Times* reporter how this happened.

> In 1972, the German courts ruled that any graduate of a gymnasium, the more academically oriented part of the German high-school system, had a right to a university education entirely paid for by the state. At Heidelberg this led to a jump in enrollment, from fewer than 10,000 students to more than 30,000, before it settled to its current

level [26,000]. "The whole notion of an elite was practically taboo," Mr. Hommelhof said.[36]

Concerned that German universities were deteriorating academically, Chancellor Gerhard Schröder and the education ministers of the sixteen German states announced a plan to form a group of outstanding universities (and outstanding departments at other German colleges) financed by about $300 million from the German government, starting in 2006.

"It is our common goal to raise the performance of German universities and research to an international top level in the next few years," said the federal education minister, Edelgard Bulmahn, acknowledging that in fact, they are not at the international top level at the moment.[37]

German university students denounced this plan as violating the egalitarian ideals of the welfare state. Their opposition was undermined, however, by a realization that these egalitarian entitlements had given rise to overcrowded classes and difficulties of gaining personal supervision from professors.

As bad as the situation has become in the universities of European welfare states from the point of view of maintaining high academic standards in the face of rising enrollments, it is much worse in some Latin American and African countries, partly because they have much less money available to support higher education and partly because publicly supported universities tend to provide an ideological rather than a marketable education. In Mexico, for example, Mexico's jumbo national university in Mexico City [UNAM] enrolls 275,000 students! They pay tuition of two cents per year. When the government attempted in 1999 to raise tuition to $75 a year—the government subsidy per student was at the time $4,420 per student—the students launched a strike in April 1999 to preserve what was essentially free tuition and open admissions.[38] The strike closed the university for nine-and-a-half months even though the government backed down on its proposed increase in tuition and its attempt to raise lax academic entrance standards. Here is how a Mexican journalist described higher education at the Mexican National University:

> Only four out of every ten students at UNAM ever graduate. This is partly due to the fact that the professions they have chosen, at public expense, are already saturated. If students were asked to pay part of their tuition, they would be more likely to choose careers that are in demand. Another reason graduates have trouble finding work is that their competitors from private universities usually have much higher qualifications . . . . Some newspaper employment ads advise UNAM graduates to abstain from applying and others simply refuse to hire them. . . .[39]

At the same time that UNAM-educated political scientists, architects, physicians and lawyers drive taxis or wait tables in growing numbers, jobs for mid-level technicians with a basic understanding of mathematics, electronics, computers, and English go unfilled.[40]

Most African countries are equally lax at requiring diligent students. In 1994 the University of Dakar in French-speaking Senegal became so expensive to the government and so remote from its educational mission that the government felt compelled to attempt reform. Here is the report of the *New York Times* correspondent who observed on the scene the struggle for reform:

> Since independence, not only has tuition been free, but student benefits have included restaurant prices frozen for over 30 years at about 10 cents a meal. Health care and housing have also been entirely free. A result, administrators say, is that for years, students have been defrauding the system by deliberately delaying their graduations year after year so that they can retain student housing and health care for relatives.[41]

The government finally attempted in 1994 to restore some academic standards for admission, reduce enrollment, and require students to pay some of the costs of their education. The result was that students battled riot police on the University of Dakar campus and went on strike for a week. The situation is similar in most of the other African universities; higher education is an entitlement that these poor nations cannot afford. Strangely enough, the efforts of the World Bank to promote educational opportunity in African countries seem to have worsened the situation at the university level. In Senegal, for example, Western money poured into primary and secondary education and, as a result many more youngsters completed high school and aspired to college educations. In 2000, 9,000 high school graduates passed the competitive baccalaureate that entitled them to college admission; in 2006 there were twice as many, and Senegalese universities became so overcrowded that meaningful education was impossible for most students.[42]

A stressful higher education system requiring academic excellence for its incoming students is rare in Latin America, but there are at least two: Chile and Brazil. Unlike the Mexican system of higher education, the Brazilian university system is selective and resembles the Japanese system of higher education; both employ very difficult entrance examinations for which students study intensively, sometimes for an additional year after graduating from high school.[43]

It is a dreaded rite of passage, known to generations of Brazilian high school students as "the funnel." Every December, just as the rest of the country is starting to ease into the relaxed rhythms of summer vacation, graduates who want to go on to college are forced to prove themselves in a series of exhausting, ferociously competitive and all-important college entrance exams.[44]

Exams with important outcomes at stake are necessarily stressful. If there were no consequences of success or failure on the exams, youngsters would have less motivation to study diligently in high school.

Part of the reason that foreign students are eager to do graduate work in the United States despite the language hurdle is that the alternative, universities in their own countries, usually offer them second- and third-rate graduate programs, especially in scientific fields. The National Center for Education Statistics reported that in 2002–2003 more than 60 percent of the doctorates in engineering were awarded to non-U.S. citizens with either a temporary or permanent visa, 49 percent of the mathematics doctorates, and 43 percent of doctoral recipients in all of the physical sciences were non-U.S. residents on either permanent or temporary visas, while the number of U.S. students studying abroad in graduate schools was nowhere close to that figure.[45] American citizens predominated among doctorate recipients in less demanding fields. Doctoral recipients are only a fraction of the universe of *graduate students*, but educational statistics identifying foreign nationals by field were not available for the larger pool of graduate *students*, only for doctoral degree recipients.

The mediocrity of most graduate schools outside of the United States is not only a result of inadequate funding and too many students; it is also the result of antimeritocratic admissions policies on the undergraduate level that undermine achievement standards on all levels.

IS UNIVERSAL "ACCESS" SUCH A GOOD IDEA?

A possibility worth considering is that, even apart from the financial problems, broad entitlements to higher education undermine academic excellence, but this possibility is rarely considered, especially by politicians. Former New Jersey Chancellor of Higher Education Edward Goldberg announced in a speech that he believed so strongly in a *right* to higher education that he favored amending the New Jersey constitution to include that right explicitly. The student publication of Rutgers University reported the Chancellor's speech on the *right* to higher education that he gave on the New Brunswick campus.[46] He was honest about his motivation. He believed that the New Jersey legislature was not providing enough financial support for higher education, and he reasoned that the courts could force the legislature to do so once the right to higher education was in the State constitution. Public higher education is costly—$1,955,510,000 for the State of New Jersey in the fiscal year 2005 budget proposal[47]—and State legislators do not want to impose tax increases lest voters turn them out of office at the next election, as happened to former Governor James Florio after he supported an unpopular tax increase.[48] New Jersey is not unique. Most states provide considerable financial support to higher education, which is reflected in the taxpayer expenditure per enrolled college student. Furthermore, these data do not include capital expenditures.

Chancellor Goldberg did not get the constitutional amendment he desired. Not long after he made this proposal, Republican Christine Whitman campaigned vigorously against high taxes and was elected Governor of New Jersey. Governor Whitman dismissed Chancellor Goldberg and also abolished the New Jersey Department of Higher Education, distributing its functions to other parts of the State government. What makes it worthwhile to recall Goldberg's notion that higher education should be a right, however, is that many influential Americans hold the same conviction. During the 1992 campaign for the presidency, for instance, candidate Bill Clinton stressed the importance of *investing* in higher education to help make the United States more productive in the twenty-first century. After becoming president, President Clinton continued to talk and to act as though almost any measure to increase college attendance was good for the country. He gave a speech on March 1, 1993, at the Rutgers University Athletic Center to an enthusiastic New Jersey audience, including 9,000 students, in which he returned to his campaign theme of investment in education. In return for tuition loans to make college attendance more affordable, "we'll ask you to . . . help control pollution and recycle waste, to paint darkened buildings and clean up neighborhoods, to work with senior citizens and combat homelessness and help children in trouble."[49] The students cheered.

Congress went along, passing in the fall of 1993 a measure establishing AmeriCorps, a community service program for young adults within the United States that provided an educational benefit.[50] The national service plan called for a ten-month residential program for American citizens 18 to 24 years of age working on community service jobs. In return for completing a year of service, participants receive "education awards," funds that can be used either to pay tuition or repay student loans. According to a Fact Sheet on AmeriCorps's Web site prepared by a research contractor for AmeriCorps, Abt Associates, in 2005, "In exchange for a year of full-time service, AmeriCorps members earn an education award of $4,725 that can be used to pay for college or graduate school, or to pay back qualified student loans. Since 1994 more than 350,000 Americans have served in AmeriCorps." In September 1994 the first class of 20,000 AmeriCorps volunteers started working on community service projects in the United States in more than one thousand communities. In 2004 there were more than 70,000 AmeriCorps volunteers.

Compared with the 14.5 million students enrolled in degree-granting colleges or universities in the fall of 1997 and the more than 18 million in 2007, AmeriCorps is a modest program.[51] But the symbolism is noteworthy; AmeriCorps treats a college education as a reward for participating in community service. After prodding from President Clinton, Congress also passed a measure that revamped the loan program for college students. The intention was to make loans simpler for college students to obtain—and easier to pay back. Total federal aid to students in inflation-adjusted 2007 dollars was only $1.57 billion in the 1964–1965 academic year; federal student aid grew rapidly to $29.8 billion by 1974–1975, then more slowly to $30.4 billion by 1984–1985, and to $48.9 billion by 1994–1995.[52] Federal student aid leaped to $88.4 billion by 2004–2005 and to $96.0 billion by 2007–2008.[53]

Only occasionally is the assumption questioned that universal access to higher education is better both for the individual and for society. Are the consequences of virtually *universal* access to higher education a good "investment" for American society? Although the United States is a rich society, it costs taxpayers a lot to send everyone to college with substantial government grants and loans. True, educated citizens make a society more productive in an information-greedy economy. This assumes, however, that everyone has to be *college* educated in order to maintain a knowledge-based economy. Could it be that having half of the population college educated would support a knowledge-based economy adequately? If a knowledge-based economy does not require universal access to higher education, the question becomes whether universal access is worthwhile in cost-benefit terms. Most youngsters want to go to college, mainly because they have been told that education pays off in lifetime earnings and more interesting jobs. For example, the Bureau of Labor Statistics reported that in 2006, the median weekly earnings of those with a bachelor's degree was $962 versus $595 dollars for those with a high school diploma.[54] Over the span of a lifetime, this difference could really add up, amounting to literally hundreds of thousands of dollars, far more than the cost of the education. Moreover, college attracts youngsters because it is a good place to socialize with other attractive young people. Why not encourage everyone to go college despite doubts that everyone is capable of making good intellectual use of the opportunity?

This chapter considered a little noticed educational consequence of moving toward universal access to college: how easy access to college undermines primary and secondary education. This cost is borne most immediately by our primary and secondary schools, although eventually it shows up at the higher educational level in the form of underprepared college students. Low standards at primary and secondary schools mean that many students attending college cannot do college-level work without extensive remediation. (Chapter 2 will consider the consequences of underprepared college students in detail.) Although the American educational system is not perfectly integrated, what happens at the college level in admission of and financial aid to students affects the incentives to learn at lower levels. If it is easy to get into college for 80 to 90 percent of the students who wish to attend college, primary and secondary schools cannot dangle before students admission to college as an incentive for doing homework conscientiously and learning what they are supposed to learn.

CONCLUSION

In the face of the hard and stubborn fact that some high school graduates have not learned enough in high school to profit intellectually from enrolling in college, what are the policy choices for government? One possibility is to embrace the type of opportunity program for higher education announced by former President Lawrence Summers for Harvard College. President Summers promised that *talented* applicants for admission from low-income families would receive enough financial aid from the University so that they could enroll without *any* financial contribution from their parents.[55] Of the 22,796 applicants for the Harvard class of 2009, only 9.1 percent were notified that they had been admitted.[56] Harvard's selectivity insures that only extraordinarily well-qualified applicants even seek admission. Other elite colleges have followed Harvard's lead so that now the educational expenses of academically excellent students from lower-income backgrounds admitted to such colleges are fully covered by college grants.[57] Presumably though, students cannot take advantage of this opportunity without their having developed appropriate talents over many years. Such trained capacities are needed for doing the work required at Harvard or other selective colleges. Poverty does not preclude parental supervision and encouragement, but lack of the emotional support of one or both parents does. President Summers was offering what is in effect a merit-based program, and a merit-based program, even for students with good genetic endowments, requires years of self-disciplined preparation. Youngsters without parents who inculcate self-discipline in them don't get this opportunity.

The other possible way to think about higher education is to regard it as so valuable that it should be made available to every youngster who wishes to attend college. Higher education becomes a free public service that taxpayers ought to provide. This approach treats higher education essentially as available even for students who failed to learn much of what their teachers tried to teach them in high school and earlier. Its proponents argue that students often have talents that fail to develop because of the inadequacies of their parents or of the schools that they attended. Since life is not fair, maybe government ought to try "to level the playing field."

Which of these two policy options does American higher education embrace? To place these options in perspective, consider that a person need not behave in special ways to qualify for police protection. Drug dealers are *entitled* to redress if someone tries to rob or murder them. Contrast police protection with education. Unlike police protection, education is contingent on effort on the part of both teachers and students. Consequently a person cannot be *given* an education, only the opportunity to work for one. Even in the lower grades, though we speak of "compulsory education," that term is an oxymoron. Voluntary effort is necessary. Calling higher education a right, as former Chancellor Goldberg wished to do, minimizes the role of student effort in learning and suggests that, if students fail to learn, the fault must lie with the professor and the college. Higher education becomes a valuable public service that taxpayers ought to provide. This approach treats higher education essentially as a welfare benefit.

Until fairly recently, the United States treated higher education as an opportunity, subsidized partly by parents, partly by the individual attending college, and partly by private and state scholarships. Who should receive this subsidy? The traditional answer was that those with superior aptitude for learning should receive it, partly because Western society values knowledge as a good in and of itself, partly because a knowledgeable workforce will enhance the productivity of an economy that depends on information technology, and partly because it is the fairest way to allocate this benefit. A different justification for subsidizing college attendance is to use higher education to promote a more egalitarian society. If children from economically or ethnically disadvantaged families are educated to the same extent as children from more privileged backgrounds, they may not be trapped in the underclass. Unfortunately, as the next chapter will show, some youngsters cannot profit intellectually by attending college without extensive remediation; they have not built up the background in primary and secondary schools that solid college work entails. Others are unwilling to put in the effort that study requires. Whether unwilling or unable to learn much at college, many students are underprepared for higher education. Should American society refuse to take "no" for an answer? Should taxpayer support for postsecondary education be granted on the same automatic basis as police protection without requiring aptitude or diligence? Perhaps nearly universal access to higher education has produced unintended consequences that no one anticipated.

The chapters that follow lead to my conclusion that treating undergraduate enrollment as an entitlement is questionable public policy. Doing so miseducates most college students and ultimately harms American society. Here is an overview of this case:

- This chapter, "How Colleges Undermine High School Education," considered the unintended consequence of low academic standards for admission to American undergraduate colleges—and the easy access that results—on the U.S. educational system as a whole, particularly high schools.
- Chapter 2, "Maximizing Access to College Maximizes the Enrollment of Underprepared Students," discusses the problem of students underprepared for college courses. The underprepared impose heavy costs of remedial education on colleges optimistic enough to admit them, although many drop out in disproportionately large numbers, take six or more years to graduate, or fail to learn enough to obtain the business or professional careers to which they aspired.
- Chapter 3, "How Grade Inflation Undermines Academic Achievement," considers the causes and the consequences of grade inflation at colleges: the willingness of professors—for both altruistic and prudential reasons—to award high grades for mediocre performance.
- Chapter 4, "Goofing off at College" examines how college students spend their time and its consequences for "retention rates" of colleges. College administrators consider a low retention rate a blot on the college as well as a financial problem, and they try to raise it—even though a low retention rate might reflect high academic standards.
- Chapter 5, "Is College Graduation Enough for a Good Job, or Do College Graduates Have to Know Something?" looks at the job market for college graduates. Does attending college necessarily improve prospects for a highly remunerative career—apart from the noneconomic benefits that a college education may produce?
- Chapter 6, "The Perils of the Financial Aid Labyrinth," describes the labyrinth of programs of federal grants and loans—seventeen at present from the United States Department of Education alone—that essentially universalized "financial aid" to college students. "Financial aid" is a mutation of nonfederal scholarship programs based on academic performance.

- Chapter 7, "How a Change in Public Policy Can Improve American College Education" brings together the strands of the public policy argument of the foregoing chapters. What Congress might do is to continue the current practice of providing *grants* to students who are from lower-income families and wish to attend college. Grants are gifts from taxpayers; they do not have to be repaid. But *loans* are required to be repaid; consequently loans to underprepared students are often personal disasters for them as well as detrimental to the financial system. Chapter 7 suggests that eligibility for government-guaranteed student loans be made contingent on superior academic performance both in high school and college as well as on other clues to the ability of students to repay their loans. Doing so would give applicants to college an incentive to study harder at all educational levels and avoid problems similar to those caused by sub-prime mortgages.

NOTES

1. Robert Maynard Hutchins, *The Higher Learning in America*, New Haven, CT: Yale University Press, 1936.

2. Albert Shanker, "Who Sets the Standards?" American Federation of Teachers sponsored column, *New York Times*, March 21, 1993.

3. According to the National Center for Education Statistics of the Department of Education, 15 percent of the public four-year American colleges offering the B.A. degree and 17 percent of the private colleges accepted less than 50 percent of their applicants. U.S. Department of Education, National Center for Education Statistics, *Digest of Education Statistics 2008*, Table 316: "Number of Applications, Admissions, and Enrollees; Their Distribution across Institutions Accepting Various Percentages of Applications; and SAT and ACT Scores of Applicants, by Type and Control of Institution: 2006–07." Web site accessed in April 2009: http://nces.ed.gov/pubs2009/2009020_0.pdf

4. Susan Dominus, "Tense Times at Bronxville High," *New York Times Magazine*, September 30, 2007; Naomi Schaefer Riley, "The College Try May Not Get You into College," *Wall Street Journal*, September 28, 2007; Alan Finder, "Ivy League Crunch Brings New Cachet to Next Tier," *New York Times*, May 16, 2007.

5. E. D. Hirsch, Jr., *Cultural Literacy: What Every American Needs to Know*, Boston: Houghton Mifflin, 1987.

6. Michael Winerip, "SAT Pressure Is On, and Even Online Prepsters Noodge," *New York Times*, November 14, 2008.

7. James S. Coleman et al., *Equality of Educational Opportunity*, U.S. Government Printing Office, 1966.

8. U.S. Department of Education, National Center for Education Statistics, *Digest of Education Statistics 2008*, March 2009. Table 35. "Enrollment in Public Elementary

and Secondary Schools, by Level, Grade, and State or Jurisdiction: Fall 2005." Web site accessed in April 2009: http://nces.ed.gov/pubs2009/2009020_0.pdf.

9. Laurence Steinberg, *Beyond the Classroom: Why School Reform Has Failed and What Parents Need to Do*, New York: Simon & Schuster, 1996.

10. *Ibid.*, p. 195.

11. This was a very elaborate undertaking; the William T. Grant Foundation, the Spencer Foundation, the Lilly Endowment, the Carnegie Corporation of New York, and the Office of Educational Research and Improvement of the U.S. Department of Education contributed funds. *Ibid.*, p. 8.

12. *Ibid.*, p. 15.

13. "Worse Than You Think," *Wall Street Journal*, October 24, 2007.

14. See James S. Coleman, Thomas Hoffer, and Sally Kilgore, *High School Achievement: Public, Catholic, and Private Schools Compared*, New York: Basic Books, 1982, and James S. Coleman and Thomas Hoffer, *Public and Private High Schools: The Impact of Communities*, New York: Basic Books, 1987.

15. United States Census Bureau, *The 2009 Statistical Abstract*, Table 4: "Cumulative Estimates of the Components of Resident Population Change for the United States, Regions, States, and Puerto Rico: April 1, 2000 to July 1, 2008." Web site accessed in April 2009: www.census.gov/popest/states/tables/NST-EST2008-04.csv; Department of Homeland Security, "Estimates of the Unauthorized Immigrant Population Residing in the United States: January 2005," *Population Estimates*, August 2006, accessed January 2006: www.dhs.gov/xlibrary/assets/statistics/publications/ILL_PE_2005.pdf.

16. Ginger Thompson and Sandra Ochoa, "By a Back Door to the U.S.: A Migrant's Grim Sea Voyage," *New York Times*, June 13, 2004.

17. Brink Lindsey, "The Culture Gap," *Wall Street Journal*, July 9, 2007.

18. Peter D. Salins, "The Test Passes, Colleges Fail," *New York Times*, November 17, 2008.

19. U.S. Department of Education, National Center for Education Statistics, *Digest of Education Statistics 2008*, March, 2009, "Table 188: Total Fall Enrollment in Degree-Granting Institutions, by Attendance Status, Sex of Student, and Control of Institution: Selected Years, 1947 through 2007." Web site accessed in April 2009: http://nces.ed.gov/pubs2009/2009020.pdf.

20. In 1970, 32 percent of males 18 to 24 were enrolled in college compared with 20 percent of females 18 to 24. By 1988, 33 percent of females 18 to 24 were enrolled compared with 30 percent of males in that age group. By 2003, 41 percent of females 18 to 24 were enrolled compared with 34 percent of males. Source: U.S. Census Bureau, Current Population Surveys (CPS), October, various years, unpublished tabulations. Web site accessed in April 2009: http://nces.ed.gov/programs/youthindicators/Indicators.asp?PubPageNumber=22&ShowTablePage=TablesHTML/22.asp.

21. U.S. Census Bureau, Census 2000 Special Reports, Series CENSR-4, *Demographic Trends in the 20th Century*, U.S. Government Printing Office, Washington, D.C., 2002, "Table 5. Population by Age and Sex for the United States: 1900 to

2000," p. A-9. Web site accessed in April 2009: www.census.gov/prod/2002pubs/censr-4.pdf.

22. Justin Pope, "More Colleges May Close in Ailing Economy," *Boston Globe*, November 17, 2008.

23. U.S. Department of Education, National Center for Education Statistics, *Digest of Education Statistics 2008*, March 2009, Washington, D.C., March 2009, Table 142, p. 208. See also Figure 3.2 in Chapter 3.

24. The survey can be found at: www.horatioalger.org/pdfs/state05.pdf. Accessed in January 2006.

25. Sungha Park, "On College-Entrance Exam Day, All of South Korea Is Put to the Test; Noisy Flights Can't Land; Offices Open Late to Avoid Traffic; Mothers Pray a Lot," *Wall Street Journal*, November 12, 2008.

26. "National Higher Education Entrance Examination," in *Wikipedia, the Free Encyclopedia*. Web site accessed in April 2009: http://en.wikipedia.org/wiki/National_Higher_Education_Entrance_Examination.

27. William C. Kirby, "On Chinese, European, and American universities," *Daedalus: Journal of the American Academy of Arts and Sciences*, vol. 137, No. 3 (Summer 2008); Howard W. French, "China Luring Scholars to Make Universities Great," *New York Times*, October 28, 2005.

28. *Ibid.*

29. Thomas P. Rohlen, *Japan's High Schools*, Berkeley, CA: University of California Press, 1983.

30. John Hechinger, "When $26 Billion Isn't Enough," *Wall Street Journal*, December 17, 2005; "Oxford Blues," *Financial Times*, November 4, 2006; John Redwood, "If Oxford Wants to Remain World-Class, It Has to Change," *Telegraph*, November 14, 2006; Kim Burgess, "Cambridge Turns to City to Lead Fund," *Financial Times*, November 26, 2006.

31. The number of hours per week that a student would have to work for a year at the minimum wage to be able to afford to attend a four-year university (average tuition and fees and room and board) has increased dramatically for both public and private American universities. In 1964, a student needed to work 17.6 hours a week at minimum wage to pay tuition at a public university and 36.8 hours a week to pay tuition at a private one. By 2004, those hours per week had jumped to 47 (an increase of 167 percent!) for a public and 129.5 (an increase of 252 percent!) for a private university. Nevertheless, American students continued to enroll in ever increasing numbers, in large part because governmental grants and loans helped them pay these higher costs. Sources: Digest of Education Statistics, 2006, "Table 319: Average Undergraduate Tuition and Board Rates Charged for Full-time Students in Degree-Granting Institutions, by Type and Control of Institution, 1964–65 through 2005–06"; United States Department of Labor, History of Federal Minimum Wage Rates Under the Fair Labor Standards Act, 1938–2006.

32. Patrick E. Tyler, "Blair Narrowly Prevails in a Vote to Raise Tuition," *New York Times*, January 28, 2004.

33. *Ibid.*

34. Katherine Zoepf, "Across Europe, An Outcry over Paying for College," *New York Times*, February 4, 2004.

35. *Ibid.*

36. Richard Bernstein, "Halls of Ivy May Receive Miracle-Gro in Germany," *New York Times*, May 9, 2004.

37. *Ibid.*

38. Julia Preston, "University, Mexico's Pride, Is Ravaged by Strike," *New York Times*, January 20, 2000.

39. Sergio Sarmiento, "UNAM: Mexico City's Giant School for Scandal," *Wall Street Journal*, February 25, 2000.

40. *Ibid.*

41. Howard W. French, "Ending Free Ride at Senegal University Brings Turmoil," *New York Times*, September 27, 1994.

42. Lydia Polgreen, "Africa's Storied Colleges, Jammed and Crumbling," *New York Times*, May 20, 2007.

43. Larry Rohter, "For Brazil's College-Bound, a Brutal Test of Mettle," *New York Times*, December 29, 2000.

44. *Ibid.*

45. U.S. Department of Education, National Center for Education Statistics, *Digest of Education Statistics 2005*, "Table 295: Statistical Profile of Persons Receiving Doctor's Degrees, by Field of Study and Selected Characteristics, 2002–2003," Web site accessed in April 2009: http://nces.ed.gov/programs/digest/d05/tables/dt05_295.asp

46. *The Daily Targum*, "Goldberg Says NJ Constitution Should Include Right to College," April 22, 1992. The student publication of Rutgers University reported on a speech the Chancellor gave on the New Brunswick campus.

47. This number includes $496,129,000 in "fringe-benefit" costs not included in the direct appropriations from the state to institutions of higher education. Office of Budget and Resource Studies, Rutgers University (unpublished data).

48. Kimberly J. McLarin, "The 1993 Election: Governor Whitman Triumphantly Pledges Income-Tax Cut by 1994 Budget," *New York Times*, November 4, 1993.

49. Thomas Friedman, "Clinton Offers Tuition Aid Linked to National Service," *New York Times*, March 2, 1993.

50. This quotation came from a Fact Sheet on AmeriCorps Web site in 2005 prepared by a research contractor for AmeriCorps, Abt Associates.

51. U.S. Department of Education, National Center for Education Statistics, *Digest of Education Statistics 2008*, March 2009. p. 269." Web site accessed in April 2009: http://nces.ed.gov/pubs2009/2009020_0.pdf.

52. College Board, *Trends in Student Aid 2008*. Web site accessed in April 2009: www.collegeboard.com/html/costs/aid/1_1_total_aid.html.

53. *Ibid.*

54. U.S. Department of Labor, Bureau of Labor Statistics, "Education Pays . . ." Accessed in April 2009: www.bls.gov/emp/emptab7.htm

55. "Overcoming Economic Barriers to College," *The [Harvard] Gazette*, April 2004, pp. 1, 6. Harvard College is the most selective college in the United States.

56. Harvard Club of New Jersey, *Newsletter*, Summer 2005, p. 4.

57. Rimer, Sara, "Elite Colleges Open New Door to Low-Income Youths," *New York Times*, May 27, 2007.

Chapter 2
Maximizing Access to College Maximizes the Enrollment of Underprepared Students

I retired after fifty years as a professor of sociology at Rutgers University. Then I offered a deal that my department could not refuse: to teach for free every other semester a seminar course limited to fifteen juniors and seniors. I was surprised by what happened.

Since one of the first classes I taught after retiring was small, I gave the students weekly writing assignments based on that week's readings and class discussions in lieu of examinations. I graded their short papers for the ideas they contained. I could not address all the shortcomings in the clarity, structure, and expression of basic ideas, but I felt morally obliged to correct errors of spelling, punctuation, and grammar—often five to ten errors per page in a 500-word paper. I learned that although they had computers equipped with spell-check, spell-check did not prevent them from using the wrong homophone. Thus, the majority could not keep straight when to use "there" rather than "their" or "they're." Spell-check ought to have suggested in other cases that their attempted spelling did not correspond to any word known in the dictionary, but rather than expend time finding the correct spelling in a dictionary—difficult unless the correct spelling is similar to the incorrect spelling—they simply let it go. I found the following misused words—in addition to pure spelling errors:

"weather" instead of "whether"
"prey" instead of "pray"
"threw" instead of "through"

"sight" instead of "site"
"aloud" instead of "allowed"
"were" instead of "we're" or "where"
"accel" instead of "excel"
"aid" instead of "aide"
"write" instead of "right"
"peaked" instead of "peeked"
"personal" instead of "personnel"
"quite" instead of "quiet"
"souly" instead of "solely"
"Ivy" instead of IV (intravenous)
"stranglers" instead of "stragglers"
"lose" instead of "loose"
"pass" instead of "past"

Very rarely could I find a student who knew when to use "principle" rather than "principal" or "effect" rather than "affect." But some errors were startling in their ignorance. One Rutgers senior tried to say that she was appalled at the views of a professor at CCNY and wrote, "I was up hauled [sic] and emotionally upset reading [his] beliefs. It's displeasing [sic], the way he brainwashes young adults and instills in them frustration."

Although I did not reduce the grade on their papers for misspellings, I tried to shame those who had misspelled or misused words by indicating that their words did not convey their intended meaning. I put the two words in the margins, separated by an equal symbol with a slash through it. If I had expected this procedure to improve spelling and word usage on student papers as the semester went on, I was mistaken. Perhaps students were doing as well as they could. Apart from errors in spelling, word usage, and grammar, a few of the papers were clearly written, and I gave them A grades. But the majority of the papers were so muddled that I felt that the Cs and Ds I awarded should have been Fs. After a few weeks, five of the fifteen enrolled students in my course dropped it for fear of failing or getting a low final grade.

This was in the spring of 2003, and these Rutgers students were majoring in sociology or psychology; some were even planning to become teachers. My experience with future teachers was not unique. Professor Sheila Schwartz, having retired from the English education faculty of SUNY–New Paltz after teaching there for thirty-five years, wrote an op-ed piece describing her former students.

Over time, I saw a steady decline in the quality of these future teachers. Many had writing skills that ranged from depressing to horrifying, especially when we remember that these same people eventually went on to teach writing to high school students.[1]

By comparison with other American universities, Rutgers is somewhat selective. In 2002 at the main campus in New Brunswick where I was teaching, 55 percent of the applicants for the freshman class and 37 percent of the transfer applicants were admitted.[2] The mean SAT score in 2002 for registered first-year students in the University as a whole, which includes the Newark and Camden campuses, was 610 for math and 578 for verbal, quite a bit better than the 516 math and 504 verbal mean scores for all American first-year students.[3] Rutgers, like other American colleges, has remedial writing courses for freshmen. More than 600,000 freshmen entering American colleges in 2002—29 percent of entering freshmen— were required to take at least one remedial reading, writing, or math class.[4]

But some colleges are more deeply involved in remediation than others. In the California State University system of four-year public colleges— with 360,000 students in 1998—50 percent of them took one or more remedial courses. The public community colleges had a bigger problem; 96 percent of them offered remedial courses in 1998, compared with 72 percent at four-year colleges.[5] The need for remedial work at college is not new. In 1978 the New Jersey Board of Higher Education tested the basic skills of 42,984 students admitted to New Jersey colleges in the fall of that year. The Basic Skills Council concluded that "a substantial number of the students entering colleges in New Jersey are not adequately prepared in the basic skills of reading, writing, and mathematics and are thereby hindered from doing college-level work in a broad variety of disciplines."[6] But mine was an advanced class, not a remedial one. Presumably my students had been given remediation if their screening tests had revealed a need for it.

In my frustration, I assumed that professors at much more selective colleges did not have to teach underprepared students. However, a recently published memoir of a senior professor at Emory University, Patrick Allitt, demonstrated to me that even selective universities taught substantial numbers of underprepared students.[7] Professor Allitt, who holds the Arthur Blank Chair for Teaching Excellence at Emory University, did not complain. In fact, he begins his fascinating memoir of a semester of college teaching as though he reveled in the give-and-take of Socratic dialogues with smart, diligent undergraduates: "It's a great job being a professor, and the best part of the job is the teaching." But his chronological account of 42 consecutive meetings of his history course at Emory, "The Making of Modern America: 1877–2000," provides scant evidence of these qualities. Professor Allitt's students, although they must have gotten high enough grades in secondary schools to be admitted to Emory, come across as too ignorant to participate in meaningful dialogue. One, having never read a novel, believed that "novel" and "book" were synonyms. In addition to these misapprehensions, Professor Allitt faulted various weaknesses of his students on written assignments: their inability to construct a logical argument, the unnecessarily complicated language that they used, and their elementary grammatical mistakes. He gave the reader some specific illustrations.

> Hardly any students know the past participle of the verb *to lead*. In a group of thirty papers, twenty-five will say something like this: "Sherman was a tireless commander and he lead his army to victory" . . . . [E]ven rarer is it to find students who know the rules for apostrophes. Picking up at random a paper that the student failed to collect, my eye at once falls upon this sentence, "American's eagerly snatched up all the manufactured good's they could afford." Confusion is absolute when it comes to *its* and *it's* and on the question of whether the apostrophe goes before or after the s when making possessive and plural a singular noun that ends with s.[8]

By the twenty-third meeting of the class, the day of the midterm, Professor Allitt had covered the life and presidency of Theodore Roosevelt and had assigned part of the book Roosevelt wrote about his role in the Spanish-American War in 1898, *The Rough Riders*. He had also discussed in class President Franklin Delano Roosevelt's New Deal that began after the later Roosevelt's election in 1932. Consequently Professor Allitt was disappointed—though not surprised—by the following confused answer to his question about the historical significance of Theodore Roosevelt:

> Theodore Roosevelt was the author of the *Rough Riders* and also the president during the Depression and up to the Second World War. He led a group of soldiers from all around the country to fight with him in the Spanish-American War of 1898. He enacted the New Deal; he had gotten polio at the beginning of his political career and was paralyzed from the waste [sic] down.[9]

Whatever the knowledge deficiencies of Professor Allitt's students, they expected high grades.

> The aftermath of distributing grades every semester . . . is a series of visits from the students who didn't get straight A's . . . . "I'm a straight-A student. Why didn't I get that A?" . . . I've always found it difficult to stand up to their browbeating.[10]

Professor Allitt tried to forestall such browbeating by giving higher grades than students deserved.

> Look at the students I've been teaching this term. In an ideal world I would give about a quarter of them F's. Why? Because they have no aptitude for history, no appreciation for the connection between events, no sense of how a historical situation changes over time, they don't want to do the necessary hard work, they skimp on the reading, and can't write to save their lives. That's grounds enough for an F, surely.[11]

But if so many undergraduates at a selective college like Emory seem so underprepared to be students, what about students in the unselective colleges that most American students attend, and what do the colleges do about them? What happens in the "basement of the ivory tower," as an adjunct professor of English in a community college called it?[12]

WHAT DO COLLEGES DO WITH UNDERPREPARED STUDENTS?

As Chapter 1 demonstrated, underprepared undergraduates are inevitable in unselective colleges with low or nonexistent admission standards for high school graduates. Since American high school students don't *have* to work very hard to get into college, most high school students who plan to attend college do *not* work very hard in their courses, as the longitudinal study of nine American high schools, cited in Chapter 1, demonstrated. Hence, a large proportion of them arrive on campus without the level of reading, writing, and mathematical skills that college-level work ought to require.

Given the low level of academic achievement on the part of a considerable proportion of the high school graduates who go on to two-year and even to four-year colleges, the system of higher education as a whole must deal with large numbers of students not prepared to read demanding texts or to write coherent papers. But colleges vary greatly in the proportions of underprepared students that they admit, depending mostly on the selectivity of their admissions standards. Even selective colleges like Emory admit small numbers of comparatively underprepared students—athletes, members of minority groups eligible for preferential selection, the offspring of alumni or major donors ("legacies"), or applicants with special talents or experiences. "Special admits" at these elite colleges are only underprepared by comparison with students admitted in accordance with the academic standards of their colleges. Nevertheless, they present problems. Professors are reluctant to give failing or even low grades to an undergraduate class containing appreciable numbers of athletes and minorities. To avoid unpleasantness, professors tend to give high grades to everyone, which makes grades increasingly unreliable as an indication of what students have learned at college, even at selective colleges.[13] While it is very difficult to get into colleges like Emory or Harvard, once in, grade inflation usually enables both well-prepared and poorly prepared students to survive. (In the next chapter I discuss grade inflation in greater detail; apparently it is even more prevalent in the highly selective colleges than at less selective colleges.)

Grade inflation at Yale, for example, produced a small scandal in 1995. In that year Yale expelled a senior transfer student, Lom Grammer, for forging an outstanding transcript from Cuesta Community College in California as well as his California high school transcript, two glowing letters of recommendations from fictitious professors at Cuesta Community College, and a phony letter of recommendation from a Cuesta dean—in addition to taking $61,475 in loans and scholarships under false pretenses. What was remarkable was that although Mr. Grammer actually had had a C average at Cuesta Community College that his forgeries disguised, he was able to obtain over three semesters at Yale as many As and Bs as Cs and Ds. Grade inflation helped him to maintain his deception.[14] He was unmasked only a month before he was scheduled to graduate with a degree in political science because a former roommate reported to Yale authorities that Grammer had boasted that he got admitted to Yale with fake documents.

American colleges where virtually every applicant is accepted for admission have a much more serious problem than selective colleges do. Colleges have three options of how to handle underprepared students. They can maintain high academic standards and ask students who fail to measure up to leave; they can relax standards drastically in order to pass everyone who attends class three-quarters of the time; or, they can strike a compromise, attempting to remediate the deficiencies of underprepared students to enable them to read and write well enough to learn college-level material. Unfortunately, remediation is no small task. Overall, about a third of the entering freshmen in American colleges now require remediation in reading, writing, or mathematics.[15] As Table 2.1 shows, the remediation problem is more serious in two-year colleges than in four-year colleges. In the fall of 2000, 42 percent of the freshmen at public two-year colleges had to enroll in one or more remedial courses, 20 percent in reading, 23 percent in writing, 35 percent in mathematics. Not shown in Table 2.1 are those enrolled in more than one remedial program nor that 63 percent enrolled in remedial courses had to remain enrolled in them for a year or more.

In public four-year colleges, 38 percent of freshmen were enrolled in remedial courses, and in private four-year institutions, 17 percent were

Table 2.1

Percentage of Entering Freshmen Enrolled in Remedial Courses at College, 2000

	Other	Reading	Writing	Mathematics
Public Two-Year	42%	20%	23%	35%
Private Two-Year	24%	9%	17%	18%
Public Four-Year	20%	6%	9%	16%
Private Four-Year	12%	5%	7%	8%
All	28%	11%	14%	22%

Source: U.S. Department of Education, National Center for Education Statistics, *Remedial Education at Degree-Granting Postsecondary Institutions in Fall 2000*, NCES 2004-010, by Basmat Parsad and Laurie Lewis, Washington, D.C.: 2003, Table 4, p. 18. http://nces.ed.gov/pubs2004/2004010.pdf.
Note: Although these data were from 2000 and were issued in a report of the National Center for Education Statistics in 2003, as of April 2009 no later national data on remedial education in American colleges were available.

enrolled.[16] Of course, colleges had to establish and staff such remedial classes. Table 2.2 reports how often colleges responded with formal remedial courses in addition to the informal remedial help provided by instructors.

The remedial problem was greater for some students than others, as would be expected. Presumably the reason why remedial courses were almost universal in the public two-year colleges according to Table 2.2 is that the public two-year colleges contained the highest proportion of students with the weakest academic preparation from high school. These statistics

Table 2.2

Percentage of Higher Educational Institutions Offering Remedial Courses to College Freshmen, 2000

	Other	Reading	Writing	Mathematics
Public Two-Year	98%	96%	96%	97%
Private Two-Year	63%	37%	56%	62%
Public Four-Year	80%	49%	67%	78%
Private Four-Year	59%	30%	46%	49%
All	76%	56%	68%	71%

Source: U.S. Department of Education, National Center for Education Statistics, *Remedial Education at Degree-Granting Postsecondary Institutions in Fall 2000*, NCES 2004-010, by Basmat Parsad and Laurie Lewis, Washington, D.C.: 2003, Table 1, p. 8. http://nces.ed.gov/pubs2004/2004010.pdf.
Note: Although these data are from 2000 and were issued in a report of the National Center for Education Statistics in 2003, as of April 2009 no later national data on remedial education in American colleges were available.

ignore the tremendous financial burden of remediation for colleges that enroll a majority of students with serious academic deficiencies. Obviously, students assigned to remedial classes were underprepared to begin with. But the whole point of remediation is to enable students to overcome their initial handicaps and take advantage of the educational opportunities that higher education offers.

The crucial question is whether remediation succeeds. Frequently it doesn't, judging by the number of students who require remediation and, after getting it, do not complete their college program. The more remedial courses students needed to take at college, the less likely they were to complete college and obtain a degree. Thus, among 1992 twelfth graders who enrolled in postsecondary education and were followed for ten years, 57 percent of students who needed no remedial courses at college obtained at least a college degree within eight years of high school graduation whereas only 19 percent of students who had to enroll in three or four remedial courses obtained a college degree within eight years.[17] Remedial courses in reading were most predictive of dropping out of college, which is not surprising since reading is necessary to do course work.

Data from the National Center for Education Statistics strongly suggest that remediation at college was insufficient for the task. Despite assistance offered through remediation, other studies confirm the finding that students enrolled in remediation courses were less likely to earn a degree or certificate than students who needed no remediation.[18]

The "Diploma to Nowhere" report of the Strong American Schools program of the Rockefeller Philanthropy Advisors documented the remediation problems of American colleges in excruciating detail. In public two-year colleges, 995,077 students needed remedial courses, which cost those colleges between $1,880,000,000 and $2,350,000,000; in public four-year colleges 310,403 students needed remedial courses, which cost those colleges between $435,000,000 and $543,000,000 in 2004–2005.[19] The explanation given by the report was that the high schools did not prepare students adequately for college-level courses. According to the latest National Assessment of Educational Progress, only one-fourth of high school seniors are proficient in math, only half of high school seniors are proficient in science, and less than three-quarters of high school seniors possess basic reading skills.[20]

As might be expected, differences in family background produced differences in the need for remediation, although the differences were not very large. Students from higher-income families needed less remediation than students from lower-income families; students from families where the parents had a bachelor's degree or more required less remediation than students from families where the parents had a high school education or

Table 2.3

Percentage Distribution of the Highest Postsecondary Degree Eight Years after High School Graduation, 1992, by Highest Level of Mathematics Completed in High School

	No Postsecondary Degree	Certificate	Associate's	Bachelor's	Incomplete Graduate Degree	Graduate Degree
Calculus	13.3%	0.3%	3.7	49.3	16.6	16.8
Precalculus	19.0%	0.9%	5.2	51.5	12.9	10.5
Trigonometry	29.7%	2.6%	5.6	45.7	9.2	7.2
Algebra 2	42.5%	6.1%	11.1	31.5	5.7	3.1
Geometry	55.0%	9.0%	13.8	17.1	3.9	1.2
Algebra 1	67.0%	11.8%	11.0	8.3	1.2	0.7
Less than Algebra 1	68.9%	18.1%	8.9	3.8	0.3	*

Source: U.S. Department of Education, National Center for Education Statistics, National Education Longitudinal Study of 1988 (NELS:88/92/2000): "Second Follow-up, High School Transcript Study, 1992," and "Fourth Follow-up, Postsecondary Education Transcript Study (PETS), 2000." http://nces.ed.gov/programs/quarterly/Vol_5/5_3/4_2.asp#Table-C. (Taken from Table 11, p. 19 of the complete report from which the second article is excerpted.)

Note: The universe consists of all known postsecondary participants for whom the highest level of mathematics completed in high school could be determined. Weighted n = 2.0 million. Detail may not sum to totals because of rounding.

* Rounds to zero.

only some college; students from black, Hispanic, or Native American families required more remediation than students from non-Hispanic white families or Asian families.[21] An interesting point made in the report was that high school seniors who required remedial courses in college were not aware of the deficiencies of their high school preparation. They thought they were ready for college. The report asserted that the courses students took in high school were not rigorous enough. Supporting this assertion was the finding that among students assigned to remedial courses at college, only 1 percent said that their high school courses were "very difficult" and only 13 percent found them "somewhat difficult;" the rest said that their high school classes were "very easy," "somewhat easy," or "right at my level."[22] Unwillingness to fail high school students in courses in which they deserved a failing grade exports the problem to the colleges. *New York Times* reporter Samuel G. Freedman found at the High School of Arts and Technology in Manhattan [New York City], that a well-deserved failing grade was changed by the principal to a passing grade in order to allow the student to graduate. The principal explained her action in writing to the journalist as part of a "standard procedure" of "encouraging teachers to support students' efforts to achieve academic success."

The difficulty of large-scale remediation is usually attributed to lack of money committed to remedial programs. True, remedial programs are costly, and the colleges that accept virtually all applicants also tend to be the ones with negligible endowments and chronic financial problems. In the year 2008 the cost of remediation at all American colleges, not just public colleges, for students who had not learned in high school what they should have learned was estimated at $2.3 billion to $2.9 billion annually.[23] Another difficulty is the attitude of students taking remedial classes. Students who score low on placement tests and are assigned to remedial writing or math classes don't necessarily believe that they need help to overcome academic deficiencies. Having gotten through high school and having been admitted to college, they think they are prepared for college. Test failures? A fluke. They simply believe that they are no good at taking tests. Severely underprepared students are not necessarily motivated to put in the work they must put in if they are to catch up, especially when they have plenty of company on campuses where remediation programs are extensive and fully prepared students are the exception. Even if underprepared students recognize that they have goofed off in high school and need to improve their reading and writing skills in order to succeed in college courses, remedial college courses may be too little, too late. Keep in mind the difficulty of stimulating the development of reading and writing skills over the relatively brief period of time—a few semesters—during which underprepared students are assigned to remedial courses.

Such skills are normally developed over many years during preadolescence and adolescence. Just as it is usually too late to become a professional ballet dancer or a concert pianist if one starts at 18, it is usually too late to become a successful college student without trained capacity to read, write, and compute. Anecdotal examples of "late bloomers" can be cited, youngsters who did poorly at one level and brilliantly at the next level. Albert Einstein, for example, was reputed to have been a mediocre secondary school student. But "late bloomers" are rare. Most students find it discouraging when they are told that their academic deficiencies are serious and require putting in considerable time and effort in order to catch up. Moreover, foregoing the fun side of college and devoting prodigious effort to improving reading and writing skills will not pay off quickly in better grades. Like dieting and exercise to shed extra weight, the results are slow in coming.

Statistically, colleges enrolling large proportions of underprepared students have lower graduation rates than colleges enrolling fewer underprepared students. Professor Vincent Tinto, a leading expert on student attrition at college, has calculated that in highly selective colleges with average SAT scores of more than 1100, the first-year attrition rate is 8.0 percent; in colleges with average SAT scores of less than 700—that is, warm-body institutions—the first-year attrition rate is 45.5 percent.[24]

These statistics suggest that when large numbers of enrolled students require remedial courses in order to cope with college work, many students, presumably the least well prepared, get discouraged, give up on higher education of their own accord, and drop out. More rarely, the colleges ask them to withdraw for a semester or two or permanently. A superb ethnographic study of the day-by-day experiences of underprepared students is at least as convincing as these statistics, which might be interpreted as due to other factors than students underprepared for higher education. James Traub, a journalist, took advantage of the "natural experiment" in open admissions that New York City's City College undertook in order to provide greater educational opportunities for minorities and the economically deprived.[25]

WHAT CAN BE LEARNED FROM THE CCNY EXPERIMENT?

The "open admissions" experiment that Traub studied took place at the City College of New York (CCNY), which had been until 1969 a highly selective public college whose graduates went on to prestigious graduate schools and had earned eight Nobel Prizes. CCNY had proudly offered free college educations to all New York City high school graduates who demonstrated academic aptitude. By the late 1960s, the demography of

New York City had changed as African Americans and Hispanics moved in and Caucasians left for the suburbs. Despite the shift in city demographics, the able students selected for enrollment at CCNY continued to be mostly Caucasian. In 1969, African American and Puerto Rican students chained the gates of CCNY closed and mounted raucous, sometimes violent demonstrations demanding that the College admit vastly more minority students. The protestors would not accept the argument that the College was searching hard for minority students able to do college-level work in, for example, its SEEK program, but could not find enough of them.[26]

Under the pressure of these demands, the administration and faculty of City College yielded and suddenly established "open admissions" for a very different clientele. Pressure did not wholly explain the capitulation to the demand for less selective admissions. Many faculty members and administrators were liberals like Traub himself and were uneasy about serving an overwhelmingly white clientele in a city with a large minority population. They wanted to help African Americans and Puerto Ricans move into the middle class through educational achievement, as Jews, Irish, and Italians had done in previous generations. "Open admissions" was not a complete abdication of standards. Most faculty members believed, at least initially, that their new clientele could catch up educationally. They did not plan to hand out an empty credential. This is how Traub, a staff writer at the time for the *New Yorker* magazine, described the liberal attitude toward these open-admission students that he shared with faculty members at City College, an attitude that made them optimistic about the possibilities of remediation. "I *wanted* City College to work . . . . I had grown up with the civil rights movement and the war on poverty . . . . I took it as a premise that a humane institution focuses an important part of its energy on bringing the poor into the mainstream."[27]

Open admissions at CCNY had been in operation for more than two decades when Traub began in 1992 eighteen months of in-depth observation of what happened as CCNY tried to cope with a flood of underprepared students. He conducted several hundred interviews with current City College students, professors, administrators, and alumni. He also attended many classes, listening intently to the interactions between professors and students. For example, here is what happened on the first day with a new group of students in Professor Rudi Gedamke's remedial class in basic skills:

> In the spring of 1992 [Gedamke] presented a new batch of kids with a headline from *The Campus*, the student newspaper: STUDENT TURNOUT NIL AT GAMES. He asked for a simple translation.

Gedamke had cut out the answers and pasted them one on top of another. One student wrote, "he/she is not good for nothing." Others tried, "Students spend most of their studies time as their leisure times" and "Students are getting addicted toward it." Others made a real stab at translation but did not know what to make of *nil*, and so wrote "Students act uncivilized at games" or "Students turnout facinate [sic] at games." There was only one answer he could deem correct: "no one didn't go."[28]

In the fall of 1992, Traub sat in on another of Gedamke's remedial classes. Gedamke started by asking questions about his students that enabled him to gauge the extent of their problems. He learned that although only nine of the twenty-six students in the class could name a book or a magazine article lately that had impressed them, they spent on the average 17 hours a week watching television and some spent as much as 40 hours. One student in the class replied to his question, "What are your strengths and weaknesses in reading/studying?" as follows: "My strength in reading is finishing the book. My weakness is I can't remember what I have read."[29] Many of the students admitted that they could not understand what they read.

If Traub had begun his study at the start of the experiment in 1970 when 2,752 new students registered for class or in 1971 when the freshman class peaked at 3,216 (as compared with 1,752 in the fall of 1969), he could be accused of using a bad sample, that is, of studying an understandably chaotic situation unrepresentative of the remediation problem in most colleges.[30] But Traub did not start his investigation until 1992, two decades after it began. By that time CCNY had a manageable enrollment, partly because it had begun charging tuition. It also had years of experience with educating underprepared students—as well as carefully selected teachers to address their difficulties. CCNY established the following remedial programs, each staffed with dedicated teachers committed to readying their students for regular courses:

- An English as a Second Language (ESL) program for recent immigrants from African, Asian, Eastern European, Mid-Eastern, or Latin American countries unable to read or write English comprehensibly. Some had very good secondary education in the countries from which they came; others were virtually illiterate. Immigrant students were assigned to one of three levels of ESL classes in order to give them a chance to learn English gradually so that they could move into regular classes.
- A Language Arts program for students—mostly products of New York City schools—who had not done well enough on a writing assessment

test given to incoming students. There were two levels of remediation in Language Arts depending on assessment scores. Students assigned to one of these Language Arts remedial courses were in the SEEK program, which had been established to locate students from New York City neighborhoods with large concentrations of minorities and recruit them for admission to CCNY. By 1970, SEEK students had to come from families below the poverty level and have an academic record that would *not* qualify them for regular admission to a senior college.[31] Traub sat in on a Language Arts class to get an idea of the magnitude of the remedial task for such students. He observed students who flirted, whispered, or avoided eye contact with the teacher, and could not or would not answer the teacher's very simple questions.[32] Traub concluded that they had not been socialized into the student role; they continued to behave according to the implicit contract that they had made in high school: not to bother teachers who did not bother them. A Basic Writing program had originally been a separate program to improve writing skills, but after budget cuts in 1976, it was folded into the Language Arts remediation efforts. (Traub implies that in view of the communications difficulties of open-enrollment students, they needed more help than they could get in the more general Language Arts program.)

- Math remediation classes that attempted to address deficiencies identified on incoming students' math assessment tests. These courses were especially important for students who hoped to obtain a degree in engineering.
- A tutoring and counseling program that tried to address the unique problems of individual students.

While CCNY's experiment in open admissions was the largest attempted in the United States, it was not the first. Midwestern public universities had for decades admitted as freshmen all high school graduates from their states in accordance with requirements imposed by their legislatures—and failed about half who failed to meet academic standards by the end of the first year. CUNY's experiment was different because it guaranteed a much longer period during which academic consequences were postponed. Here is how Traub put it:

And while half of each freshman class routinely flunked out at many Midwestern universities that functioned under a state-mandated open enrollment system, CUNY agreed to give all incoming students a one-year grace period. In other words, CUNY committed itself not only to accepting a vast cadre of new students but to advancing them toward a bachelor's degree.[33]

For several reasons, though, CUNY's version of open admissions was different in important ways. In the first place, high school graduation was more selective in Midwestern high schools a half-century ago than in New York City in the 1960s and later; most students who persevered until graduation in Michigan or Wisconsin at that time were more capable of doing college-level work if they were motivated to do it. Second, Midwestern college faculties were unhesitant—some might say "brutal"—about failing students who did not perform well. Consequently students knew that flunking out was a realistic possibility. Third, unlike the native-born Midwestern high school graduates, many of the open-admission students at CCNY were recent immigrants from African, Asian, or Latin American countries, too recent to be able to read or write English comprehensibly.

Studying CCNY's experience with open admissions might be criticized as an inappropriate way to learn about underprepared students at *other* American universities. After all, CCNY changed suddenly from a highly selective college to one swamped with thousands of underprepared students, necessitating radical changes in the way professors taught. Most colleges are not suddenly transformed into institutions where three-quarters of the entering students require remedial courses. Nevertheless, the open-admissions experiment at CCNY was reasonably comparable to the remedial task that other American colleges and universities face. After all, most colleges have similar commitments to minority students and foreign-born students, both of whom tend to be underprepared for college. New Jersey, for example, enacted in 1968 the New Jersey Educational Opportunity Act as a response to urban riots in neighborhoods with large African American populations. The EOF program, still in operation, provides special scholarships for students from low-income families to attend both public and private colleges within the State of New Jersey, but like the SEEK program at City College, EOF scholarships are awarded to *educationally disadvantaged* students.[34] "Educationally disadvantaged" is a delicate way of describing students unprepared for college.

I shall return to the subject of special scholarships that provide financial aid to unprepared students more extensively in a later chapter. For now, consider the possibility that remediation problems, endemic in American colleges, may be an unintended consequence of state and federal financial-aid programs intended to enable low-income students to attend college. While some middle-class students are underprepared also, underpreparation is much more common among low-income students, many of whom come from low-achieving schools, do not benefit from sound educational advice from their parents, and move frequently from one school to another.[35] A major reason why students in public schools serving a low-income neighborhood learn so little is that families in such neighborhoods tend to move around frequently, forcing their children to transfer from school to school. Under these conditions of midterm transfers, students have difficulty learning. In addition, constant population turnover in classes demoralizes teachers who face the prospect of starting over with new arrivals instead of building on what has already been taught. None of this is the fault of the children themselves, but the consequence is that even if they get through high school, they are underprepared for college.

In 1972 Professor Irving Kristol, a distinguished alumnus of City College, expressed skepticism about the remedial task that the open admissions program had set for itself.

> To think that you can take large numbers of students from a poor socioeconomic background, who do badly in high school, who do badly on all your standardized tests . . . who show no promise, and who do not show much motivation—to think that you can take large numbers of such students and somehow make them benefit from a college education instead of merely wasting their time and their money, I say this is demonstrably false . . . . Schools just cannot do that much and colleges simply cannot accomplish this mission.[36]

Despite his initial hopes, Traub's eighteen months of careful observation tended to confirm Kristol's skeptical view of remediation. *City on a Hill* revealed many, many cases of students with academic handicaps too severe to be repaired by their efforts or the efforts of their teachers, and this anecdotal evidence was confirmed in statistical studies. One study of 155 SEEK students who had also been placed in the ESL program found that only seven had graduated after six years and another half-dozen or so after seven years; projection over a decade yielded an estimate of 15 percent completing college.[37] If remediation does not solve the problem of underprepared students, an obvious strategy is to say, in effect, "We are admitting you even though our experience suggests that you fall into a statistical category of students not likely to succeed at college. Be warned. It would not be surprising if you did not graduate." But as far as I know, such a message was never given to underprepared students.

Colleges sometimes talk about "high-risk admissions," which shows their intellectual recognition of the lower chance of success for underprepared students. But colleges have, by and large, recoiled from the implications of high-risk admissions: low "retention" rates. "Retention" is a peculiar word that suggests that the college rather than students bears the responsibility for students leaving before graduating. Yet the evidence is clear that the worse the academic preparation of admitted students at a college, the lower the college's retention rate on the average. Many deficiencies are difficult to repair. Some references in speech or writing are not fully understandable without what E. D. Hirsch, Jr. calls "cultural literacy"—such as knowledge of characters in one of Shakespeare's plays. For instance, "John considers himself a Romeo," is not clear unless the listener knows a little about *Romeo and Juliet*. Without a rudimentary knowledge of the Old Testament, a student hearing a resort described as a "Garden of Eden" might be baffled. Yet many students enroll in college without significant knowledge of the Bible or of Shakespeare's plays or of nineteenth-century novels like those of Charles Dickens.[38] Journalist Russell Baker tells the story of asking a college-age Greenwich Village bookstore clerk for a copy of *David Copperfield*. "'Who's the author?' the clerk asked. 'Dickens,' I said. 'What's his first name?'"[39] Baker thought that a college-age bookstore clerk should have known.

Admitting students should not be an assurance that they will graduate. Nevertheless, in trying to maximize "access," the system of higher education arouses expectations in admitted students that they *will* graduate. Whereas the traditional response of students who failed was to accept suspension or expulsion meekly, high-risk students nowadays, especially those who belong to socioeconomic or ethnic groups considered victims of bad educational institutions, may refuse to accept responsibility for failure or loss of interest and accuse colleges of discrimination.

Once they have given remedial courses to underprepared students, colleges feel obliged to graduate them even though they may not have corrected their initial weaknesses. Graduating such students exacerbates the problem, because other underprepared students infer from their graduation that everyone who is admitted can make progress toward a degree without committing himself or herself to repairing weaknesses in preparation. They lack a strong incentive. CCNY and indeed the rest of the City University system have abandoned the open-enrollment experiment and are seeking to return to more traditional academic standards for admission and retention.[40]

Getting back to my last teaching experience at Rutgers University, I attempted to remediate the grammatical, word usage, and punctuation mistakes of the fifteen students initially enrolled in the class and of the ten who did not drop out. Perhaps I lacked the skills of staff members who specialize in remedial writing courses. But I did not notice any improvement as the semester wore on. I suspect that the problems could not be fixed at this stage of their lives, at least not until they had stronger incentives than I was able to mobilize to improve their writing. My students would have had to have read a great deal more than they did in the years leading up to college enrollment to be familiar with how English words are spelled and used.

UNDEMANDING COURSES FOR UNDERPREPARED STUDENTS

An almost universal consensus exists in the United States that education, like freedom and democracy, is desirable and necessary. As novelist H. G. Wells put it, "Human history becomes more and more a race between education and catastrophe."[41] Yet with so many students unprepared for intellectually demanding course assignments, colleges tend to cope with the problem by trivializing part of the curriculum. Many activities called educational in American colleges and universities are educational mainly in the broad sense that one learns from most life experiences such as serving in the Army, living in a high-crime neighborhood, getting along with roommates, growing up in a broken home, or trying to cope with a drug habit. Although many colleges now give some credit toward graduation for "experiential learning," the traditional assumption is that mastery of a body of knowledge—that is to say, intellectual learning—should be the primary basis for a B.A. degree. Nevertheless some colleges are generous in awarding college credit for life experiences. The Adult Degree Program at James Madison University, a public university in Harrisonburg, Virginia, gives students as much as thirty credits—a fourth of the number of credits needed for graduation—for life experiences.[42] The Baccalaureate for Unique and Interdisciplinary Studies, an individualized program of the City University of New York, gives a maximum of fifteen credits.[43] For example, Kim J. Hartswick, academic director of that program, gave fifteen credits for proficiency in "fund-raising and development," "creative art for the classroom" and "Web page design."

Where should the line be drawn in awarding or not awarding college credit for courses that are broadly educational in a street-smart sense but do not involve intellectual mastery of traditional subjects? In an effort to satisfy the student appetite for "stimulating" courses that are intellectually undemanding, otherwise-qualified scholars have begun to offer courses that are only marginally more scholarly than television soap operas. For example, Bloomfield College, a small four-year liberal arts college a few miles west of Newark, New Jersey, offered in 1993 a four-credit course called "Introduction to Circus Arts" and may still offer it.[44] Students take it not to become clowns, but to fulfill their humanities and fine arts requirement for graduation. The midterm in 1993 consisted of juggling three balls for forty throws and balancing a six-foot pole on their chins for twelve seconds. Their final grades were based on a paper ("Explain how to juggle") and on their performance in a show at the end of the semester. The then President of the College, John F. Noonan, explained the rationale of the course: "Basically, this course is about teaching people that they can do what seems at first to be impossible."

"Introduction to Circus Arts" lacked the intellectual content usually associated with college courses, but the Bloomfield College administration justified this intellectual flabbiness partly by the changing ethnic composition of the student body. As the journalist who wrote the story about the school put it, "The 125-year-old institution has increasingly been accepting eager but sometimes unprepared students who come from nearby tough towns like East Orange, Irvington, and Newark with more desire than preparation for learning." The students in the class were satisfied; they felt that they had learned more than they thought they would. The teacher, John H. Towsen, an associate professor of performing arts, felt that the course "really does seem to give the students confidence, in the sense that they come to school often with lower SAT scores, lower self-esteem, and without necessarily feeling that they're destined for success." "Introduction to Circus Arts" may indeed raise self-esteem, but at one time college professors would have been reluctant to grant college credit for this or other ways of raising self-esteem, e.g., personal psychotherapy. In short, they would question whether students in such a course gain enough cognitive mastery of a body of knowledge for college credit to be awarded. A related problem is posed by a fall semester three-credit course taught by history professor David M. Jacobs at Temple University entitled, "Unidentified Flying Objects in American Society."[45] Professor Jacobs, a Ph.D. in history from the University of Wisconsin, is doubtlessly qualified to evaluate historical material and to teach history courses. But what is he doing teaching undergraduates in the Temple University History Department that extraterrestrial invaders of planet Earth kidnap men and women at night, put them into a trance, and steal eggs and sperm for their own purposes?

This course sounds so bizarre that it might be thought to be the quirk of a particular professor. Apparently, however, many colleges and universities permit courses to be offered that stretch the boundaries of intellectual respectability. A conservative organization compiled a list of courses it regards as bizarre curriculum offerings. Although they are probably not representative of what is taught at those colleges, some of which are selective colleges, the fact that they are taught at all is surprising.[46]

- Occidental College's "The Phallus" covers a broad study on the relation "between the phallus and the penis, the meaning of the phallus, phallologocentrism, the lesbian phallus, the Jewish phallus, the Latino phallus, and the relation of the phallus and fetishism."
- "Queer Musicology" at the University of California–Los Angeles explores how "sexual difference and complex gender identities in music and among musicians have incited productive consternation" during the 1990s. Music under consideration includes works by Franz

Schubert, Holly Near, Benjamin Britten, Cole Porter, and Pussy Tourette.

- Students enrolled in the University of Pennsylvania's "Adultery Novel" read a series of nineteenth and twentieth century works about "adultery" and watch "several adultery films." Students apply "various critical approaches in order to place adultery into its aesthetic, social, and cultural context, including: sociological descriptions of modernity, Marxist examinations of family as a social and economic institution" and "feminist work on the construction of gender."
- Occidental College—making the list twice for the second year in a row—offers "Blackness," which elaborates on a "new blackness," "critical blackness," "post-blackness," and an "unforgivable blackness," which all combine to create a "feminist New Black Man."
- "Whiteness: The Other Side of Racism" is Mount Holyoke College's attempt to analyze race. The class seeks to spark thought on: "What is whiteness?" "How is it related to racism?" "What are the legal frameworks of whiteness?" "How is whiteness enacted in everyday practice?" And how does whiteness impact the "lives of whites and people of color?
- "Native American Feminisms" at the University of Michigan looks at the development of "Native feminist thought" and its "relationship both to Native land-based struggles and non-Native feminist movements."
- Duke University's "American Dreams/American Realities" course seeks to unearth "such myths as 'rags to riches,' 'beacon to the world,' and the 'frontier,' in defining the American character."
- Swarthmore College's "Nonviolent Responses to Terrorism" "deconstruct[s] terrorism" and "build[s] on promising nonviolent procedures to combat today's terrorism." The nonviolent struggle Blacks pursued in the 1960s is outlined as a model for tackling today's terrorism.

Should students who learn about extraterrestrial invaders of planet Earth earn three credits toward graduation? Professor Jacobs claims to have evidence for his assertions; he has hypnotized about sixty people and discussed with them their experiences with extraterrestrial beings. But as a historian Professor Jacobs doesn't have expertise in social research or in the special problems of the suggestibility of research subjects when interviewed under hypnosis. Some of his colleagues in the history department are deeply skeptical; others want to promote him on the basis of the book he has written about his "research." Students in his course give him high ratings as a teacher.

Resolving the issue of whether higher education is high enough is not just one of academic freedom, although in the name of academic freedom, professors teach very strange courses. Increasingly, higher education is not merely a private transaction between student customers and college vendors of educational services. Higher education, like medical care, increasingly involves a third party, federal or state governments or private foundations, which underwrite some or all of the cost, especially at public institutions. Taxpayers and private donors, who are indirectly paying part of student tuition and living costs, may, understandably, be less willing to pay for students to enroll in courses like "Introduction to Circus Arts" or "Unidentified Flying Objects in American Society" than in courses like "Introduction to Organic Chemistry."

Some college officials argue that governments and even private donors should support anything that colleges and their students wish to call higher education because to do otherwise is an infringement on academic freedom. Students are entitled to study whatever they like and professors to teach whatever pleases their students. This sounds like Humpty-Dumpty's reasoning in *Through the Looking Glass.* "When *I* use a word," Humpty Dumpty said in a rather scornful tone, "it means just what I choose it to mean—neither more nor less."[47]

JUGGLING UNDERPREPARED AND EXCELLENT STUDENTS

In 1980, Harvard Professor David Riesman identified a force associated with some of the intellectual downgrading of American higher education that started in the late 1960s and the 1970s.[48] That force was "student consumerism:" the gradual transfer of power to student customers as both public and private colleges came to realize that rising costs forced them to compete more aggressively for freshman enrollment than they had done in the past. Colleges started hiring market research firms to advise them about how to court students more successfully.[49] This trend has continued ever since, and colleges now compete for students relentlessly, especially for students likely to do well academically. They send out glossy brochures; they advertise in newspapers, magazines, and radio; they court high school counselors. Counselors can potentially steer high school seniors to one college rather than to another. A newspaper article reported on the practice:

> The colleges themselves seem uncertain as to what is, or is not, appropriate. Some say theater tickets are all right, but professional sporting events are questionable. Others say massages are obviously out of bounds, but fancy dinners and waterfront cruises that feature a city's skyline are fine.
>
> "Where is the line? That's a tough one," said John J. Gladstone, associate academic vice president for enrollment services at John

Carroll University in Cleveland. "For many years, schools just lived on their known reputation, but nowadays we're much more aware that this is a buyer's market, and we want to show our best side."[50]

With so many colleges competing for student enrollments, high school graduates and their counselors are courted. They are told about student centers, gyms, comfortable dorm rooms, and an attractive campus. For students who are looking for four years of pleasant peer group experiences with no more than a bachelor's degree in hand to certify that they have pursued "higher education," such amenities may be enough. But for high school graduates for whom it is not enough, colleges try to be perceived as academically excellent in order to attract admission applications. Those students and their parents have to believe that they are enrolling in an educational institution, not merely a recreation center. Colleges also need some claim to academic excellence in order to recruit faculty, especially productive scholars who can validate a college's claims to educational excellence and help in future faculty recruitment.

So at the same time that most colleges admit, remediate, and graduate underprepared students, they also feel compelled to recruit and teach excellent students. Colleges award merit scholarships for excellent students, and they establish honors colleges for good students with separate courses and even separate dormitories.[51] More than a thousand colleges and universities have honors programs, although each has distinctive features. "Honors students at Illinois State, for example, have separate housing, their own advisors, and sometimes a private lab bench for research; they are eligible for a variety of special scholarships; at registration, honors students and varsity athletes pick their classes ahead of the rest of the university, scooping up the popular courses before they fill."[52]

Wilkes Honors College of Florida Atlantic University goes a step further than most honors colleges. Wilkes opened in 1999 on a separate campus in Jupiter, Florida, about forty miles from the main campus of Florida Atlantic University. In order to promote a student culture supporting its academic aspirations, Wilkes requires all of its unmarried students to live on campus in single rooms of modern suites. Wilkes provides a liberal arts education for a small student body taught in small classes by a small faculty. Here is how Wilkes describes itself for prospective applicants on its Web site:

A number of universities offer honors programs or honors colleges. But unlike the *honors options* at almost all of these other universities, at the Wilkes Honors College you are able to take all your classes within the Honors College, and your professors are faculty whose full-time appointments are to the Honors College: we provide an all-honors education at an all-honors college.

I visited Wilkes Honors College in 2007 and led a guest discussion with students in one class. The students were friendly, lively, intelligent—and they seemed to all know one another. The honors programs at public colleges and universities generate stratification despite a formal institutional commitment to equality. To be in an honors program is to be part of an elite group with rules and privileges separate from those governing ordinary students at the same institutions. Just as airlines sell first-class, business-class, and coach seats, each class with its own amenities, colleges treat honors students better than ordinary students. What is noteworthy about college stratification, though, is that honors students pay *less* rather than more for the privileges they receive; the merit scholarships they are often given constitute a substantial discount to full tuition and room and board.[53] Colleges believe that they *must* establish these bargain-priced honors programs in order to compete for excellent students with more prestigious and expensive private colleges and universities. In effect, they claim to provide all the educational benefits that private institutions offer at cut-rate prices. Not only a successful marketing ploy, honors colleges do provide excellent educations for their students. Ironically, the City University of New York, which nearly ruined CCNY with its notorious open admissions experiment, now has an outstanding honors college, Macaulay Honors College, whose students have an average SAT score of 1399, compared to 1132 in CUNY's eleven senior colleges.[54] In addition to free tuition—tuition is not free in the City University's colleges now—Macaulay students can receive up to $7,500 each year to study abroad or to defray living expenses during an unpaid internship.[55]

Even colleges of last resort need excellent students for their public relations. They do not want to be perceived as academically weak. National magazines like *U.S. News and World Report* rank colleges in accordance with the SAT scores and high school GPAs of the average entering freshman. College administrators deny the validity of these ratings. Nevertheless, they feel they must do well in the rankings or lose out in the competition for student applicants.[56] Whether the rankings are valid or not, parents, students, and faculty members pay attention to them. Rankings influence potential recruits to the faculty also. If higher-quality new faculty can be recruited, the reputation of the college is enhanced, which gets reflected in higher college rankings. The addition of a Nobel-prize winner to a faculty helps the attractiveness of a college to freshmen applicants even if his or her responsibilities are laboratory research and teaching graduate students, not teaching undergraduates. Academic excellence may be located in segregated enclaves: in certain departments, schools, programs, or in honors colleges separate from the main undergraduate teaching enterprise, but the perception of academic excellence is one basis for competing for students. Thus, colleges work both sides of the street: recruiting good students as well as underprepared students.

Claiming a concern for academic excellence is not just a marketing ploy. Oftentimes there is a genuine commitment to academic excellence on the part of most faculty members. However, in colleges where the student culture does not encourage students to try to learn much, where students do the minimum amount of work to pass, professors cannot demand much in the way of performance or even interest from undergraduates who are not enrolled in an honors program. Many professors teach such undergraduate classes with reduced enthusiasm. Or, if they are in a university, they try to avoid teaching undergraduates at all; they find it more enjoyable to teach graduate students who are more likely to share their values and interests.

Some professors, however, such as Professor Allitt, maintain enthusiasm for teaching undergraduates, deriving satisfaction from the handful of responsive, conscientious students in their classes. But it is not a simple matter to deal with a mix of students: one tier consisting of students who did well in grade school and high school and come to class with a zest for learning and another tier consisting of unprepared, half-asleep catatonics who drift in late and leave early. Should a dedicated teacher like Professor Allitt concentrate on his best students and ignore those who do not and perhaps cannot keep up? Or should he try to incorporate enough entertainment for students not interested in learning the course material so that they feel that taking the class is worthwhile? Most professors make compromises between the two alternatives. But the more the professor tries to be a popular entertainer, the less the best students have to study to get high grades on tests and an A in the course. Easy courses foster a belief among the engaged students that they are intellectually better than they actually are and feed their expectations of high grades in every course they take. Believing as they do that they *deserve* an A in every course, they are tempted to bring pressure on professors to give them A grades; student pressure is one factor in grade inflation, the subject of the next chapter.

CONCLUSION

The individual professor cannot avoid having underprepared students in his classes. They result from the admissions process. The professor can only evaluate student success or failure to learn what is taught. The admissions office too has limited options. The financial solvency of the institution depends on sufficient enrollment. At the same time that some colleges are desperate to fill their classes and dormitories, others, usually public institutions with relatively low tuition, are seriously overcrowded, because they happen to be located in states like Arizona and Nevada that receive massive in-migration.[57] To argue by analogy, American colleges are like American farmers and American business corporations; they expanded too much in good times and the overhead has become a burden.

In the modern era of higher education, fear of academic failure, a fear that used to persuade students with no great commitment to academic achievement to read assignments and to attend classes, is no longer credible, particularly in the less selective colleges. Financially weak colleges cannot afford to lose many students, even students who don't attend regularly, don't study, and don't do well on easy tests. Such colleges cannot afford massive remedial programs either, and their students don't clamor for such help; many are unaware of how little they know, and those who are aware don't think that their ignorance will be a career handicap. But even if colleges were financially able to engage in a greater emphasis on remedial courses, no evidence exists that they are effective.

Since many college students did not study diligently in high school because they did not think they had to in order to be admitted to college, they are not only unprepared intellectually for college, but they lack much interest in courses that they need to take in order to graduate. Most colleges can survive with a lower stratum of poorly prepared students who cannot learn much and who drop out in disproportionately large numbers, along with an upper tier of honors students—most of whom flourish. The National Assessment of Adult Literacy, given in 2003 by the Department of Education, found that the literacy of college graduates had declined over the past decade, especially for Hispanic college graduates. There were 26.4 million college graduates in 2003. Eight hundred thousand of these were unable to perform even the simplest verbal skills, like "locating easily identifiable information in short prose."[58] This is not an ideal situation from an educational standpoint.

Although colleges talk about "remediation" as though it addresses the problem of underprepared students, remediation programs may be an elaborate charade to disguise the reality that most underprepared students remain underprepared until they either drop out or graduate. What colleges do is to establish honors programs for their best students in which genuine higher education can take place. As for the underprepared students, colleges do not completely give up on them; they create courses that amuse them and extracurricular programs that please them.

I shall return to the issue of what kind of financial subsidies to poorly prepared students taxpayers *ought* to provide in Chapter 7.

NOTES

1. Sheila Schwartz, "Teaching's Unlettered Future," *New York Times*, August 6, 1998.

2. Rutgers, the State University of New Jersey, Office of Institutional Research and Academic Planning, *2002–2003 Rutgers Fact Book*, p. 1. Web site accessed in April 2009: http://oirap.rutgers.edu/instchar/factbook08.html

3. *Ibid.*, p. 35.

4. John Cloud, "Who's Ready for College?" *Time Magazine*, October 14, 2002.

5. Karen W. Arenson, "Classes Are Full at Catch-Up U." *New York Times*, May 31, 1998.

6. Alfonso A. Narvaez, "Basic Skills Tests Point Up Deficiencies in College Freshmen," *New York Times*, December 17, 1978.

7. Patrick Allitt, *I'm the Teacher, You're the Student: A Semester in the University Classroom*, Philadelphia: University of Pennsylvania Press, 2005. My review of the book was published in *Contemporary Sociology: A Journal of Reviews*, Vol. 34, No. 5, September 2005, pp. 459–461.

8. *Ibid.* pp. 84–86.

9. *Ibid.*, p. 150.

10. *Ibid.*, p. 222.

11. *Ibid.*, p. 219.

12. Professor X, "In the Basement of the Ivory Tower," *Atlantic*, June 2008.

13. For some data on the grade inflation problem at elite colleges, see Chris Hedges, "An A for Effort to Restore Meaning to the Grade," *New York Times*, May 6, 2004; Craig Lambert, "Desperately Seeking Summa," *Harvard Magazine*, May–June, 1993, pp. 36–40; Harvey C. Mansfield, "Grade Inflation; It's Time to Face the Facts," *Chronicle of Higher Education*, April 6, 2001, p. B24; Jackson Toby, "In the War against Grade Inflation, Dartmouth Scores a Hit," *Wall Street Journal*, September 8, 1994.

14. Raymond Hernandez, "Yale Student Pleads Not Guilty to a Fraud," *New York Times*, April 21, 1995.

15. Ronald Phipps, "College Remediation: What It Is, What It Costs, What's at Stake," Institute for Higher Education Policy: Washington D.C., 1998.

16. "Remedial Education at Degree-Granting Postsecondary Institutions in Fall 2000," National Center for Education Statistics, November 2005.

17. Rockefeller Philanthropy Advisors, Strong American Schools, "Diploma to Nowhere," Report issued on September 15, 2008, p. 7. See also Clifford Adelman, *Principal Indicators of Student Academic Histories in Postsecondary Education*, 1972–2000, United States Department of Education, January 2004. The full Adelman report, including a longitudinal follow-up of 1992 high school graduates was accessed in April 2009 at the following Web site: www.ed.gov/rschstat/research/pubs/prinindicat/prinindicat.pdf.

18. Ronald Phipps, op. cit.; U.S. Department of Education, National Center for Education Statistics, The Condition of Education 2004, *Remediation and Degree Completion*, Web site accessed in April 2009: http://nces.ed.gov/programs/coe/2004/pdf/18_2004.pdf

19. "Diploma to Nowhere" (note 17), p. 3.

20. *Ibid.*, p. 7.

21. *Ibid.*, p. 12.

22. *Ibid.*, p. 8.

23. Justin Pope, "Remediation Nation: Millions of College Students First Have to Catch Up on High School Work," Associated Press, September 14, 2008.

24. Vincent Tinto, *Leaving College: Rethinking the Causes and Cures of Student Attrition,* 2nd ed., Chicago: University of Chicago Press, 1993, p. 16.

25. James Traub, *City on a Hill: Testing the American Dream at City College,* Reading, MA: Addison-Wesley, 1994.

26. The SEEK program is described as follows on the official CCNY Web site: "The 'Search for Education, Elevation and Knowledge' (SEEK), is a program funded by New York State. It is a program designed to meet the needs of students who are considered to be economically disadvantaged and academically underprepared."

27. Traub, *op. cit.,* p. 18

28. *Ibid.*, p. 136.

29. *Ibid.*, p. 139.

30. *Ibid.*, p. 69.

31. *Ibid.*, p. 94.

32. *Ibid.*, p. 96.

33. *Ibid.* p. 67.

34. Jackson Toby, "Ill-Advised Guidelines Put Students at Disadvantage," *Star-Ledger,* October 10, 1993.

35. See Sam Dillon, "When Students Are in Flux, Schools Are in Crisis," *New York Times,* July 22, 2004.

36. Traub, *op. cit.* 79.

37. *Ibid.*, p. 106.

38. E. D. Hirsch, Jr., *Cultural Literacy: What Every American Needs to Know.* Boston: Houghton Mifflin, 1987; Adam Nicholson, "The Bible Tells Me So," *Wall Street Journal,* September 23, 2005, p. W13.

39. Russell Baker, "Is That Charles with a 'C'?" *New York Times,* January 24, 1995.

40. Karen W. Arenson, "CUNY Plans to Raise Its Admission Standards," *New York Times,* July 28, 2007.

41. Herbert G. Wells, *The Outline of History,* New York: Macmillan. 1921, Chapter 41.

42. Rachel Aviv, "Turning Life Experience into College Credit," *New York Times,* October 30, 2008.

43. *Ibid.*

44. Anthony DePalma, "When Students Try to Achieve Perfect Balance," *New York Times,* March 10, 1993.

45. Michael DeCourcy Hinds, "Taking U.F.O.'s for Credit, and for Real," *New York Times,* October 28, 1992.

46. The list is taken from Young America's Foundation, "The Dirty Dozen: America's Most Bizarre and Politically Correct College Courses," December 22, 2006.

47. Lewis Carroll, *The Annotated Alice: Alice's Adventures in Wonderland & Through the Looking Glass.* New York: Clarkson N. Potter, 1960, p. 269.

48. David Riesman, *On Higher Education: The Academic Enterprise in an Era of Rising Student Consumerism.* San Francisco: Jossey-Bass, 1980, especially Chapter 4, "College Marketing and Student Customers," pp. 105–161.

49. Edward B. Fiske, "The Marketing of the Colleges," *Atlantic,* October 1979, pp. 93–98.

50. Greg Winter, "Wooing of Guidance Counselors Is Raising Profiles and Eyebrows," *New York Times,* July 8, 2004.

51. Sam Hooper Samuels, "With Honors," *New York Times,* August 5, 2001; Karen Arenson, "CUNY Finds a Way to Lure the Brightest," *New York Times,* May 26, 2005.

52. *Ibid.*

53. William G Bowen and David J. Breneman, "Student Aid: Price Discount or Educational Investment?" *Brookings Review* 11(1), Winter 1993, p. 28–31.

54. Marc Santora, "A Brownstone Becomes an Ivory Tower, and New York City is the Campus," *New York Times,* September 7, 2008.

55. *Ibid.*

56. Alan Finder, "College Rating Race Roars on Despite Concerns," *New York Times,* August 17, 2007.

57. Alan Finder, "Sun Belt Growth Is Playing Out on Campus," *New York Times,* October 6, 2007.

58. Sam Dillon, "Literacy Falls for College Graduates, Testing Finds," *New York Times,* December 16, 2005.

Chapter 3

How Grade Inflation Undermines Academic Achievement

When students observe many professors giving equally high grades to mediocre performance and outstanding performance, it probably reduces their incentive to maximize effort in the courses that they take. Grade inflation was not always as common as it is nowadays. In order to put the phenomenon in perspective, consider grading in 1951 when I joined the Rutgers University faculty as a young assistant professor. I can cite the grade distribution from that era because I retained in my files a report dated June 1, 1955, that Rutgers prepared for the Middle States Commission on Institutions of Higher Education, the accrediting agency, on various academic activities. The report included the grade distribution at Rutgers College during the first semester of the 1954–1955 academic year. During that academic year, A grades constituted 10 percent of the final grades awarded to students in elementary courses at Rutgers College, Bs 25 percent, Cs 35 percent, Ds 14 percent, and Fs 8 percent.[1] The report separated the grades in elementary courses from grades in advanced courses, and I am reporting only the grades in elementary courses. The grades in advanced courses were higher, partly because the grades in the elementary courses included grades for freshmen who later dropped out of college, whereas the grades for the advanced courses included only juniors and seniors; these juniors and seniors may have been better students to begin with. In 1971, 52 percent of Rutgers grades were A or B in elementary courses, seventeen percent higher than grades for elementary courses in 1954; by 1991, the percentage climbed 15 points more to 67 percent.[2] Grades in the elementary courses show more clearly the extent of grade inflation, although grades in advanced courses rose also.

An informal consensus existed at that time between professors and students that C was an average grade and A was awarded for extraordinary accomplishment. The traditional grading system depended on different professors in most disciplines making essentially the same judgment of student performance when awarding grades. Professorial standards varied somewhat; some professors were considered "tough graders" and some "easy graders." Nevertheless, grades had approximately the same meaning to everyone. Grade inflation undermines that structure of common meanings and thereby encourages each professor to make idiosyncratic decisions about upward departures—or, much more rarely, downward departures—from the traditional interpretation of grades. When some professors give everyone or nearly everyone an A in their courses, students who enroll in a course taught by a professor old-fashioned enough to give Cs, Ds, and Fs are at a competitive disadvantage. Students in such a course receiving a C can ruin their averages and jeopardize their chances of getting into law or medical schools even though it does not mean what readers of the transcript may think it means. Consequently, although students were always motivated to prefer courses where the professor had a reputation for giving unusually high grades, grade inflation exacerbates this tendency. Due to grade inflation, many courses exist now where high grades are so automatic that, particularly for students planning to apply for admission to graduate or professional schools, the prudent decision is to select courses with good prospects for boosting their GPA. In a statistical study that will be discussed at length later in this chapter, Professor Valen Johnson demonstrated the impact of grade inflation at Duke University. One effect on undergraduates was to make them more likely to shop around for easy courses.[3]

During the 1960s the grade point average started moving upward at most colleges and universities, and since then it has continued to climb. Figure 3.1 shows grade inflation from 1991 to 2007, but it started much earlier, according to data on grade point averages collected by Professor Stuart Rojstaczer on a Web site devoted to grade inflation.[4] While grade inflation has been greater in private than in public colleges, it occurred in both categories, as Figure 3.1 shows.

In the most selective colleges and universities grade inflation brought grade point averages to greater heights than in relatively unselective ones, especially private colleges and universities. In 1966, Harvard awarded 22 percent of its grades in the A range and 50 percent in the B range; by 1991–1992, Harvard awarded 43 percent of grades in the A range and 48 percent in the B range.[5] And in 2005–2006, half of the grades awarded in Harvard College were A or A–.[6] Grade inflation continues to characterize not only selective colleges like Harvard but most, if not all, American colleges and universities, as Figure 3.1 shows.

Recent GPA Trends Nationwide

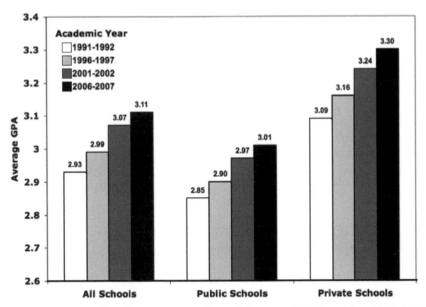

Figure 3.1.   Grade Inflation at American Colleges and Universities, 1991–2007 [www.gradeinflation.com, a Web site constructed and maintained by Professor Stuart Rojstaczer. Reprinted by permission.]

The impression that grade inflation is a problem only in the selective private colleges and universities is partly due to the fact that the public colleges and universities started with lower average grades in the 1960s than the private selective ones. Consequently, inflating grades did not bring them so conspicuously to the top of the grade distribution by the 1990s. A second reason for the impression that grade inflation has characterized only elite colleges like Harvard, Yale, Princeton, and Stanford is that they receive much more media attention than grade inflation at less expensive and less prestigious public schools.[7] The *New York Times* reported that about 90 percent of the grades at Stanford are As and Bs, that some elite colleges—Stanford, Brown, Oberlin—abolished the F grade altogether, and that Brown and Oberlin abolished the D grade for good measure. Brown went an extra mile to avoid negative reports about students on its transcripts, according to a story published in the *New York Times*.

> Brown University remains intent on making transcripts reflect only achievement. Any grade below a C does not appear on transcripts, and students are permitted to withdraw from classes at any point in the semester. Only 20 percent of a class, however, can graduate with honors.

"When you send in your resume, do you put down all the jobs you applied for that you didn't get?" said Sheila Blumstein, Brown's dean. "A Brown transcript is a record of a student's academic accomplishments."[8]

Dean Blumstein would have us believe that a transcript for a student who failed fifteen courses, was on disciplinary probation for drinking and drug infractions for several semesters, and took seven years to graduate should include only courses in which he or she received good grades. That generous attitude makes Brown transcripts virtually worthless for potential employing organizations or graduate schools if they seek to give the best opportunities to the best candidates. Students who behave responsibly while at Brown may not look better on paper than students who were a source of endless problems for teachers and administrators.

IS GRADE INFLATION REALLY OCCURRING, AND IF SO, DOES IT MATTER?

In spite of the statistical evidence showing that grade inflation progressed over the past half-century in American colleges and universities, some professors deny that it exists or, if it exists, that it has a detrimental effect on higher education. For example, Donald Kennedy, the former president of Stanford University, taught large undergraduate biology courses until 1977 and then returned to teaching in 1992. He argued that it is not grade inflation when Stanford students get higher grades than Stanford students used to get because they deserve their higher grades.

> Stanford undergraduates are significantly brighter and better-prepared than their 1977 counterparts. They work harder, and we expect more of them. If they are receiving B-plus as against their predecessors' C-plus, that is an improvement of about 10 points on a 100-point scale. So we should ask whether these students are 10 percentage points better. My time-lapse answer is "at least."[9]

Dr. Kennedy was reacting to a *New York Times* editorial on June 5, 1994, deploring grade inflation and praising Stanford University for restoring the F to the grading system. One of Dr. Kennedy's colleagues at Stanford, English professor Ronald Rebholz, was even more critical of the change. He wrote as follows in a letter to the editor of the *Times*:

> If, in a class of a reasonable size, I can't get achievement up to a level where students deserve a B or an A, I am a poor teacher . . . . Students know when they have failed . . . without needing it inscribed on a piece of paper.[10]

Professor Rebholz argued that love of learning should motivate students to study, not fear of failure. However, in a higher-education system so structured that students have no concern that they might fail or get lower grades than their classmates, would they be motivated to work as hard as they could to learn the course material? Perhaps a few might. The evidence suggests that the great majority would not. Consider the large number of college students—perhaps a majority—who do not keep up with their assignments until a test is scheduled and then "pull all-nighters" to study material that they should have been studying all along, even though this requires ingesting many cups of coffee or Benzedrine tablets in order to stay awake. Why would they subject themselves to what is clearly an unpleasant experience if they were not afraid of failing a test? Or consider the large number of college students who admit on anonymous surveys to cheating on tests, plagiarizing material for a required paper, or buying a paper from an online service that supplies custom-written papers.[11] Why would they engage in behavior that could result in being suspended or expelled unless they feared failure? Professor Rebholz is asserting a proposition that at least unconsciously he knows to be unrealistic.

The other argument—advanced by Professor Kennedy—is similarly flawed. If students are truly more prepared than a generation ago, and thus actually deserving of higher grades, then shouldn't their higher level of preparedness be reflected in higher SAT scores? The College Board publishes scores on Scholastic Aptitude Tests taken by high school seniors as part of their college applications over decades.[12] Average math SAT scores dipped for between 1967 and 1987 before rising until 2007, when they were about the same as average math scores in 1967. On the other hand, average critical reading SAT scores have declined steadily between 1967 and 2007, as shown in Figure 3.2.

Other studies confirm this decline. Recent data released by the National Assessment of Educational Progress in early 2007 showed that "the reading skills of 12th graders tested in 2005 were significantly worse than those of students in 1992, when a comparable test was first given, and essentially flat since students previously took the exam in 2002."[13] In view of these data, Professor Kennedy must exercise a leap of faith to believe that the rise in grades is simply a result of better students working harder. True, Professor Kennedy was referring to his experience at Stanford, which was always a very selective college, but might be even more selective now than it used to be. That is conceivable, but it is not plausible that the considerable increase in the number of A grades bestowed on Stanford students now can be explained by a modest increase in selectivity—and certainly not on greater studiousness on the part of contemporary students. (The next chapter will show that students at very selective colleges like Swarthmore and the University of Pennsylvania manage to "goof off" quite a bit, as students have always done.)

Average SAT Scores 1967-2008

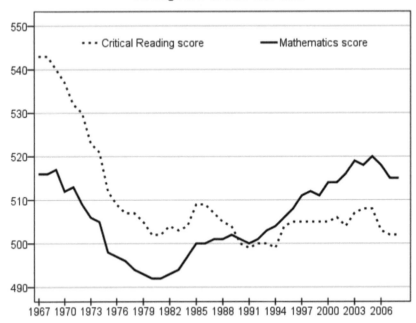

Figure 3.2. Average SAT Scores of College-bound High School Students, 1967–2008. [Thomas D. Snyder, Sally A. Dillow, and Charlene M. Hoffman, (2009). *Digest of Education Statistics 2008*, National Center for Education Statistics, Institute of Education Sciences, U.S. Department of Education, Washington, DC, March 2009, Table 142, p. 208.]

Other commentators admit that grades have gotten higher without student improvement, but do not think it problematic. They argue that it makes no difference if students now get Bs for levels of learning that would have received Cs in their parents' time because there is nothing sacred about the letters we use. As long as grades distinguish better from worse students, they say, grades can still provide meaningful evaluations. The flaw in this view is that the bunching up of grades at the A and B levels eliminates the distinction between good and outstanding. In other words, treating grade inflation as essentially harmless glosses over the disadvantages of grade "compression," the term coined by Professors Rosovsky and Hartley in a study of grade inflation for the American Academy of Arts & Sciences.[14] Grade compression refers to the tendency for student grades to cluster at the top of the distribution, thereby making it difficult to disentangle an average student who receives an A from a brilliant and hard-working student who receives an A. This prevents the best students in a class from receiving a clear communication from the professor that they are learning very well what they are supposed to be learning and for graduate schools and others looking at their transcripts from recognizing their real accomplishments. At the same time, grade inflation also prevents the worst students in the class from receiving a low or failing grade, which keeps them from realizing that the professor does not believe that they have learned what they should have. Grades are not simply rewards and punishments; they are communications between professors and students.

Grade inflation has had a different impact on different curricula. Some departments—business, computer science, engineering, biology (pre-med)—have more students than they can handle so that they are able to adhere, more or less, to traditional standards; those departments find it useful to give poor grades for poor performance in order to determine whom to accept as majors in their programs. Students can receive low grades and fail courses in those departments in appreciable numbers. Other departments fear that giving too many low grades will jeopardize their future enrollments; hence their budgets will suffer and they will not be authorized to recruit new faculty members or to promote to tenure existing junior faculty. In short, grade inflation protects some students who, compared with other students taking harder courses, are disproportionately penalized. Students who do only middling well in Computer Science usually realize that they are fighting a losing battle. Had they majored in Criminal Justice or Education, their overall college record might have been stronger.

The existence of different grading standards in different fields has a redeeming virtue. It informs students who initially make an inappropriate choice of major of their mistake. Students who receive failing grades in engineering or computer science do not necessarily leave school; some of them are reincarnated as journalism, history, sociology, or English majors. These are not necessarily weak students, only weak students in the curriculum they initially chose. That said, if journalism, history, sociology, or English courses award high grades to virtually everyone, then students who mistakenly chose those fields won't realize that there is a better fit for them in the math or physics programs. Of course, some of these reincarnated students *are* mediocre or lazy. The greater grade inflation in English or journalism makes it possible for mediocre students to get much better grades than they received in engineering or computer science and to graduate.

THE UNDERLYING CAUSES OF GRADE INFLATION

College faculties became more diverse in the second half of the twentieth century than they were in the eighteenth and nineteenth centuries. When faculties were small and socially homogenous—Jewish, black, and

even Italian professors were rarities—consensus on the meaning and purpose of grades was more readily achievable. Professors believed that it was
their responsibility to evaluate student performance clearly and honestly—
even when poor evaluations caused students pain. They felt that students
needed to discover early whether they were wasting their time and money
in college because they lacked either the intellectual ability or the motivation to learn enough to justify taking four years out of their lives. An A
would encourage the student to continue studying; he was learning what
he was supposed to be learning; a D or an F would tell him that he may be
in the wrong field or the wrong college. Or maybe a low grade told him
that he should stop fooling around and start studying. Society—including
parents—also needed grades. Was the expense of sending a student to college for four years likely to pay off? Shouldn't students justify the subsidy
to their sponsors? High grades suggested that the investment of parents,
governments, or the college itself was justified. Low grades suggested that
the student should quit school and take a full-time job. One possible reason that the consensus about the meaning of grades broke down is that
professors as well as students began to come increasingly from previously
disadvantaged economic, ethnic, and racial groups, and they carried with
them different ideologies.

The breakdown of the consensus about the meaning of grades became
apparent when some colleges tried to rein in grade inflation in the early
1990s. For example, in order to reduce the incentive to give inflated grades,
the Dartmouth faculty voted that the Registrar should start to include on
the student's transcript not only the grade in each class but the size of the
class and the median grade of all of its students. The rationale of the new
Dartmouth policy was to clarify the meaning of grades without compelling professors to change their previous grading practices. Some Dartmouth professors objected to the change in policy precisely because they
did not wish the comparative aspect of grades made clear. Dartmouth
physics professor Delo Mook told *The Dartmouth*, the student newspaper,
that this would "pit one student against another. I don't think [competi-
tion] is something we want to encourage."[15] Similarly, when the Stanford
Faculty Senate voted 37 to 3 to bring back a failing grade in 1995–1996—
although called NP for "not passed" instead of a more straightforward F—
three faculty members thought this action morally wrong.[16] The same
English professor whose letter to the editor of the *New York Times* I quoted
earlier was one of the three; he accused the Faculty Senate of falling into a
"punitive mode" that involved "branding students."[17] These professors
subscribed to an egalitarian ideology that overrode the view that grading
the academic performance of students is a responsibility of college professors, despite the unhappiness that students may feel over bad grades. Ide-

ology drives some college teachers into giving excessive numbers of As and Bs and never giving Fs. However, if student transcripts reveal that the modal grade in the class is A, as the Dartmouth approach now requires, their students might have been less pleased to receive an A, especially the better students who had mastered the material of the course.

Why do some professors have an ideological objection to failing students who have performed poorly? Some believe that students do the best they can or that fear of failure is an illegitimate pedagogical tactic or, pragmatically, that positive and negative sanctions (grades) do not constitute incentives for learning. They may be mistaken in their assumption that getting good or poor grades will not influence student effort. Incentives motivate even pigeons, as learning expert B. F. Skinner demonstrated.[18] But a college from which it is almost impossible to fail out does not give its students much incentive to meet appropriate intellectual standards. Even without *failing out* a high proportion of students, colleges that enroll students with little aptitude for intellectual achievement get low retention rates almost automatically because their students lose interest in attending classes that present material beyond their ability to comprehend. Giving short assignments and easy examinations does not solve this problem.

A poll of Stanford's undergraduates, taken in 1994 (the year in which the faculty had voted to reinstate the somewhat disguised failing grade) revealed that 48 percent of the student sample opposed the return of the possibility of failure against 40 percent who approved.[19] Were students even more ideologically egalitarian than the faculty? Perhaps. But another possibility is that the weaker students were voting their self-interest; possibly the more able and diligent students favored a tougher grading policy whereas the lazier and less able students preferred the status quo. The more able and diligent students at every college, not just at Stanford, may prefer that the grading system reward their achievements differently from their less able or less diligent peers. They do not shy away from competition for grades. Most students would agree that one reason for going to college instead of being educated at home is to find out how one compares with peers in ability to learn what is important for adults to know.

Actually, when the Stanford faculty Senate voted to reinstate the failing grade, which had been gone from the grading system since 1970 in the wake of student demonstrations, the issue was broader than the failing grade. The issue was restoring meaning to the transcript of Stanford undergraduate grades. Professor Gail Mahood, a geologist who was chair of the faculty committee that drafted the resolution mandating a variety of changes to be implemented in the 1995–1996 academic year, put it this way: "These changes send a strong message to students that we want them to take their intellectual lives at Stanford very seriously. If they're dropping classes just before the final exam, that's a sign of lack of seriousness." What Professor Mahood was referring to was a system by which Stanford students manipulated their transcripts so that transcripts appeared to show outstanding performance. Students did this by shopping around for classes and dropping those in which they did not expect top grades—even just before the final exam in the course. The result was that ninety percent of grades at Stanford had been As and Bs. Stanford regulations permitted students to take the same course again and again until they felt they were going to get the grade they wanted; no indication on their transcripts indicated what they had done. The *New York Times* journalist who covered the faculty senate decision explained that it went far beyond reinstating a failing grade:

> Beginning in the 1995–96 academic year, students who drop classes between the fifth and eighth weeks of a quarter will have a W placed on their transcripts to mark the withdrawal. Students who are still in courses after that point will be in them for keeps, with the prospect of a failing grade if they do poorly. The changes will also bar students from retaking a course more than once, and all repeated courses will be recorded as such on transcripts.[20]

The faculty Senate had voted overwhelmingly—37 to 3—to attempt to restore honesty to Stanford transcripts; many students were not pleased. "We've lost the freedom for academic exploration, which I think is the central mission of the University," said one student. The new president of Stanford, Gerhard Casper, *was* pleased. "To fail in some endeavor is something we all go through, and it is not unseemly to remind people that it also happens in a university. Unless you dare something and admit that you may fail, you are living in an illusionary world, and that is not something that should be part of the notion of an education." Nevertheless, President Casper, who had been Dean of the University of Chicago Law School before coming to Stanford, was not optimistic that the new policy would curb grade inflation, which he attributed at least in part to student efforts to manipulate their transcripts. "Students are very transcript-conscious. Anyone who has ever sat on a law school admissions committee knows that."[21]

Students are on both sides of the grade-inflation issue. On the one hand, they recognize intellectually that grade inflation erodes the incentive to work hard for an A, and they sometimes decry "grade inflation" in letters to the editor of student newspapers as lowering the value of their degrees. On the other hand, they care so much about grades for themselves that, in their daily behavior, they promote grade inflation by being unwilling to accept the grades their professors give them. They want high grades because they believe that their futures depend on getting high grades. If they wish to apply to professional or graduate schools after receiving a bachelor's degree, which is increasingly the case, especially in selective colleges, they calculate—correctly—that the higher their grade point averages, the better their chances for admissions, fellowships, and scholarships, although federal financial aid would not be affected. Since their futures are at stake, grades are not a trivial issue. Anxiety about their futures underlies the pressure many students put on their professors to give them higher grades than their professors think that they deserve as well as the illegitimate tactics some students employ to get better grades, such as cheating on exams or submitting plagiarized papers. Numerous professors have complained about student preoccupation with "making the grade" over the past half century.[22]

When professors decry this pressure from students to give high grades and lament the rarity of students interested in learning for its own sake rather than for grades, they underestimate the anxiety of many students that without good grades, they will be unable to find a job that will permit them to maintain a middle-class style of life. True, they can study harder and more consistently. However, even for those who have done their best, given their level of previous preparation, they are often dissatisfied with the resulting grade. In the short run, begging or demanding a higher grade is another option.

Those students who feel that they *need* the highest grades they can get are tempted to put pressure on their teachers. Sometimes the pressure is anonymous. The following was an anonymous note slipped under my office door after I posted the grades in my criminology course several semesters ago: "How can you justify giving 13 A's in a class with over 200 people. You are just an old fucking asshole. I could have had a 4.0 for three straight semesters . . . . Burn in hell." At the bottom of the note was a drawing of a middle finger raised in an obscene gesture. The author of the note felt *entitled* to an A, whether he deserved it or not.

A great deal of student pressure is not anonymous; it is confrontational. Here is an example from an article in the official journal of the American Association of University Professors:

A young man we know received a "C" on a term paper that he thought deserved an "A." Like many a disgruntled student, he went to see his professor, but instead of arguing the merits of his paper, he badgered and cajoled her. He used her first name as if to say, "come on, we're friends: give me a break," and when that didn't work, he threatened to show the paper to another professor. No doubt there were several reasons why the student thought his approach would work, but we believe that the professor's status was one of the most important. The student knew that the professor was an adjunct. He probably hoped that because she had no job security and could ill afford unfavorable teaching evaluations, she would be vulnerable to his pressures. But whatever the student's reasoning was, we suspect that incidents like this are becoming increasingly common, and it is not as easy as one might think to know what professors who find themselves in such situations should do.[23]

A journalism professor at Tufts wrote an article in the *Boston Globe* decrying the pressure a student brought to bear on him for a B grade.

The student deserved a B-minus. Maybe even a C-plus, I had decided. One paper was especially weak; another was late. But then I began to rationalize. The student had been generally prepared and contributed to class discussion, so I relented and gave what I thought was a very generous B. At least I wouldn't get a complaint about this grade, I figured. Then came the e-mail. "Why such a 'low grade'?" the indignant student wrote.[24]

Students press for A grades for several reasons. First, they are competing with other students for excellent transcripts of their grades to send to graduate or professional schools and they know that other students are coercing professors, often successfully, for high grades. In the more selective schools, students are more likely to seek graduate school or professional school admission. That is probably why grade inflation is more rampant at Harvard and Stanford than at all but the most selective state universities like the University of California at Berkeley. Second, students have already learned from their experiences in primary and secondary schools about the existence of grade inflation and about the possibility of pressuring teachers to ratchet up a lower grade to a higher grade. These experiences foster a sense of entitlement. Secondary school teachers report that the parents of some students call and send e-mails complaining about the grades assigned—unjustly, of course—to their children. The Association for Supervision and Curriculum Development, a nonprofit organization dealing with educational issues, devoted a blog in the fall of 2008 to the issue of grade inflation. Here is what one sixth grade teacher wrote in response to a published article about grade inflation in college about combined student and parent pressure for high grades:

The sense of entitlement that the author mentions begins at an early age. As a 6th grade teacher, I see it with my students. They expect to get an A on everything and are disappointed when they do not. They rarely take into account the fact that their efforts do not match their expectations. This is being reinforced by parents who also expect A's and will fight and complain also without looking at the effort their child is making. An A stands for excellence, yet it has become a mark of participation. When I started teaching in my town, and I live here and have children in the middle and elementary schools, a colleague explained to me how grades work here. If they pass they get an A, and if they fail they get a B. Teachers are inflating grades rather than dealing with parents who may be at best unrealistic and at worst irate over grades.[25]

Another teacher posted in her blog that she felt like tearing her hair out every time she gets a call from a parent saying she would like to "discuss" a score assigned to a paper that her child submitted.

Why are teachers and professors susceptible to student pressure? For several reasons. Besides normal human sympathy, self-interested motives tempt professors to give high grades to students whom they don't believe deserve them. Young professors without tenure fear that giving low grades will result in poor student evaluations that could jeopardize their promotions. Anonymous student evaluations at the end of a course are now almost universal in undergraduate colleges. Students who want high grades and fear that they may not get them are not dispassionate observers of their teachers. When students receive lower grades than they would like, they may prefer to believe that the professor is not a good teacher rather than that they themselves did not perform adequately in the course; they can retaliate on the course evaluations. Poor course evaluations may influence department decisions for tenure and promotion.[26] Furthermore, professors with a reputation for being "tough graders" find that many students avoid their courses. Thus, prudential considerations tempt some professors to give higher grades than they feel students deserve, as Professor Allitt did. It is also very easy to rationalize. After all, everyone else is giving high grades, why should I jeopardize the employment prospects of students in my class by not giving them inflated grades? Given an ambiguous situation, where the only guidance is one's own standards about the appropriate distribution of grades, student pressure is difficult to resist.

Another motive for professors to give higher grades to students than professors think they deserve is to avoid unpleasant hassles with disgruntled students. Giving high grades leads to fewer confrontations in which students insist that they deserve a higher grade or that, deserve it or not, they need a higher grade in order to remain in school or to graduate. About six years ago I felt compelled to give a grade of F to a student who had failed the midterm and the final exam in my spring criminology class. After submitting my grades to the Registrar in May, I left for a short vacation at the New Jersey shore. I took my laptop with me in order to check my e-mail. I soon received an e-mail from this student, pleading with me to change the F grade to a D. He explained that he was a graduating senior and that relatives were coming long distances to attend his graduation. Luckily, I had records of the grades in this large criminology class on my laptop, and although I had not met this student personally, I was able to find out how badly he had done. I replied by e-mail, explaining that I was sorry about interfering with his graduation but that I did not have a basis for changing his grade. He wrote back an anguished email, redoubling his pleas and offering to write a paper. I replied that it was much too late to give him the opportunity to write a paper but that I had fuller records of the course in my office and that I would be returning to New Brunswick in a day or two and would see whether there was some basis for changing his grade to a D. When I returned, I consulted the attendance records. Perhaps, if he had been faithful in attending the class—I required students to sign in on class rosters—I could justify giving him a D. When I checked the attendance rosters, I found to my surprise that, although he had taken the midterm and the final exam, he had *never* attended the lectures at all! Not even on the first day when I explained the requirements of the course. I wrote what I thought would be a final e-mail, pointing out that in view of his attendance record, I had no basis for changing the grade. I said that I could not understand his behavior. How had he expected to pass the course without attending classes? What was he doing when he was supposed to be at lectures? Why didn't he come to see me when he failed the midterm? He tried once more to beg for a D. He explained in another e-mail that he was an Administration of Justice major and that he had believed that he knew the material in the criminology course from the courses he had already taken in his major. I stood firm and refused to change the F to a D. But I pointed out in my final e-mail reply that he could retake criminology in the Rutgers Summer Session—with a different instructor— and, upon passing it, would graduate later in the year. In *his* final e-mail message he said that he had enrolled in the Summer Session criminology course. His last words were, "I don't need your help." He didn't. He passed the course in the summer. I did not inquire about his attendance.

THE CONSEQUENCES OF GRADE INFLATION

I have pointed out that grade inflation (1) confuses students about where their strengths and weaknesses really lie, (2) prevents graduate and professional schools from readily distinguishing brilliant college graduates unequivocally deserving of the opportunity for professional training from more pedestrian graduates with equally high grades and (3) gives employing organizations a more difficult task distinguishing the best prospects among job candidates.

The consequences for faculty are also noteworthy. Suppose that students reciprocate the high grades they receive by awarding higher evaluations to faculty members who give or are expected to give high grades to them, and suppose that promotion decisions are influenced by this input from students. Then the best scholars and the best teachers may be disadvantaged in competition for tenure and promotions. If this is true, grade inflation not only diminishes student achievement; it can diminish faculty excellence also.

Is there empirical evidence on some of these issues, or must we rely only on speculation? Fortunately, Dr. Valen Johnson, a Duke University professor of statistics and decision sciences, conducted a rigorous empirical study of the consequences of grade inflation on undergraduate behavior at Duke University during the academic year 1998–1999. Professor Johnson, a fellow of the American Statistical Association, published his analysis of survey data collected under the aegis of a Duke faculty committee that wanted to study grade inflation at Duke.[27] The study dealt only with the behavior of *Duke* undergraduates, but it is reasonable to assume that undergraduates at Duke responded to grades in pretty much the same way as students at other selective colleges would have responded.

What were Professor Johnson's conclusions? First, and perhaps most important, students gave, on the average, higher ratings to instructors who had or probably would have given them high grades. (Since these were instructors whom the *same* student rated in comparison with different instructors in both the same and in different departments, Professor Johnson concluded that the higher ratings were probably due to student satisfaction with teachers who would give them high grades, deserved or not.) Professor Johnson's second conclusion was that students tended to take courses where they knew or suspected it was easier to get a high grade than in courses where hard work was necessary and the results uncertain. Again, this is an unsurprising conclusion, but keep in mind that there is a difference between suspecting that something is true and *knowing* that it is true. Professor Johnson said, "Differences in grading practices have a substantial impact on student enrollments, and cause fewer students to enroll in those fields that grade more stringently."[28]

What this means is that grade inflation is a factor in the growth and decline of departments within a college or university. If students perceive the grading to be more difficult in chemistry, physics, and math than in geology, sociology, or criminal justice, they are less likely to enroll in the more difficult subjects for a single course—or to choose them as a major. When enrollment falls in a department, it does not have an immediate effect on the number of faculty in the department if a majority of the faculty is tenured, but ultimately, budget and faculty lines are allocated in response to student demand. Meanwhile, professors in departments with declining enrollments do not need a weatherman to see which way the wind is blowing. They redouble efforts to attract students: redesigning courses, adding interesting slide shows to their lectures, and giving higher grades. Professor Johnson could not expect to draw such unflattering conclusions about student motivations from direct questions like, "Why did you enroll in this course?" And perhaps most students were not even consciously aware that grading had such a strong influence on their course choices. What he had to do was to infer motivation from aggregate data.

Consider how the planning and executions of his study—called the Duke University Evaluate Teaching (DUET) experiment—contributed to its validity. The dean of the college sent personalized letters to all full-time undergraduates asking for their participation in a survey designed to study the feasibility of collecting course evaluation data over the Web. The students were told that their individual responses would not be accessible either to their current instructors, to other members of the faculty, to other students, or to university administrators. Here are five of the thirty-eight questionnaire items asked of students who agreed to participate in the experimental survey about a course they were taking or had taken:

20. How was this course graded?
    1) very leniently
    2) more leniently than average
    3) about average
    4) more severely than average
    5) very severely
    6) not applicable
22. What grade do you expect (or did you get) in this class?
    1) A+
    2) A
    3) A–
    4) B+
    5) B
    6) B–
    7) C+
    8) C
    9) C–
    10) D+/D/D–
    11) F
    12) not applicable

23. How much did your knowledge of how the course would be graded positively affect your decision to enroll in it?
    1) no effect or negative effect
    2) slight effect
    3) moderate effect
    4) significant effect
    5) very significant effect
    6) not applicable
34. How good was the instructor(s) at communicating course material?
    1) very bad
    2) bad
    3) fair
    4) good
    5) very good
    6) excellent
    7) not applicable
37. Would you take another course from this instructor?
    1) yes
    2) no
    3) not applicable

Temptation requires tempters. Who does the tempting and why? Professor Johnson's research throws light on this issue. He demonstrated that responsibility for grade inflation does not lie with individual professors alone; some departments graded much more leniently than others. Taking the transcripts of the approximately 15,000 students who enrolled at Duke between 1995 and 1999 and were still enrolled in 1999, he compared the grades each student received in courses taken in the departments in which they majored and in courses taken outside of their major departments. Biology, chemistry, economics, mathematics, and physics majors received *higher* grades in courses taken outside of their major departments than in courses in their majors. Students majoring in all other departments, such as sociology, history, English, and French, received *lower* grades in courses taken outside of their major departments than in courses in their majors. Professor Johnson concluded that professors in the biology, chemistry, economics, mathematics, and physics departments graded more stringently. Even if the student who majored in biology, chemistry, economics, mathematics, and physics were intellectually more proficient *initially* than students who majored in other fields, comparing grades that students received in their majors with grades outside of their majors took care of this potentially confounding variable. (Studies at other universities confirmed that students who majored in fields where the grading was more stringent were indeed intellectually *more* proficient initially than students who majored in other fields.) Nevertheless, weaker Duke students tended to get higher grades than their more able peers because they chose to major in departments with easier grading practices. Professor Johnson did not explain why these systematic differences between departments occurred. His data did not permit such an explanation since his survey was conducted among students, not professors.

The desire of some students to take easy courses instead of difficult ones is not the only student motivation in selecting courses or majors. Students who wish to become engineers will enroll in the engineering curriculum even if they know that the courses will be difficult. Students who wish to become lawyers will take political science courses. Students who plan to become physicians or dentists or veterinarians will major in one of the biological sciences. But if grade inflation has an appreciable impact on enrollments, as Professor Johnson's research appears to demonstrate, it gives some departments larger faculties than they would have if the course choices of students were not being influenced by the effects of grade inflation.

One might argue that permitting student interest to influence course offerings and the size of departments is desirable. Let the market for educational services determine what services the colleges provide. But a market-driven student choice between Coca-Cola and Pepsi Cola is different from a market-driven student choice between chemistry and black studies. Society subsidizes higher education. These subsidies from taxpayers, parents, and college endowments are justified by benefits not only to students but to American society. The implicit contract that Duke students made when they enrolled is that they take some courses they may find difficult or boring because the representatives of society, the faculty, regard chemical literacy, for example, as important. When students give way to the temptation that grade inflation offers them—to take the easier courses regardless of educational benefits—they violate the contract. Of course, this excellent study was conducted at one university—Duke—and a highly selective one at that. At less selective colleges, which by definition enroll students of lesser intellectual abilities, choosing to take more difficult courses and major in more difficult curricula would be more challenging for such students—and perhaps unrealistic.

The bulk of American undergraduates matriculate at relatively *unselective* public colleges. Grade inflation has been greater at selective private colleges than at unselective public ones, perhaps partly because a higher proportion of students at selective colleges plan to attend graduate or professional schools than do students at unselective colleges. This might suggest that Professor Johnson's findings at Duke would apply less strongly to unselective colleges. On the other hand, the fact that a school is unselective does not mean that it does not have excellent students who could have been admitted to selective schools. Students choose schools for many reasons—geographic location, financial constraints, climate, or friends or relatives who go to a school. In short, some excellent students at unselective colleges want to attend graduate and professional schools just as students at selective schools do, and they may be even more concerned with getting high grades, coming from colleges with mediocre reputations. In addition, the unselective colleges contain students so deficient in academic skills that easy courses in easy majors are almost obligatory for them if they are to pass enough courses to graduate; they need easy courses more than Duke students do. Thus, the conclusions about student preferences for easy courses in easy majors based on data collected about grade inflation at Duke University would probably be supported by similar studies at most other American colleges.

Professor Emeritus of Religion at Hamline University in St. Paul, Minnesota, Walter Benjamin, wrote about a demanding freshman English teacher, Dr. Doris Garey, whose course he had taken in 1946, in an article entitled "When an 'A' Meant Something." Professor Benjamin praised the memory of Dr. Garey and expressed gratitude for what her demanding standards had taught him.

> Even though she had a bachelor's degree from Mount Holyoke and a doctorate from Wisconsin, Miss Garey was the low person in the department pecking order. And physically she was a lightweight—she could not have stood more than 4-foot-10 or weighed more than 100 pounds. But she had the pedagogical mass of a Sumo wrestler. Her literary expectations were stratospheric; she was the academic equivalent of my boot camp drill instructor . . . .
>
> The showboats had long since faded, along with their banter, jokes and easy grades. It was the no-nonsense Miss Garey whose memory endured.[29]

Karl Borden, professor of finance at the University of Nebraska, commented in a letter to the editor that such a teacher with high expectations and rigorous standards would not survive in today's colleges and universities; half the students would drop her course before the end of the semester, and those that remained would give her poor evaluations on the anonymous forms filled out at one of the last meetings.

> Whether her annual contract would be continued to the point of a formal tenure review (four to five years into her career) is questionable, but without strong student evaluations it is extremely unlikely

that she would survive the tenure process. Her colleagues and depart-
mental administrators would doubtless insist they are fully in support of rigorous standards, and that student evaluations are only one
of many sources of data considered by the tenure review process. But
in practice a professor with consistently poor student evaluations
and a reputation such as Miss Garey's would have little chance of
success.[30]

Government professor Harvey Mansfield considers the problem of
grade inflation serious and devised a playful way to criticize it:

> This term I decided to experiment with the grading of my political-
> philosophy course at Harvard. I am giving each student two grades:
> one for the registrar and the public record, and the other in private.
> The official grades will conform with Harvard's inflated distribution,
> in which one-fourth of all grades given to undergraduates are now
> A's, and another fourth are A–'s. The private grades, from the course
> assistants and me, will be less flattering. Those grades will give stu-
> dents a realistic, useful assessment of how well they did and where
> they stand in relation to others.[31]

Professor Mansfield's method of shaming his colleagues and ridiculing the
tendency for grades to lose all meaning because of grade inflation received
mostly favorable media attention. A few colleges and universities have
attempted to deal with the problem, as Dartmouth has, by providing not
only the grade of the individual student but the grade distribution in the
class where the grade was received. Yet no one claims that the problem has
been solved. An extremely pessimistic report on grade inflation by the
American Council of Trustees and Alumni has not been refuted.[32]

CONCLUSION

It is difficult to estimate precisely the burdens that grade inflation places
on American higher education. True, grade inflation distorts the selection
process by which undergraduates choose teachers and courses and thereby
indirectly results in greater popularity of some disciplines than they
deserve on educational grounds. True also, grade inflation distorts the
process by which teachers evaluate student learning and the complementary process by which students assess the teaching skills of their professors.
What is unclear, however, is the extent to which these distortions constitute a crisis in undergraduate education, as Professor Johnson believes.
The subtitle of Professor Johnson's book on grade inflation, "A Crisis in

College Education," suggests that the burdens grade inflation imposes on higher education are very, very heavy. Here is how he put it on the last page of his research report:

> Current assessment practices are flawed, and both students and faculty know it. Unregulated grading practices change student enrollment patterns and penalize students who pursue demanding curricula. They permit students to manipulate their GPAs through the judicious choice of their classes rather than through the moderation of their performances in those classes. Disparities in grading also affect the way students complete end-of-course evaluation forms, and so result in inequitable faculty assessments. As a consequence, academic standards are diminished.[33]

His pessimistic view is that grade inflation is undermining the very foundations of higher education. Conceivably, he exaggerates the problem. Grade inflation may be merely a nuisance, causing some confusion but permitting undergraduate education to be conducted pretty much as it would be conducted in the absence of grade inflation. He is correct that high grades have become less meaningful than they used to be. Is it still possible to distinguish college graduates who have obtained a first-rate education from those who have simply gone through the motions? Perhaps, with difficulty. More ambiguity is present in the evaluation process than there used to be when grades were more meaningful and when letters of recommendation could be taken at face value. What is worse is that, unless incentives and disincentives mean nothing, grade inflation probably undermines the motivation of able students to do their best and learn as much as they can.

NOTES

1. Unpublished report, pp. 42, 44.

2. These data come from an unpublished internal Rutgers document dated November 4, 1971, on the distribution of final grades at Rutgers College for the spring semester of the 1970–1971 academic year.

3. Valen E. Johnson, *Grade Inflation: A Crisis in College Education*, New York: Springer, 2003.

4. Professor Stuart Rojstaczer started the Web site www.gradeinflation.com when he was on the faculty of Duke University.

5. Craig Lambert, "Desperately Seeking Summa," *Harvard Magazine*, May–June 1993, p. 37.

6. Brittney L. Moraski, "Report: Grade Inflation Persists," *Harvard Crimson*, May 9, 2007.

7. Chris Hedges, "An A for Effort to Restore Meaning to the Grade," *New York Times*, May 6, 2004; Alison Schneider, "At Harvard, a Veteran of the Grade-Inflation Wars Launches a Guerrilla Offensive," *New York Times*, February 6, 2001; Stuart Rojstaczer, "Where All Grades Are Above Average," *Washington Post*, January 28, 2003.

8. Davidson Goldin, "In a Change of Policy, and Heart, Colleges Join Fight against Inflated Grades," *New York Times*, July 4, 1995.

9. Donald Kennedy, "What Grade Inflation?" New York *Times*, June 13, 1994.

10. Ronald A. Rebholz, Letter to the Editor, *New York Times*, June 12, 1994.

11. Charles McGrath, "Outsourcing Homework: At $9.95 a Page, You Expected Poetry?" *New York Times*, September 10, 2006.

12. College Board SAT, 2008 College-Bound seniors: Total group profile report. Web site accessed in July 2009: http://professionals.collegeboard.com/profdownload/ Total_Group_Report.pdf

13. Diana Jean Schemo, "Grades Rise, but Reading Skills Do Not," *New York Times*,: February 23, 2007.

14. Henry Rosovsky and Matthew Hartley, *Evaluation and the Academy: Are We Doing the Right Thing? Grade Inflation and Letters of Recommendation*, Occasional Paper of the American Academy of Arts & Sciences, Cambridge, MA: 2002, p. 16.

15. "Truth in Grades, Dartmouth Style," *New York Times*, August 24, 1994.

16. "Failing Grades Are Restored at Stanford University," *New York Times*, June 3, 1994.

17. David Margolick, "Stanford U. Decides to Make Courses Harder to Drop but Easier to Fail," *New York Times*, June 4, 1994.

18. B. F. Skinner, "'Superstition' in the Pigeon," *Journal of Experimental Psychology*, 38, 168–172.

19. Margolick, *op. cit.*

20. *Ibid.*

21. *Ibid.*

22. Howard S. Becker, Blanche Geer, and Everett Hughes, *Making the Grade: the Academic Side of College Life*, New York: John Wiley, 1968; Helen Lefkowitz Horowitz, *Campus Life: Undergraduate Cultures from the End of the Eighteenth Century to the Present*, Chicago: University of Chicago Press, 1987.

23. David Foster and Edith Foster, "It's a Buyer's Market: 'Disposable Professors,' Grade Inflation, and Other Problems," *Academe*, January–February, 1998, p. 29.

24. Phil Primack, "Doesn't Anybody Get a C Anymore?" *Boston Globe*, October 5, 2008.

25. ASCD Community Blog, post by Dave, "InService," Comments Section, October 14, 2008. Accessed in July 2009: http://ascd.typepad.com/blog/2008/10/ grade-inflation.html#comment-135559227

26. Randal C. Archibold, "Give Me an 'A' or Else," *New York Times*, May 24, 1998.

27. Johnson, *op. cit.*

28. *Ibid.*, p. 237.

29. Walter W. Benjamin, "When an 'A' Meant Something," *Wall Street Journal*, December 3, 1997.

30. Karl Borden, "Teachers Must Dance to Students' Tune," *The Wall Street Journal*, December 16, 1997.

31. Harvey C. Mansfield, "Grade Inflation: It's Time to Face the Facts," *Chronicle of Higher Education*, April 6, 2001.

32. George C. Leef, "Degraded Currency: The Problem of Grade Inflation," American Council of Trustees and Alumni, October 2003

33. Johnson, *op. cit.* p. 200.

Chapter 4

GOOFING OFF AT COLLEGE

Pope John XXIII, when asked how many people work at the Vatican, is reported to have answered, "About half." That may sound like a cynical papal evaluation of the commitment to their calling by members of religious orders; after all, they took vows of poverty and chastity and do not have responsibility for an immediate family. It would not be cynical, however, if a *college president* replied "About half" to the question, "How many students at your college take seriously the work of acquiring knowledge?" Many faculty members would think one-quarter closer to the mark. Yet that same college president would be delighted to report a six-year "retention rate" of 90 percent or more, as Harvard, Yale, Princeton, Williams, and Dartmouth do, meaning that at least nine out of ten of the freshmen who started six years earlier persisted to the point of graduation at these highly selective private institutions. He would probably consider a "retention rate" of 70 percent or less a black mark against his college, a sign that more remedial efforts are necessary. Although the meaning of retention rates is far from unambiguous, they vary considerably from college to college. Table 4.1 shows the four-year graduation rate and the six-year graduate rate for the cohort of students entering four-year public and private colleges with more than 5,000 students. I include the four-year graduation rate in this table because four years used to be the expected length of time for undergraduates to obtain a bachelor's degree. Nowadays, however, undergraduates interrupt their educations so commonly that it is more realistic to present data for six-year graduation rates, which is how they are presented in most official education reports.

Consider the contrast between Harvard and Yale, with four-year graduation rates of at least 87 percent and six-year graduation rates of more than 90 percent, and Chicago State University with a four-year-graduation rate

Table 4.1

Graduation Rates of Four-Year Public and Private Colleges, 2006–2007

Private Schools with the Highest Graduation Rate,* 2007		
	Four-Year Rate	**Six-Year Rate**
Florida College	100%	100%
Chester College of New England	100%	100%
MedCentral College of Nursing	100%	100%
Baker College of Cadillac	100%	100%
Charles Drew University of Medicine and Science	97%	97%
Williams College	91%	95%
Carleton College	91%	93%
Swarthmore College	91%	94%
Princeton University	89%	95%
Art Center College of Design	88%	94%
Harvard University	88%	97%
Vassar College	88%	93%
Cleveland Institute of Music	88%	95%
Yale University	87%	96%
Babson College	87%	89%
Dartmouth College	87%	93%
University of Pennsylvania	87%	95%
Washington and Lee University	87%	89%
Pomona College	86%	94%
Northwestern University	86%	93%
Brandeis University	86%	89%
Mount Holyoke College	86%	89%
Bucknell University	86%	89%
Haverford College	86%	91%
Claremont McKenna College	85%	89%

of 4 percent and a six-year graduation rate of 16 percent. Do nearly all the students at Yale and Harvard study conscientiously, learn a lot, and consequently deserve a prestigious Ivy League degree? True, Ivy League colleges are extremely selective; 22,769 high school graduates applied for admission to the class of 2009 at Harvard, including 3,200 valedictorians in their high schools and over 12,750 with combined scores on their SATs of 1400 or more.[1] (There is room for only about 1,500 freshmen.) However, some students at Harvard, like students at other colleges, flounder in the four years following admission, experience identity crises, suffer from depression and other psychiatric illnesses, and even kill themselves.[2] If Ivy League students, like students in other colleges, experience problems that adversely affect their academic performance, how can the high retention rate of selective

Table 4.1 (*continued*)

Public Schools with the Highest Graduation Rate,* 2007		
	Four-Year Rate	Six-Year Rate
College of William and Mary	84%	91%
University of Virginia–Main Campus	84%	93%
United States Naval Academy	82%	82%
United States Military Academy	80%	81%
United States Coast Guard Academy	78%	81%
St Mary's College of Maryland	75%	83%
University of North Carolina at Chapel Hill	71%	83%
University of Michigan–Ann Arbor	70%	88%
The College of New Jersey	68%	83%
University of Mary Washington	68%	76%
Miami University–Oxford	67%	80%
University of California–Los Angeles	66%	90%
United States Merchant Marine Academy	66%	79%
James Madison University	65%	81%
University of Delaware	64%	78%
University of Illinois at Urbana–Champaign	63%	82%
Maine Maritime Academy	63%	64%
SUNY at Geneseo	63%	79%
SUNY at Binghamton	62%	77%
University of California–Berkeley	61%	88%
University of New Hampshire–Main Campus	59%	74%
Citadel Military College of South Carolina	59%	65%
University of Maryland–College Park	58%	80%
Pennsylvania State University–Main Campus	58%	84%
University of California–San Diego	56%	84%

continued

colleges be explained? Perhaps because of their students' reluctance to give up a prized achievement: admission to these prestigious colleges. No matter how unhappy or unmotivated they become, leaving a selective college without graduating is a comedown. An additional explanation may be the benevolence of Ivy League professors and administrators, illustrated so forcefully at Stanford in the previous chapter. Despite rumors of unbearable academic pressure, Harvard, like Stanford, is extremely generous in grading students. By the academic year 2000–2001, 48.5 percent of Harvard grades were As and A-minuses, compared with 33.2 percent of grades in 1985. Grades in the three C categories fell from 10 percent in 1985 to 4.9 percent the 2000–2001 academic year; Ds and failing grades accounted for less than 1 percent each.[3] In short, it is very difficult to get into Harvard, but, once in, considerable leeway is given for poor performance.[4]

Table 4.1 (*continued*)

Private Non-Profit Schools with the Lowest Graduation Rate,* 2007

	Four-Year Rate	Six-Year Rate
Northeastern University	1%	66%
Pratt Institute–Main	1%	1%
Universidad Del Turabo	1%	15%
David N Myers University	2%	21%
Universidad Metropolitana	2%	17%
Universidad Del Este	2%	16%
College of Visual Arts	3%	40%
American University of Puerto Rico	3%	19%
Wilmington University	4%	35%
Heritage University	4%	13%
Alaska Pacific University	5%	35%
Gallaudet University	5%	25%
National–Louis University	5%	12%
Bellevue University	5%	17%
Universidad Politecnica de Puerto Rico	5%	18%
Kettering University	6%	56%
East–West University	7%	9%
Clarkson College	7%	9%
Long Island University–Brooklyn Campus	7%	20%
Mountain State University	7%	12%
Caribbean University–Bayamon	7%	40%
Unity College	8%	41%
Caribbean University–Carolina	8%	38%
Southeastern Bible College	9%	22%
Mitchell College	9%	9%

As for the *low* graduation rates of some colleges, it is unlikely that they result from the severity of the faculty in insisting on high standards. Their grade distributions are not distinctive. As in high-retention colleges, grades are skewed toward the high end of the distribution. Whatever it is that motivates students to drop out or to transfer to other colleges, it is probably not the onerousness of grading policies. More likely, competition from the large number of colleges in the Chicago metropolitan area explains a high transfer rate for Chicago State University and other colleges in that metropolitan area.

WHY DO STUDENTS ENROLL IN COLLEGE?

To get back to the question of how many students take seriously the work of acquiring knowledge, bear in mind that education is not necessarily a college student's first priority. Few freshmen are motivated predominantly

Table 4.1 (*continued*)

Public Schools with the Lowest Graduation Rate,* 2007		
	Four-Year Rate	Six-Year Rate
United States Air Force Academy	1%	77%
Northeastern Illinois University	2%	19%
Purdue University–North Central Campus	2%	13%
University of Maryland–University College	2%	4%
University of Houston–Downtown	2%	16%
University of Alaska Southeast	3%	15%
Southern University at New Orleans	3%	8%
Bemidji State University	3%	50%
West Virginia University at Parkersburg	3%	20%
University of Puerto Rico–Utuado	3%	16%
Macon State College	4%	14%
Idaho State University	4%	20%
Chicago State University	4%	16%
Purdue University–Calumet Campus	4%	20%
University of Maine at Augusta	4%	10%
SUNY College of Technology at Delhi	4%	36%
The University of Texas at Brownsville	4%	16%
The University of Texas at El Paso	4%	29%
West Virginia State University	4%	25%
California State University–Dominguez Hills	5%	28%
University of the District of Columbia	5%	17%
Indiana University/Purdue University–Fort Wayne	5%	23%
Western New Mexico University	5%	14%
CUNY Medgar Evers College	5%	10%
Ohio University–Southern Campus	5%	11%

Source: United States Department of Education, National Center for Education Statistics, Integrated Postsecondary Education Data System. http://nces.ed.gov/IPEDS/.
* Graduation tables are derived from the colleges that supplied graduation data for the 2006–2007 academic year to the IPEDS data system.

by intellectual curiosity and come for the liberal education that colleges such as the undergraduate college at the University of Chicago, Reed College, and St. John's of Annapolis offer. A large proportion—probably the majority—seek opportunities for business and professional careers; they go to college to avoid low paying, uninteresting jobs. They believe, correctly, that most of the better jobs require a college degree. Consequently, more or less grudgingly, they fulfill the requirements for the degree. A majority of high school graduates enroll in college; in the fall of 2007, 68.3 percent of female and 66.1 percent of male high school graduates enrolled at either two-year or four-year colleges.[5]

Since obtaining an education is only one of their motives, a convenient schedule may be more important than the content of a particular course. And even after having selected classes that meet at convenient times, a sizable minority cuts a fifth of their classes or more; and many arrive ten or fifteen minutes late.[6] Whatever the reasons, legitimate and illegitimate, for cutting classes and tardiness, academic work suffers. This may be an explanation for a growing phenomenon: students taking far longer to graduate from college than the "normal" four years, while some never graduate at all. Longitudinal studies of high school graduates show that dropout rates are high not only in the first year but throughout college.[7] In 1977, 45.4 percent of American undergraduates received a bachelor's degree within four years or less; by 1986 it was down to 34.5 percent; and by 1990, it fell to 31.1 percent, with more students graduating in six or more years than in four or fewer.[8] In 2003, the number of four-year graduates rose slightly to 34 percent.[9] The administrators of public colleges, where tuition covers a smaller portion of the costs of each student than in private colleges, are concerned that students meander through college for six or more years.[10]

The image of students flunking out of low-retention colleges by failing too many courses or by not maintaining a high enough GPA distorts the circumstances underlying dropping out of college without graduating. Sometimes students fail courses for no apparent reason beyond neglect and disinterest, sometimes as a result of drug and alcohol habits, psychiatric and physical illness, failed love affairs, identity crises, incompatible roommates, or full-time employment. Colleges vary in the extent to which academic symptoms of nonfulfillment of academic obligations results in separation. In private colleges with poor academic reputations, financing is often precarious. Consequently committees on academic standing dare not flunk out very many of the small number of students who fail or the larger number of students who shirk their academic obligations so blatantly as to bring themselves to the attention of deans for persistent low grades. In such colleges, being asked to leave for academic reasons is little more than official recognition of the student's desire to give up on a college education for personal reasons. Formally, a few students still are asked to leave "for academic reasons" in most colleges, but student "failures" are almost always active collaborators in their own terminations. In practice, academic standards are flexible; students who fail have ignored multiple opportunities to make up for inadequate performance.

Because tuition and other college expenses cost as much as they do, about two-thirds of college students at four-year institutions report spending over the academic year at least some time during a typical week working for pay.[11] Nearly one-third of them report working for pay 16 hours or more during a typical week, more than the 27.3 percent report spending 16 hours or more studying or doing homework. It is not known what proportion of these working students work because they *must* in order to finance tuition and room and board costs and what proportion work mainly to finance expensive designer clothing and various recreational activities, including iPods and cell phones. Certainly a visitor to an American college campus does not get the impression that students are just scraping by. They appear affluent. But the sources of their luxuries are unclear. And while it is true that some students take unpaid or low-paying internships during summer vacations from college and some take adventurous foreign trips, other students take summer jobs at which they work very, very hard to help with college expenses.[12]

Unlike students who work for pay during the academic year, where they must submit to employer supervision, students who do not take paid jobs have a great deal of freedom. Although they are supposed to study, they are not *compelled* to study. Moreover, if they live in campus dormitories or in off-campus housing rather than commuting from home, they do not have parents supervising their comings and goings. American college students were never subjected to the rigorous discipline administered to recruits at the Marine boot camp at Parris Island. Yet before the campus rebellions of the 1960s, most colleges supervised not only classroom behavior, such as attendance, but also student life, including behavior in the dormitories. Administrators and deans, if not professors, believed that they were acting in place of parents. However, according to a former senior professor and dean at Yale and Princeton, student life changed in the 1960s and 1970s.[13] The doctrine of *in loco parentis* was discarded in the 1960s and 1970s in deference to student rights. Nowadays, those students who do not live at home with their parents are free of most external constraints. No one will interfere if a student invites a member of the opposite sex—or the same sex—to sleep with him in his dormitory room. If a female student wishes to party on a Thursday evening, get drunk, and sleep through her Friday classes, nothing except her own conscience prevents her from doing so. Consequently, many students pursue "fun" relentlessly during the academic year.

HAVING FUN AT COLLEGE

The pursuit of fun includes uninhibited expression of profane language, especially by student fans at athletic events.

CBS sportscaster Billy Packer recounted to a reporter how, calling a University of Maryland vs. Duke basketball game, he found himself drowned out by a chorus of foul-mouthed kids . . . . Mr. Packer was later told that the school was loath to impinge upon the First Amendment by policing students' language. Soon such language was ritualized into obscene chants . . . . A small army of Maryland students could be heard shouting "F— you, J. J.!" at Duke guard J. J. Redick. The audio wasn't the only problem—the network's cameramen had trouble steering away from the obscene (and remarkably legible) T-shirts in the stands.[14]

Pleas do not seem to alleviate the problem. Neither do appeals to consider the reputation of the college. Some student fans apparently believe that the freedom to express themselves is unlimited at athletic events.

Hockey fans are among the worst offenders. At University of Michigan games, fans cheer "See ya, m—— f——r" as opponents enter the penalty box. . . . When the University of Denver plays archrival Colorado College, fans routinely chant "CC sucks!" Cornell fans . . . at a recent game in New Haven . . . chanted "BU sucks, BU sucks, BU sucks . . . and so does Yale."

The Algonquin Roundtable this is not.

College basketball has its share of louts as well . . . Duke's [fans] . . . once taunted Maryland's Herman Veal, who had been accused of sexually assaulting another student, by tossing women's underwear and inflated condoms onto the court. One sign in the student section read: "Hey Herm, Did You Send Her Flowers Afterward?"[15]

The balance between the pursuit of education and the pursuit of fun varies from college to college. Students in the selective colleges and universities are less likely to goof off than in unselective institutions for at least two reasons. First, the selective colleges admit high-achieving high school graduates, the bulk of whom have the *ability* to meet high standards of academic performance. Second, a large proportion of their students are not content merely to graduate; they intend to pursue graduate work in academic disciplines or in professional schools. Since they know that professional schools are selective and that it is important to learn as much as possible to prepare for aptitude exams and establish an impressive undergraduate record, they are motivated to meet the standards of their professors. Despite these two favorable conditions, some students are not necessarily *motivated* to meet professorial standards at selective colleges. And when students in an undergraduate course are not motivated to do their reading assignments, whether it is a selective college or not, their professor can do little about it. Theoretically he could flunk half the class. In practice, however, the professor would fail only a few of them. (Failing half of the students in a class would be a public-relations disaster for the professor.) Thus, even in selective colleges, standards depend on what students are willing to learn as well as on what professors believe they *ought* to learn. The students in a class and the professor set the standards of academic performance by an implicit process of collective negotiation.

In the unselective colleges there is an additional complication: some students are so badly underprepared for college-level work that they *cannot* perform well even if they were motivated to do so. Here the negotiation process is affected by professorial resignation to the limitations of their clientele. Furthermore, some professors have ideological objections to failing students who have performed very poorly. Some believe that positive and negative sanctions (grades) do not work. Although unselective colleges have a higher proportion of underprepared students than the selective colleges, even moderately selective and highly selective colleges contain underprepared students—some of them deliberately admitted for nonacademic reasons.

Students recruited because of their athletic prowess constitute one conspicuous group of academic underperformers, especially football and basketball players. Initially they need lower academic qualifications in order to gain admission, although the National Collegiate Athletic Association attempts to set minimum standards for playing eligibility as well as for athletic scholarships. Sometimes these reasonable standards are evaded by high school athletes who present credentials from diploma mills that are not scrutinized carefully enough by college officials responsible for admissions.[16] Especially in such cases, they neglect their studies because, having been chosen for physical prowess rather than intellectual potentialities, they find their courses difficult to master. They have been given preference in admission decisions like members of ethnic and racial minorities, although in class they must now compete with normal-admit students. They are strongly tempted to work at the sport at which they win success and popularity rather than to work at studies in which they are on the edge of comparative failure. In addition, the physical demands of practice and travel to and from games make it more difficult for athletes, regardless of their academic potentialities, to keep up with their studies compared to nonathletes, although it should be recognized that students who work twenty or thirty hours a week to help finance their education are in a similar situation. Adding to these objective handicaps of athletes is a subjective one: the goal of some varsity football and basketball players is not college graduation, or going to professional schools, or learning enough at college to get a job in a business organization. They hope—unrealistically in most cases—to be selected for a professional basketball or football team with the big money that this implies. This is also true, albeit to a lesser extent, among baseball, tennis, and golf athletes.

Are members of varsity athletic teams expected to adhere to the same academic standards as ordinary students? In most colleges they are, at least theoretically, but they are beneficiaries of special dispensations. Coaches have access to funds with which to provide academic advisors who perform two roles. One is to make available tutoring and other academic support services to pressure and help athletes to perform as well as they can in their courses. Another is to guide them in selecting undemanding courses in which performance is largely irrelevant. When athletes in major sports have no real interest in learning, they may cut classes and not read the books assigned for the courses they are taking. They don't do well academically, yet they are prestigious members of the campus community; their exploits and their photographs are in the student newspaper and even in general-circulation newspapers. Insofar as they are role models, their presence on campus may undermine the prestige of students who take their studies more seriously.

Grade inflation usually saves fun-seekers—as well as other academic underperformers—from being forced to leave college. In order to fail, a student has to work hard at defying academic norms. Not attending classes is usually not enough, because many professors have stopped taking attendance and those who do rarely use attendance as a basis for grading. In addition to online services that offer for a fee custom-written papers that students can buy and hand in to their professors, most colleges have local note-taking services whereby students can buy notes taken by academically excellent students hired by the services to attend courses and make detailed notes. Thus, students can obtain the material from the lectures without attending them.[17] Not taking any tests, including the final exam in the course, and not handing in required papers, may do it.

If students come to college to have fun, many colleges have provided features that enable them to do so in style. The University of Houston, for example, offers hot tubs, waterfalls, and pool slides, a five-story climbing wall, and a new $53 million Wellness Center.[18] Other colleges offer equally lavish amenities:

> Students now get massages, pedicures and manicures at the University of Wisconsin in Oshkosh, while Washington State University boasts of having the largest Jacuzzi on the West Coast. It holds 53 people.
>
> Play one of 52 golf courses from around the world on the room-sized golf simulators at Indiana University of Pennsylvania—which use real balls and clubs.
>
> Only about 100 miles away, Pennsylvania State University's student center has two ballrooms, three art galleries, a movie theater

with surround sound and a 200-gallon tropical ecosystem with newts and salamanders. Oh, and a separate 550-gallon salt-water aquarium with a live coral reef.[19]

Anecdotal accounts as well as some statistical data show that students spend a great deal of time on having fun, which usually includes consuming large amounts of alcohol. For a significant proportion of students, "partying"—a euphemism for long weekends of continuous alcohol consumption and occasional recreational drug use—competes successfully with academic obligations. Some colleges have nation-wide reputations as "party schools." *The Princeton Review* named Ohio State University in 2006 as the sixth best party school in the United States, whereas *U.S. News and World Report* rated Ohio State as 110th on its list of the top 124 universities in America.[20] Partying is ubiquitous at colleges, even at selective colleges with deserved reputations for academic seriousness. A 1994 graduate of the University of Pennsylvania's Wharton School wrote the following comment about partying in a letter to the *New York Times:*

> To understand the severity of this problem, all you have to do is walk by a fraternity party at an average college campus. Partying starts on Thursday—and you must understand that partying and getting drunk are synonymous to a college student. The answer to "What did you do last night?" that is most likely to get someone to smile and pat you on the back is, "Oh man, I got so drunk."[21]

A surprisingly large proportion of students play drinking games such as "beer pong," where the game involves lobbing ping-pong balls across a table into mugs of beer. "It's awesome," said Chris Shannon, 22, a senior at Drexel University. "If you win, you win. If you lose, you drink. There's no negative." Drinking games have been around since Dionysus. But a whole new industry has taken off around them, making the games more popular, more intense and more dangerous according to college administrators, who say the games are just thin cover for binge drinking.[22] Each year, college students spend $5.5 billion on alcohol (mostly beer). This is more than they spend on books, soda, coffee, juice, and milk combined.

Some students, underage or not, while away many hours consuming alcohol or doing drugs with friends or alone. Alcohol and drug abuse has been a continuing problem on most college campuses. For example, in 1997 Michigan State University reported 633 alcohol-related arrests; the University of Minnesota–Twin Cities reported 555; the University of California at Berkeley reported 460; Western Michigan University reported 401; and the University of Wisconsin at Madison reported 342.[23] More recently a freshman died in his room at a fraternity house at all-male Wabash College after solitary binge drinking.[24]

The Harvard School of Public Health conducted rigorous statistical studies of alcohol consumption among a random sample of 14,000 college students in 1993, 1997, and 1999 financed by the Robert Wood Johnson Foundation; 128 nationally representative four-year colleges in 39 states and the District of Columbia participated in the studies.[25] The studies found that between fifteen and twenty percent of all students in the three sample years abstained from alcohol use completely in the year previous to the study—with a somewhat higher rate of abstention in religious colleges. The studies disregarded the abstainers and focused mainly on *binge drinking,* defined by the principal author and his colleagues to describe a style of consuming five or more drinks in a row for men and four or more for women, at least once in the two weeks preceding the surveys, although the surveys threw light onto other matters, like the proportion of students who drank moderately and at least one question about illegal drugs. The researchers asked on their questionnaires why the binge drinkers adopted this style of alcohol consumption. In response to a question asking whether *getting drunk* was their motivation for drinking, those students who responded *very important, important,* or *somewhat important,* as opposed to *not important,* were considered to have a drinking style of "drinking to get drunk." Two notable findings about binge drinking among college students were (1) how large a proportion of college students reported themselves binging on alcohol (more than 40 percent of students in the surveys) and (2) how many of the bingers did it to get drunk (about half the male bingers and even 40 percent of the female bingers).

Some findings were not surprising. More binge drinking occurred among students living in fraternity or sorority houses than in other living arrangements, more among males rather than among females, more among students who binged in high school than among students who didn't, more among younger students than among older students, and more among single than married students. Some findings *were* surprising. The prevalence of binge drinking among white students was twice as great as the prevalence among black students. Although there were some unsurprising and surprising differences in the prevalence of binge drinking, what was remarkable was that binge drinking was fairly widespread; moreover, about a third of all male students who drank had been drunk at least three times in the month prior to the survey as were about a fifth of all female students who drank. One might have expected that the most selective colleges would have the lowest prevalence of binge drinkers, enrolling as they did a high proportion of excellent students aiming for graduate and professional schools. Surprisingly, the competitive, very competitive, and highly competitive colleges had similar prevalence rates and markedly higher rates than those of the noncompetitive schools. Perhaps this was due to a higher proportion of commuter schools among the noncompetitive schools, and commuter schools had lower rates, probably because the students lived at home under parental supervision. Nevertheless, a great deal of self-destructive drinking behavior occurs among American college students at almost all colleges, including religiously oriented ones and highly selective ones, although students are aware that they engage in risky behavior when they are "wasted." What alcohol-related problems resulted from excessive drinking?

When the samples were divided into occasional binge drinkers—those who binged only one or two times in the two weeks preceding the surveys—and frequent binge drinkers—those who binged three times or more in that time frame, the frequent binge drinkers reported more problems: missing a class, falling behind in school work, doing something they regretted, arguing with friends, engaging in unplanned sexual activities and not using a condom, damaging property, getting in trouble with the campus or local police, getting personally injured, drunk driving, and requiring medical treatment for an alcohol overdose. Of the frequent bingers, 57 percent drove vehicles while drunk, and 54 percent were so drunk that they could not remember where they had been or what they had done while binging. In addition to the problems that their binging behavior created for themselves, secondhand binge effects were experienced by nonbinge drinkers and abstainers who happened to live in the same dormitories or fraternity or sorority residences with the bingers: being interrupted while studying or being awakened at night (58%), having to take care of a drunken fellow student (50%), and being insulted or humiliated (29%). About 77 percent of the nonbinge drinkers and abstainers experienced at least one secondhand effect.

Consider only the 11,160 college student drinkers—that is, ignore abstainers. Among college student drinkers, about 45 percent did not binge and were probably mostly moderate drinkers, although some of them may have gotten drunk occasionally. For example, parties, including tailgate parties at intercollegiate football games, involve for *most* students who go to them moderate alcohol consumption. The Harvard–Yale game between these traditional rivals attracts older alumni as well as current students to tailgating parties. Some attendees, however, drank not wisely but too well. On November 19, 2005, 28 young people were taken to hospitals for alcohol poisoning from parking fields around the Yale Bowl during and after the annual Harvard–Yale football game.[26] College football games on many college campuses entail convivial tailgate parties before the game starts where at least some students consume amounts of alcohol excessive enough to require medical attention.

Moderate student drinkers notwithstanding, a majority of the student drinkers in the Harvard survey were binge drinkers, either occasional binge drinkers (2,962) or frequent bingers (3,135). It is difficult to comprehend how these frequent binge drinkers could have gotten much intellectual education out of their college attendance. Different researchers used the data from the Harvard School of Public Health College Alcohol Study to throw light on other misbehavior of American college students, for example, the small percentage who used ecstasy, an illegal drug.[27]

The alcohol-related problems of students sometimes bring them to the attention of campus or local police. Whether students are arrested or are subjected to internal disciplinary procedures depends partly on the degree of outrageousness of alcohol-related behavior and partly on college policies. Princeton students developed two traditions that institutionalize alcoholic revelry. One tradition is [Paul] Newman's Day, in which students aim to consume twenty-four beers in twenty-four hours, which sometimes requires them to come to class drunk and to bring beer to class in coffee mugs. Actor Paul Newman had nothing to do with attaching his name to this Princeton tradition and, as a newspaper article indicates, objected to this use of his name.[28] Another Princeton tradition, the Nude Olympics, began in the streaking days of the 1970s. Every year sophomores and often other students drank large quantities of alcohol, removed all their clothes, and ran naked around a particular campus quadrangle at midnight after the first snow. However, in January 1999 the event included some of the 350 revelers throwing bottles as well as visibly urinating and engaging in public sexual activities; ten students were hospitalized with severe alcohol poisoning.[29] The University president, Harold T. Shapiro, appointed a committee of faculty members and students to "prevent a tragedy before it happens." The result was that the Nude Olympics was subsequently banned—although the ban bitterly disappointed some students.

When the priority of students who come to college is having fun, they are more likely to get into personal difficulties than students having a clear academic objective from the start. The result is that colleges have to implement programs to deal with alcohol abuse, drug abuse, sexually transmitted diseases, and crime. Crime? Not just high-spirited incivility but theft, assault, robbery, and forcible rape. Although crime rates have fallen over the past decade, crime rates are far higher than they were in the 1930s, 1940s, or 1950s, and college students reflect that reality.[30] In addition, colleges now place greater emphasis than they used to on admitting youngsters from poverty backgrounds who were exposed to high community crime rates during their formative years, both as victims and perpetrators. Partly as a result of these changes, colleges now need and have sizable police forces. In addition, more students behave inappropriately because of mental illness. Professor Gerald Armada, who has codirected the mental health program at the City College of San Francisco, has studied managing student misbehavior on college campuses, including classrooms. He believes that over the past several decades student misbehavior has become an increasingly serious problem.[31] Students and former students with mental health issues do not usually pose a threat to students or to faculty, only a distraction. But some lethal events have occurred, as the mass murders at Virginia Tech showed.[32]

National data on the growth of college police forces are not readily available. However, it seems likely that the growing police presence at the university where I taught for fifty years is typical. In 1951, the year I joined the faculty, Rutgers, the State University of New Jersey, had no police force. Like other colleges and universities, Rutgers relied on municipal police to deal with occasional burglaries, thefts, and assaults and to handle traffic problems at special events. A few deans were sufficient to cope with student misbehavior, including academic dishonesty. Although there were hearings, they were perfunctory by today's standards. Now the flagship New Brunswick campus of Rutgers University has a police force to deal with crime, including drug selling and under-age alcohol use in the dormitories and the neighborhoods in which the campus is located, as well as with crowd control, automobile accidents, and traffic problems. The Rutgers police are genuine police with police training and the authority to make arrests. They carry guns and arrest not only *student* offenders but also nonstudents trespassing on Rutgers property and nonstudents who commit crimes in Rutgers buildings or in the general area of the University. The Rutgers police force on the New Brunswick campus alone is larger than the forces of many municipalities, consisting of 58 officers, most of whom are assigned to specific geographic areas but five of whom are detectives assigned to investigate open criminal cases. In addition the Rutgers Police Department employs eighty-two full-time, unarmed, uniformed students to patrol the campus and twenty-five unarmed community service officers to provide parking enforcement for university lots, man stationary security posts, operate an after-hours escort service, and help maintain order at athletic and other special events.[33]

A student arrested for a crime by the Rutgers police must face not only the New Jersey criminal justice system but also internal charges that can lead to separation from the University. An Office of Student Judicial Affairs organizes formal hearings that can last several days. Charges are categorized by degree of seriousness and level of penalties that can be imposed. Outside lawyers are hired to serve as hearing officers. These procedures are fairer than the disciplinary procedures of former years, but they are also more time-consuming and more costly. Complex intramural judicial processes are now the rule at most colleges and universities. American colleges and universities have expanded student-life administrative positions as well as police positions to cope with student misbehavior.

When American students participate in junior year abroad programs in foreign colleges and universities, their fun expectations often clash with the expectations of the colleges they attend. Apparently the casual misbehavior of American students is exported to foreign colleges and universities through "study abroad" programs, which for many students are better labeled "partying abroad."[34] About 160,000 American students participate in these study-abroad programs every academic year. Originally intended to provide opportunities for students with a serious interest in the language or the culture of a foreign country, they lost this academic rationale, especially for English-speaking destinations like England and Australia. The unfortunate result was boorish behavior. Some Americans students in Amsterdam threw trash out of their dorm-room windows on passers-by on the street below. Other American students in Spain got into a knife-and-stick fight with local youths. Still others disappeared from classrooms for weeks to look for more interesting party scenes. "'I had two students in Asia who decided that they would drop beer bottles on passing cars,' said Joseph L. Brockington, associate provost for international programs at Kalamazoo College in Michigan."[35] Colleges have attempted to tighten controls on students taking study-abroad programs. One method, adopted by Middlebury College in Vermont, is to place all the grades students earn overseas on their transcripts. David Macey, director of off-campus study at Middlebury, believes that this measure "will eliminate the student who goes to Australia and just hangs out on the beach and drinks beer."[36] Partying is an obvious repudiation of studying. Not only is the time spent partying not used for studying, but the party goers are often incapacitated the following day, either sleeping most of the day or recovering from hangovers. American students who study abroad for their entire four years of higher education—now a fairly common practice—tend to be more serious students, but with a drinking age of 18 in the United Kingdom and Ireland, for example, they spend considerable time in pubs while enrolled in English, Irish, and Scottish universities.[37]

Other extracurricular activities, although worthy in themselves, sometimes absorb so much time and energy as to crowd out the educational activities for which students supposedly are enrolled. Dan Ronnen, the former editor-in-chief of the Rutgers student newspaper, *The Daily Targum*, decided on the eve of graduation that he had learned a lot during his college years but that his out-of-class learning experiences provided more of his education than formal classes. He argued that most Rutgers students had subordinated academic opportunities to volunteering for worthy community service activities or other extracurricular activities. Ronnen wrote in *The Daily Targum* as follows:

> I would venture to guess the percentage of students who do go to class, who do take notes and who do keep up in their reading are a small minority . . . [S]tudents have used their extracurricular activities, not just to round out their education, but they have made it [sic] their primary teacher. That's not the reason we're paying several thousand dollars a year to be at this university.[38]

The next question ought to be this: how is it possible for students to spend most of their four years working on the student newspaper, playing basketball, or just socializing with friends and still graduate? The answer seems to be: because there are enough undemanding courses in all colleges but especially in the unselective ones so that undergraduate students don't have to study diligently if they don't wish to. Some wish to because they plan to continue into law school, medical school, or graduate school. For the rest, no strong incentive pressures them to study diligently rather than to pursue nonacademic activities that attract them more. Is there anything wrong with the choice Mr. Ronnen made to neglect classes in order to devote a great deal of effort to the college newspaper or to heavy commitments by other students to theater productions, sports teams, music groups, and other extracurricular activities? Certainly, such activities are educational in a broad sense, although they may not provide the intellectual tools students will need in the actual careers they pursue after college. However, parents, governments, foundations, and the colleges themselves are providing funds for the *intellectual* education of students. The word, "*extra*curricular," suggests that these activities should be undertaken in addition to curricular pursuits, not instead of them.

In view of the fact that some of these extracurricular activities facilitate careers in journalism, radio and television, the theater, professional sports, and so on, it may perhaps be justifiable for colleges to provide easy courses that enable students like Mr. Ronnen to devote themselves single-mindedly to their extracurricular interests. But the idea that students are sent to college so that they can major in *fun* for four years—or more—is clearly a use of higher education that adult society did not have in mind. Johnny Lechner, a 29-year-old student in his twelfth year as a pursuer of fun at the University of Wisconsin-Whitewater campus in 2005, is unusual in the length of time he has spent avoiding serious study.[39] He has accumulated $30,000 worth of student loans during his college career. Although Mr. Lechner may be unique in lingering in college to pursue adolescent fun long after most of his peers have launched adult careers, some students do take a long time to graduate, sometimes for legitimate reasons—for instance, family problems or economic circumstances that compel them to withdraw temporarily to earn money to apply to educational expenses. Mr. Lechner does not, however, hold the record for length of time spent at college. Former U.S. Secretary of Education Margaret Spellings (2005–2008) reported in the article about Mr. Lechner that she had found a student who had been enrolled in college for 17 years.[40]

Length of time in college notwithstanding, clearly the academic curriculum on most campuses must compete with a culture of frivolity, as newspaper accounts reveal. Here is how one college athlete enjoyed himself during four years at college:

> I went to a large state school—the University of Illinois—and during my time there, I became one of the best two or three football players in the Land of Lincoln. I learned to pass deftly between my rigid players, to play the corners, to strike the ball like a cobra would strike something a cobra would want to strike. I also mastered the dart game called Cricket, and the billiards contest called Nine-ball. I became expert at whiffle ball, at backyard archery, and at a sport we invented that involved one person tossing roasted chickens from a balcony to a group of us waiting below. We got to eat the parts that didn't land on the patio.[41]

The author of this paragraph seemed to be saying that he chose freely to squander his academic opportunities at college and that athletes can still be conscientious students. For some college athletes this is true. One of my own former students, a varsity soccer player at Rutgers and for a year a player on professional soccer teams, was nevertheless an excellent student, did well in law school, and has a very successful legal career.[42] However, being a serious student may not be possible for the most professionalized college sports anymore. Professor Michael Oriard, who played football at Notre Dame in the 1960s and later was a professional football player for the NFL, specializes in the cultural history of football. He insists that today major sports like football and basketball make time and energy demands on players that are incompatible with being a diligent college student.[43] If Professor Oriard is correct, soccer, golf, swimming, wrestling, and other minor sports may provide athletes with room for academic achievement but not the two most prestigious sports on college campuses.

Students can get the opportunity for an informal major in fun at college by taking an untaxing class schedule or by changing majors in order to prolong a leisurely stay at college. Mr. Lechner meandered through four majors—education, communications, theater, and women's studies, accumulating 242 credits, more than twice the 120 required for graduation—

without concentrating in any field sufficiently to fulfill its graduation requirements.[44] Like Mr. Lechner, other students linger on the campus, although not usually for such a long time, because they regard college as a time for fun or for broad personal development and because the undemanding lifestyle suits them. According to the Higher Education Research Institute at the University of California at Los Angeles, 42.2 percent of college juniors say that they spend sixteen hours a week or more socializing with friends in addition to the 8.9 percent who say they spend sixteen hours a week or more "partying."[45] Others play computer games or download music from the Internet. A student at Swarthmore, one of the most selective colleges in the United States, reports that some of his classmates spend a lot of time looking at computer screens, though they are not necessarily doing traditional academic work:

> I have friends who have spent whole weekends doing nothing but playing Quake or Warcraft or other interactive computer games. One friend sometimes spends entire evenings—six to eight hours—scouring the Web for images and modifying them just to have a new background on his computer desktop.
>
> And many others I know have amassed overwhelming collections of music on their computers. It's the searching and finding that they seem to enjoy: some of them have more music files on their computers than they could play in months.[46]

From this Swarthmore student's description it is understandable why even some bright students perform academically less well than they could; surfing the Internet and playing computer games leave them little time for studying or writing papers.[47] Worth mentioning also are college students who spend a great deal of time and money playing poker online. One 19-year-old Lehigh University sophomore—class president, chaplain's assistant, son of a Baptist minister—lost $7,500 in a year of frantic gambling in 2006. Desperate, he held up a local bank and was arrested.[48]

The mention of "public sex" in the *New York Times* account of the Nude Olympics at Princeton sounds unusual. However, casual sex is not unusual on most college campuses; it is a recreational activity. "Hooking up," as it is called, means casual sex without commitment on either side. A *New York Times* reporter interviewed a professor who had studied "hooking up" and dating. What she told him about her research surprised him. "It turns out that everything is the opposite of what I remember. Under the old model, you dated a few times and, if you really liked the person, you might consider having sex. Under the new model, you hook up a few times and, if you really like the person, you might consider going on a date."[49] The Independent Women's Forum conducted a survey of college women on their attitudes

toward sexuality, dating, courtship, and marriage and issued a report entitled "Hooking Up, Hanging Out, and Looking for Mr. Right."[50] According to
the report, 40 percent of college women engage in "hooking up." Whether 40
percent or 20 percent or 10 percent of college females practice "hooking up"
is difficult to know with assurance; sexual surveys present serious method-
ological problems. A female anthropology professor, Cathy A. Small,
enrolled as a freshman at Northern Arizona University—where she is on the
faculty—in 2002–2003 in order to study undergraduate culture; her book
records some of the surprising behavior that she observed. "One door to a
women's dorm room had a sign up board for male classmates to say hi, and
condoms for the taking."[51]

Male "hooking up," the complementary type of sexual adventuring, has
not given rise to systematic studies, perhaps because, like dog bites man, they
are less surprising. However, nearly every college provides easy access to condoms and other prophylactic services in an effort to keep sexually transmitted diseases under control. Colleges sometimes give condoms away without
charge and also have dispensing machines in student restrooms where they
can be purchased.[52] Student health centers routinely treat students who have
contracted gonorrhea, syphilis, genital herpes, and other sexually transmitted diseases.[53] They also used to provide oral contraceptives to women students at steeply discounted prices. A recent law passed to control Medicaid
abuse included a provision that reduced this discount; female students complained bitterly at the change. Mary Hoban of the American College Health
Association said that 39 percent of undergraduate women said in a 2006
study that they relied on oral contraceptives to prevent pregnancy.[54]

CREATURE COMFORTS AT COLLEGE

Perhaps the very comfortable living arrangements that many American
college students enjoy, including private televisions, CD players, cell
phones, refrigerators, and lava lamps, encourage a culture of frivolity.
Rooms have gotten larger, more comfortable, and more private. Boston
University, for example, built an $81 million high-rise overlooking the
Charles River, which in 2003 housed 817 juniors and seniors in private
rooms within four-bedroom suites. Jarod Friedman, a senior in 2003, con-
trasted his comfortable private room with living in the same room with a
video-game addicted roommate during his sophomore year and sharing a
bathroom down the hall with 24 other underclassmen.

Mr. Friedman does share a bathroom with one of his three suite-
mates, but he is hardly complaining. The 1,200-square-foot apartment
has two bathrooms—and a kitchen and oversized dining/living room

(with spectacular views of Boston and Cambridge). All this costs Mr. Friedman $8,680 a year (on top of the $27,042 tuition), about $1,400 more than student housing where he would share a bedroom and considerably less than a similar apartment off campus. Mr. Friedman says the privacy is worth every penny.[55]

Apparently parents willingly pay for student luxuries if they can afford to, and in our affluent society many parents can. Big retail chains like Linens 'n Things, J. C. Penney, and Wal-Mart have established back-to-college gift registries so that students headed for college can indicate to parents, relatives, and friends what they want to take with them to college.[56] NPD, a market research company, estimates that "while the national average in back-to-school spending for 18- to 24-year-olds was about $550, an American middle-class family might easily spend $2,000 or more outfitting a child for freshman year in college, with purchases including a computer and other electronics."[57] Many students consider a personal microwave oven and a personal mini-refrigerator necessities. When Maria Scott-Wittenborn, an 18-year-old from Bernardsville, New Jersey, left for her freshman year at Bryn Mawr in the fall of 2003, she brought with her more than $1,000 worth of room furnishings, including new pillow shams, new rugs, and a new duvet cover.[58] These creature comforts help explain why attending college in the United States does not seem onerous to a majority of American high school graduates—except for the burden of occasional studying. Not only do many students arrive at college with lavish furnishings, computers, cameras, record collections, and cars. They continue to buy from stores and on the Internet so extensively that many colleges are forced to expand their mailrooms to store temporarily the deluge of packages until students pick them up. The mailroom at Pomona College handled an ant farm, a refrigerator, and a barbecue grill ordered by students. "The number of packages delivered to USC has nearly doubled in four years. By Dec. 31, 2007, officials [at USC] expected they will have received more than 67,000 packages in 2007."[59]

At one time colleges had cleaning women who came into the rooms while students were in class (or at least out of the rooms) and vacuumed and cleaned. That was the practice at Harvard, for example, until the cleaning service was discontinued as an economy measure and the responsibility for cleaning the rooms became that of their occupants. Some dorm rooms were never cleaned and became horrendously dirty; others were cleaned, as they were supposed to be, by their residents. At some colleges an entrepreneurial cleaning service sells its services to students who can afford to pay for it.[60] At Harvard, the University itself now operates a student-managed and student-staffed cleaning service started in 1951 to supplement the incomes of students going to college under the G.I. Bill. Here is how one member of Dorm Crew at Harvard in 2006 described his duties at one site:

> Knock on the door. Wait.
> Insert key, turn. Open slightly.
> "Dorm Crew."
> No one is home. This is a relief, as always. I locate the bathroom. I set down my bucket and mop, and get to work. Shower, toilet, sink, mirror, floor—this is my job. I work for Dorm Crew, a student-run, student-staffed division of the University's Facilities Maintenance Operations. We clean almost all the private bathrooms in the Houses and the Yard . . . .
>
> As odd as it feels to be completely ignored as you pass through the sightlines of four roommates intent on their group Nintendo game, the intermingling of manual labor and classroom interactions was somehow worse. Everyone knows that some students work hard every day just to be here, and others don't. It's just a lot more comfortable when we don't have to confront the personal realities of that gap. It's a lot more comfortable when I knock and no one's home.[61]

WHAT DO STUDENTS ACTUALLY DO AT COLLEGE?

A small professional literature exists providing statistics on the ways students spend their time at college. For example, the Higher Education Research Institute of the University of California at Los Angeles conducts an annual survey of college seniors containing some questions about student experiences at college.[62] For example, Question 9 asks respondents to fill in circles indicating how many hours per week they engaged in various activities: None, Less than 1 hour, 1–2 hours, 3–5, 6–10, 11–15, 15–20, Over 20 hours. The 20 activities were as follows:

- Studying/homework
- Attending classes/labs
- Socializing with friends
- Talking with faculty during office hours
- Talking with faculty outside of class or office hours
- Exercising/sports
- Partying
- Working (for pay) on campus
- Working (for pay) off campus
- Student clubs/groups

- Watching TV
- Housework/child care
- Reading for pleasure
- Commuting
- Prayer/meditation
- Career planning (job searches, internships, etc.)
- Playing video/computer games
- Volunteer work
- Surfing the Internet
- Online social networks (MySpace, Facebook, etc.)

One problem with this and similar studies is that they rely on retrospective reports by students. The estimations of the amount of time that students spend on various activities suffer not only from problems of recall but of *selective* recall: minimizing or omitting discreditable activities and exaggerating the amount of creditable activities like studying. An even more serious problem is that these studies depend on students being willing to fill out questionnaires or being willing to submit to Internet or telephone surveys without much incentive for doing so. The interpretation of results—what survey researchers call "response bias"—is a problem in every survey that relies on the voluntary cooperation of respondents where only a minority of those asked to participate do so.

A Rutgers colleague, Richard Tedesco, and I decided to conduct a more systematic study of the time-use of students that might provide a more accurate description of how undergraduates spend their time. We speculated that such a study might demonstrate that those students who goof off would be the ones who get low grades and fail to graduate. We paid a random sample of 80 undergraduate dormitory residents at one undergraduate college $35 each for their time and effort. The effort was considerable. Those who accepted our offer to participate in the study were required to keep logs of their time for an entire week, accounting for every ten-minute interval of time, and to hand in the logs on the following day (except for weekends when we collected the logs for Saturday and Sunday on Monday morning). Since they seem to have been punctilious in reporting even trivial details—many reported when they went to the bathroom—we are reasonably confident that we know how this group of students spent their time. We learned about all kind of activities: conversations with friends, watching television, taking showers, working out at the gym, communicating by telephone, attending classes, doing homework. We had assumed that, like adults, these college students would wake up in the morning, conduct a variety of activities during the day, and go to bed at night for seven, eight, or more hours of uninterrupted sleep before arising the next morning. Some did this. But others led extremely unstructured lives—eating, napping, TV viewing, and socializing throughout the day and the night, sometimes sandwiching in classes and studying, sometimes not. One male student usually stayed up until after 2 AM and slept until noon the next day. Some of the activities that he engaged in after midnight were watching sitcoms, playing video games, playing pool, eating at diners, and, more rarely, reading an assignment for a class.

A few students slept so extensively and got up so late that it would have been impossible for them to take morning classes. We examined the relationship between a lifestyle that we considered more appropriate for students and the grade point averages that they received to the point of their graduation. (Whether they were freshmen, sophomores, juniors, or seniors at the time they were recruited for our study, we collected from university records their GPAs for their full university careers.) We compared the thirteen students with a GPA of 3.3 or higher at graduation with the thirty students with a GPA of 2.49 or lower. The thirteen successful students spent an average of 17.0 hours a week on school related activities (reading, studying, homework) compared with an average of 13.1 hours for the academically less successful students, about thirty percent more time. In addition, the successful students averaged 10.6 hours of class attendance per week compared with 8.5 hours for the academically less successful. We had initially expected the differences between the two groups to be larger. On reconsideration, however, we hypothesized that the better students used the time they spent on academic activities more efficiently than the less competent students. Consequently the size of the quantitative difference may have been less important than the qualitative differences in study skills and ability to comprehend lecture material. Supporting this hypothesis of qualitative differences rather than mere time put in, a study at the University of Michigan did not find significant grade differences between students who studied more and students who studied less.[63] Both the thirteen successful students and the thirty less academically successful students in our study spent about the same amount of time working for pay, 8.6 hours a week for the successful students, 8.9 hours for the less successful students. They differed markedly in the average time spent on entertainment (watching television, recreation, shopping, and hobbies); the successful students averaged 12.3 hours of entertainment, whereas the unsuccessful students averaged 18.2 hours. The time devoted to socializing (conversation, eating out rather than in the campus dining hall, partying) was very large for both groups and did not differ appreciably: 20.5 hours a week for the successful students, 19.4 hours for the less successful ones. Seemingly the more successful students devoted more time to socializing than the unsuccessful ones, but this was only when socializing was the primary activity. We also tabulated secondary activities (time doing something else while mainly engaged in the primary activity). The successful students spent 10.8 hours a week socializing as a secondary activity compared with 12.4 hours for the less successful students.

Possibly the freshmen or sophomores who led relatively unscholarly lives at the time of our survey had become more studious as their college careers developed. This hypothesis was compatible with our data. The 19 seniors reported doing more schoolwork, 18.4 hours a week, compared with the 12.3 hours done by the 19 freshmen; the seniors also spent more time attending classes, 10.7 hours, than the 8.7 hours of the freshmen. The seniors engaged in less entertainment—14.6 hours for them compared with 17.5 hours for the freshmen—and drastically less socializing—18.1 hours for them compared with 25.4 hours for the freshmen. Of course, these juniors and seniors had survived three years of college. Quite possibly they were more intelligent or better prepared to be college students than students who started college at the same time as they did but who goofed off more as freshmen or sophomores and never made it to the junior and senior years.

Despite the seemingly disorganized lives that many of the students led, all but three of the eighty students in our sample eventually graduated. Here we relied on official university records rather than reports from students themselves. Part of the explanation may be that graduation is not a very high hurdle, as might be inferred from a previous chapter's discussion of grade inflation.

LOW ADMISSION AND RETENTION STANDARDS
ENCOURAGE GOOFING OFF

Overall, the academic standards for admitting students to colleges vary from high at the selective colleges and universities, low at most institutions, and nonexistent in most community colleges. Even at selective schools, some applicants for admission with substantially poorer academic credentials than normal admits—outstanding athletes, talented musicians or artists, the offspring of parents who attended the school ("legacies"), and members of certain minority groups—receive special consideration in the admissions process. Dr. William Bowen criticized the way preferences given to outstanding high school athletes create an "academic divide" that works against serious studying.[64] (Although Dr. Bowen had several collaborators in the two books he published about the role of athletics in higher education, he was the president of the Mellon Foundation that financed the study and the former president of Princeton University. As the senior author of the two books, it seems appropriate to attribute the interpretation of athletic preferences to him.) Bowen and Levin define "the academic divide" as follows: "the tendency for recruited athletes to differ systematically from students at large in academic credentials (such as SAT scores), in academic outcomes (such as majors chosen and rank-in-class), and in patterns of residential and social life." In the course of a massive study of athletics at elite colleges, Bowen and his collaborators show that these recruited athletes and also walk-on athletes—that is, students not recruited by coaches but who play on intercollegiate athletic teams while attending school—underperform the academic levels that their high school grades and SAT scores predict for them.[65] Dr. Bowen has a point. Whereas the musicians, other students who devote a large amount of time to extracurricular activities like the student newspaper or theatrical productions, and legacies get good grades and do not receive worse grades than would be expected from knowledge of their tested abilities, athletes do worse on the average than their aptitude scores suggest they are capable of doing. On the other hand, Dr. Bowen may be unduly critical of athletes. He infers that athletes underperform because they deliberately neglect their studies. This inference fuels his indignation over granting preferences to outstanding athletes at elite colleges and thereby disappointing academically better-prepared students.

A more charitable view of the underperformance of athletes is compatible with the data. Bowen and Levin point out that "athletes spend, on average, more than twice as much time on their sports than do participants in even the most time-intensive other extracurricular activities."[66] In addition to sheer time, athletes expend a lot of energy in sports, which may detract from their ability to concentrate on studies. In short, athletes may be compelled by the demands of practice, travel, and games played to do less academic work than they would prefer. That may account for the large proportion of recruited athletes who drop out of the sport for which they were recruited, some without even an initial appearance. Even if some athletes are as anti-intellectual as Dr. Bowen thinks, they also constitute a living example of an alternative prestige hierarchy to that of academic achievement. This may be why athletes do not arouse much resentment among their classmates for the known preferences they receive for admission; they are, after all, achievers, even though their achievement is not academic. Furthermore, they provide spectacles that many student spectators enjoy watching, whether or not they themselves play sports. It would be a stretch to accuse varsity athletes of "goofing off."

The scholarships reserved for blacks, Native Americans, and Hispanics differ from those awarded to athletes. Preferential consideration for disadvantaged minorities does not depend on achievement of any kind, only on presumed victimhood. Thus, their failure to live up to the academic standards applied to "regular admits" is more likely to produce resentment, even anger. Bowen and his colleagues admit that, like athletes, "underrepresented minorities" underperform their tested academic potential. Unlike the athletes, however, they do not have to be achievers in some other realm. Thomas Sowell argues that the reason for a greater upsurge of anti-black incidents on the campuses of elite colleges and universities rather than of less selective colleges and universities is that the most selective institutions have given *more* preferential treatment to minorities than the less selective institutions and have consequently generated *more* resentment of seeming unfairness.[67] Dr. Bowen does not see it this way; he is a staunch advocate of minority preferences at elite colleges and universities. He insists that minority preferences are more legitimate than athletic preferences. "The arguments in favor of recruiting minority students are entirely different from those in favor of recruiting goalies or (volleyball spikers). The two groups occupy, we would suggest, entirely different places in a mission-driven hierarchy of values and purposes. Stubborn problems of underperformance notwithstanding, the active recruitment of highly qualified minority students is justified."[68]

Inconsistencies aside, Bowen identifies a basic problem with preferences. Admitting students with fewer academic skills compared with their classmates and not requiring them to maintain normal levels of accomplishment may have unintended consequences. One unintended consequence is that these less prepared students are less likely to forge an identity based on a passionate interest in some subject in the curriculum. Instead they may develop an interest in an extracurricular activity: the Glee Club, the student newspaper, student theatricals. On the other hand, they are also more likely to drift aimlessly through the college experience, to not participate deeply either in the academic or the extracurricular opportunities offered to them. They may spend more time socializing, bullshitting with other students, getting drunk, using recreational drugs, having sex—in short, goofing off. This is only a plausible hypothesis. I could not locate empirical studies showing that less prepared students are more likely to contribute to the goofing-off culture on college campuses.

Another unintended consequence of preferences not related to academic achievement is that professors are tempted to lower their grading standards so that weak students have a chance of passing. (This unintended consequence applies, of course, not only to diversity preferences but to athletic and legacy preferences.) Remedial programs needed for such students tend to lower expectations of superior students for their own performance. If well-prepared students do not feel some competitive pressure, if good grades are available for little effort, the temptation to do the minimum may be difficult to resist. Bowen is deeply concerned that double standards of admission jeopardize a campus culture supportive of academic excellence. He is willing to pay this price, however, for minority students but not for athletes, although he and his collaborators do not attempt to explain why diversity considerations justify one exception and not the other.

CONCLUSION

Unlike the ascetic monks studying in medieval monasteries, American students expect fun, comfort, and recreation in addition to education at our colleges and universities. When Isaac Newton went to the University of Cambridge several centuries ago, he studied seven days a week, at least ten hours a day, and actively avoided the revelry that some Cambridge undergraduates engaged in even then. No one expects American undergraduates to work as hard as Isaac Newton or medieval monks. However, what seems to be happening on many American college campuses is the development of such a powerful "fun" culture that a quarter of the students or more arrive thinking that having fun is the main reason they are at college and that the pursuit of knowledge should be resorted to only when they have nothing better to do.

Professors usually think of higher education as an opportunity for students to learn what they do not know and *should* know, and some students think so too. However, learning is compelled to compete for student attention with a variety of other student interests and also with part-time work. With the cost of college high and getting higher, students say that they have to work in order to attend college at all. If the majority of the students spending 16 hours or more a week working for pay are serious students who would be studying more if they did not need the money in order to help finance their educations, the loss is not only to them but to the academic atmosphere they might help to create on campus were they more visible. On the other hand, working for pay may contribute to the academic seriousness of the college culture rather than detracting from it if student reports are to be believed. I am referring not only to students in work-study programs whose work consists of helping a professor with his research. Students who take menial jobs in the college dining hall or the building maintenance operation often say that having the discipline of a job helps them to organize their time more efficiently, including time for studying. If students working for pay would not take their academic responsibilities more seriously if they had no job, their employment is not an impediment to higher education. Paradoxically it may even help by getting them out of places where they would otherwise goof off. I do not know of empirical studies that could throw light on this issue.

By dint of numbers, the goof-off students may have more impact on the cultural atmosphere of most college campuses than serious students who are trying to learn as much as possible. Perhaps public policy can change this, at least marginally, by providing *more* incentives for serious students and *fewer* incentives for goof-off students. Chapter 7, the final chapter, will explain in detail the kind of incentives I have in mind. They involve changing the financial arrangements the United States Department of Education makes for financial aid to college students.

NOTES

1. Harvard College Admissions, 2004.

2. "The Year of Living Dangerously," *Harvard Magazine*, July–August 1995, p. 69; Tamar Lewin, "From Brother's Death, a Crusade," *New York Times*, April 25, 2007.

3. Patrick Healy and the Boston Globe Staff, "Harvard Figures Show Most of Its Grades Are A's or B's," *Boston Globe*, November 21, 2001. See also Craig Lambert, "Desperately Seeking Summa," *Harvard Magazine*, May–June 1993, p. 37.

4. Ross Douthat, "The Truth about Harvard: It May Be Hard to Get into Harvard, but It's Easy to Get Out Without Learning Much of Enduring Value at All: A Recent Graduate's Report," *The Atlantic*, March 2005.

5. U.S. Department of Education, National Center for Education Statistics, *Digest of Education Statistics 2008*, March 2009. Table 200 "Recent High School Completers and Their Enrollment in College, by Sex: 1960 through 2007." Web site accessed in April 2009: http://nces.ed.gov/pubs2009/2009020_0.pdf

6. David Romer, "Do Students Go to Class? Should They?" *Journal of Economic Perspectives*, Vol. 7 (Summer 1993): 167–174.

7. According to a study by ACT, 26.4 percent of freshmen who enrolled in 1996–1997 school year had dropped out by the following year. Source: *The Chronicle of Higher Education*, October 8, 1999.

8. Elizabeth Bernstein, "Colleges Offer Students Incentives to Finish Their Degree in Four Years," *Wall Street Journal*, April 26, 2002.

9. Table 4.1 shows the graduation rates for specific highly selective and relatively unselective colleges.

10. Maria Newman, "As Students Stay Longer, Colleges Feel the Pinch and Say, Move Along," *New York Times*, September 14, 1994, p. B9.

11. Higher Education Research Institute, *The American College Student, 1991*. Unpublished Report, University of California, Los Angeles, August, 1992, pp. 110, 126; more recent data from HERI replicates the earlier finding: Sara Lipska, "Freshmen Increasingly Discuss Politics, Worry about Money, Survey Finds," *The Chronicle*, January 19, 2007.

12. Michele Ingrassia, "A Summerful of Labor Days," *New York Times*, July 26, 2006.

13. Alvin Kernan, *In Plato's Cave*, New Haven, CT: Yale University Press, 1999.

14. Eric Felten, "Curses Not Foiled, Again," *Wall Street Journal*, September 10, 2004.

15. Mark Yost, "Dis, Boom, Bah," *Wall Street Journal*, December 26, 2003.

16. Pete Thamel and Duff Wilson, "Poor Grades Aside, Athletes Get into College on a $399 Diploma," *New York Times*, November 27, 2005.

17. Todd Gitlin, "Disappearing Ink," *New York Times*, September 10, 1999.

18. Greg Winter, "Jacuzzi U.? A Battle of Perks to Lure Students," *New York Times*, October 5, 2003.

19. *Ibid.*

20. Chrisopher Maag, "Ohio University Tries to Get Past Problems, but New Ones Emerge," New *York Times,* September 27, 2006.

21. Dan Haron, Letter to the Editor, *New York Times,* June 23, 1994.

22. Jeffrey Gettleman, "As Young Adults Drink to Win, Marketers Join In," *New York Times*, October 16, 2005.

23. "Drug- and Alcohol-Related Arrests Increase at Colleges," *New York Times*, May 23, 1999.

24. Dirk Johnson, "Rift Develops on Indiana Campus after Student Dies," *New York Times,* November 27, 2008; Michael Winerip, "Binge Nights: The Emergency on Campus," *New York Times, Education Life*, pp. 29–31, 42.

25. Henry Wechsler, *et. al.,* "College Binge Drinking in the 1990s: A Continuing Problem," *Journal of American College Health*, 48, pp. 199–210, 2000.

26. Stacey Stowe, "Yale Alumni Strike Back at Tailgating Limits," *New York Times,* November 21, 2005.

27. George S. Yacoubian, Jr., "Correlates of Ecstasy Use among Students Surveyed through the 1997 College Alcohol Study," *Journal of Drug Education,* Vol. 33, Number 1, pp. 61–69, 2003.

28. Jonathan Cheng, "Film Legend Bothered by Use of Name in Stunt at Princeton," *New York Times*, April 22, 2004.

29. "Naked Rite of Passage Defended at Princeton," *New York Times,* March 6, 1999.

30. James Q. Wilson, *Thinking about Crime,* New York: Basic Books, 1975, contains a thoughtful discussion of the cultural changes that produced this increase.

31. Gerald Amada, *Coping with Misconduct in the College Classroom: A Practical Model.* Asheville, NC: College Administration Publications, Inc., 1999; Gerald Amada, "Dealing with the Disruptive College Student: Some Theoretical and Practical Considerations," *Journal of American College Health*, Vol. 34, April 1986, pp. 221–225.

32. Christine Hauser and Anahad O'Connor, "Virginia Tech Shooting Leaves 33 Dead," *New York Times*, April 16, 2007.

33. Data from the Rutgers University Police Department, 55 Commercial Avenue, New Brunswick, NJ, 08901.

34. Greg Winter, *New York Times,* "Colleges Tell Students the Overseas' Party's Over," August 23, 2004.

35. *Ibid.*

36. *Ibid.*

37. Tamar Lewin, "Going off to College for Less (passport required)" *New York Times*, November 30, 2008.

38. Dan Ronnen, "An Extracurricular Institution," *Daily Targum*, April 8, 1992.

39. Sam Dillon, "For One Student, a College Career becomes a Career," *New York Times*, November 10, 2005.

40. *Ibid.*

41. Dave Eggers, "Serve or Fail," *New York Times*, June 13, 2004.

42. Lino DiCuollo, "The Myth of the Dumb Jock," *Wall Street Journal*, February 2, 1993.

43. Michael Oriard, "Football Glory and Education a Team No More," *New York Times*, December 23, 2001.

44. Sam Dillon, *op. cit.*

45. Higher Education Research Institute, *The American College Student, 1991.* Unpublished Report, University of California, Los Angeles, August, 1992, pp. 110, 126.

46. Nate Stulman, "The Great Campus Goof-Off Machine," *New York Times*, March 15, 1999.

47. Kate Zernike, "Students Shall Not Download. Yeah, Sure," *New York Times*, September 20, 2003.

48. Mattathias Schwartz, "The Hold-'Em Holdup," *New York Times*, June 12, 2006.

49. Charles M. Blow, "The Demise of Dating," *New York Times*, December 13, 2008. See also Kathleen Bogle, *Hooking Up, Dating, and Relationships on Campus*, New York: New York University Press. 2008.

50. "Girl Meets Boy," *Wall Street Journal*, August 3, 2001.

51. Diana Jean Schemo, "What a Professor Learned as an Undercover Freshman," *New York Times*, August 23, 2006.

52. Stephanie Rosenbloom, "Here's Your Syllabus, and Your Condom," *New York Times*, September 24, 2006.

53. *Ibid.*

54. Monica Davey, "Big Rise in the Cost of Birth Control on Campuses," *New York Times*, November 22, 2007.

55. Sara Rimer, "Colleges Offer Students Privacy," *New York Times*, January 27, 2003.

56. Katherine Zoepf, "Retailers Make Sure Freshmen Live in Style," *New York Times*, September 1, 2003.

57. *Ibid.*

58. *Ibid.*

59. Jonathan D. Glater, "Majoring in Mailroom Management," *New York Times*, November 21, 2007.

60. Pam Belluck, "At Harvard, an Unseemly Display of Wealth or Merely a Clean Room?" *New York Times*, March 22, 2005.

61. John A. LaRue, "The (Other) Crew Captain," *Harvard Magazine*, January–February 2006, pp. 71–73.

62. Higher Education Research Institute, UCLA, College Senior Survey, 2007.

63. Howard Schuman et al., "Effort and Reward: The Assumption That College Grades Are Affected by Quantity of Study," *Social Forces*, Vol. 63, Number 4 (1985), pp. 945–966.

64. William G. Bowen and Sarah A. Levin, *Reclaiming the Game: College Sports and Educational Values*, Princeton University Press, Princeton, NJ: 2003, p. 5.

65. *Ibid.*

66. *Ibid*, p. 158.

67. Thomas Sowell, *Black Education: Myths and Tragedies*, White Plains, NY: Longman, 1972.

68. Bowen and Levin, *op. cit*, pp. 238–239.

Chapter 5

Is College Graduation Enough for a Good Job, or Do College Graduates Have to Know Something?

Broadway audiences didn't necessarily have to know Shakespeare's "The Taming of the Shrew" in order to enjoy the 1948 hit musical, *Kiss Me, Kate*, with lyrics and music by Cole Porter, but it helped. Porter graduated from Yale nearly a century ago. In that era a Yale graduate—or a graduate of any American university—had to have had some exposure to the plays of William Shakespeare, because it was an era during which a college education referred to a corpus of common intellectual experiences. Colleges usually had a core curriculum that all graduates had to take, whatever their major or their interests. The lyrics of one of the hit songs of *Kiss Me, Kate*, "Brush Up Your Shakespeare," contained references to Homer, English poets, the Greek playwrights, Aeschylus and Euripides, a mention of the "Bard of Stratford-on-Avon," the town where Shakespeare was born, and puns involving titles to several of Shakespeare's plays: "Othello," "Anthony and Cleopatra," "Much Ado about Nothing," "Coriolanus," and "A Midsummer Night's Dream." Members of the audience who did not know at least the titles couldn't understand fully Porter's witticisms; they had nothing to brush up. Consider the lyrics of the song:

> The girls today in society
> Go for classical poetry,
> So to win their hearts one must quote with ease
> Aeschylus and Euripides.
> But the poet of them all

Who will start 'em simply ravin'
Is the poet people call
The bard of Stratford-on-Avon.

Brush up your Shakespeare,
Start quoting him now.
Brush up your Shakespeare
And the women you will wow.
Just declaim a few lines from "Othella"
And they think you're a heckuva fella.
If your blonde won't respond when you flatter 'er
Tell her what Tony told Cleopaterer,
And if still, to be shocked, she pretends well,
Just remind her that "All's Well That Ends Well."

Brush up your Shakespeare
And they'll all kowtow.
Brush up your Shakespeare,
Start quoting him now.
Brush up your Shakespeare
And the women you will wow.
If your goil is a Washington Heights dream
Treat the kid to "A Midsummer Night Dream."
If she fights when her clothes you are mussing,
What are clothes? "Much Ado About Nussing."
If she says your behavior is heinous
Kick her right in the "Coriolanus."[1]

Undergraduates are much less likely today to understand that *Kiss Me, Kate* took its point of departure from Shakespeare's comedy, "The Taming of the Shrew," because colleges currently don't expose their students to large dollops of the Bard of Avon, even English majors. The American Council of Trustees and Alumni recently issued a report entitled *The Vanishing Shakespeare* that took aim at this trend. The report reported a survey of the requirements for English *majors* at 70 of America's leading colleges and universities. " . . . we defined a college or university as having a Shakespeare requirement when English majors were obliged either to take a course in Shakespeare or to take two out of three single-author courses in Chaucer, Shakespeare, and Milton."[2] By this criterion, English majors at only fifteen of seventy major institutions of higher education did have to take a course in Shakespeare, including Harvard University, Catholic University, California Institute of Technology, Middlebury College, Stanford University, and Wellesley College. However, 55 of the 70 did *not* require its English majors to take a course in Shakespeare, including Princeton, Yale, Brown, Swarthmore College, Williams College, Columbia, Colby College, Carleton College, Bowdoin College, Bryn Mawr College, and Johns Hopkins. Shakespeare was not the only casualty of more permissive curricular requirements. What used to be called the core educational curriculum—what every college graduate ought to know—has faded away. Here is how the American Council of Trustees and Alumni described the disappearance of a core curriculum in a different report issued in 2004:

> Despite widespread lip service to the importance of a general education, a new survey by ACTA finds that a solid core curriculum in higher education has gone the way of the dodo. At a time when most colleges endorse the importance of a general education—a set of courses required of all students—in fact, colleges have virtually abandoned a solid core curriculum in favor of a loose set of distribution requirements. As a consequence, college students are graduating without the basic knowledge that was once considered the hallmark of a liberal education. ACTA's report of a survey of 50 colleges and universities, including all of the Big Eight and Big Ten universities, the Ivy League, and the Seven Sisters Colleges, plus an additional grouping of 13 colleges to provide institutional and geographical breadth. Each school was given a grade from A to F, depending on the number of core subjects it required.[3]

The core subjects, according to the report, were composition, U.S. Government or American History, economics, foreign language, literature, mathematics, and natural or physical science. If a college required six or all seven of these subjects, it received an A grade; if it required one or none of them, it received an F grade. Only one of the fifty schools whose curriculum requirements were examined received an A (Baylor University), whereas twelve of the fifty received an F, including Northwestern, Penn State, Wisconsin, Brown, Cornell, Mt. Holyoke, Smith, and Vassar. Whatever students were learning at these colleges, the subjects were not those traditionally considered the core of a college education. To put it another way, knowing that a person has a college degree no longer indicates what the person knows.

Another approach to assessing what college students know is by survey research. The Intercollegiate Studies Institute commissioned the Department of Public Policy at the University of Connecticut to conduct a survey

Table 5.1
Sample Questions from the Survey of the Political, Historical, and Civic Knowledge of American College Students*

5. Which battle brought the American Revolution to an end?	
a) Saratoga	19.7%
b) Gettysburg	26.0%
c) The Alamo	3.7%
d) Yorktown	47.8%
e) New Orleans	2.8%
9. The War of 1812	
a) was a decisive victory for the United States over Spain.	22.7%
b) was a stalemate.	36.3%
c) established America as the leading power in the world.	18.8%
d) enhanced Robert E. Lee's reputation as America's most talented general.	11.2%
e) was confined only to sea battles.	11.0%
10. The dominant theme in the Lincoln–Douglas debates was:	
a) treatment of Native Americans.	5.7%
b) westward expansion.	16.7%
c) whether Illinois should become a state.	7.0%
d) prohibition.	4.9%
e) slavery and its expansion.	65.7%
11. Abraham Lincoln was elected President during which period?	
a) 1800–1825	8.5%
b) 1826–1850	21.0%
c) 1851–1875	62.2%
d) 1876–1900	6.4%
e) 1901–1925	2.0%
12. In 1933, Franklin Delano Roosevelt proposed a series of government programs that became known as	
a) the Great Society.	5.2%
b) the Square Deal.	6.4%
c) the New Deal.	82.0%
d) the New Frontier.	4.8%
e) supply-side economics.	1.5%

of a sample of 14,419 freshmen and seniors at 25 selective and, in addition, 25 randomly chosen U.S. colleges and universities. The fifty multiple-choice questions that the students answered dealt with American history, government and political thought, plus international affairs and the market economy. Table 5.1 provides a sample of the questions from the survey instrument. Table 5.2 shows the results for various categories of colleges and their students. Although the sample questions displayed in Table 5.1 appear to cover topics that college students ought to know about, none of

Table 5.1 (*continued*)

18. The line "We hold these truths to be self-evident, that all men are created equal . . ." is from
a) The Federalist.	5.0%
b) the Preamble to the Constitution.	40.6%
c) The Communist Manifesto.	3.7%
d) the Declaration of Independence.	47.7%
e) an inscription on the Statue of Liberty.	3.0%

28. In his "I Have a Dream" speech, Dr. Martin Luther King, Jr.
a) argued for the abolition of slavery.	7.0%
b) advocated black separatism.	4.8%
c) morally defended Affirmative Action.	3.9%
d) expressed his hopes for racial justice and brotherhood.	81.4%
e) proposed that several of America's founding ideas were discriminatory.	2.9%

35. The Monroe Doctrine:
a) discouraged new colonies in the Western hemisphere.	27.5%
b) proclaimed America's "Manifest Destiny."	46.4%
c) was the earliest recorded agreement between the United States and France.	11.8%
d) was America's response to Aleksandr Solzhenitsyn's Gulag Archipelago.	6.1%
e) resolved border disputes among the thirteen colonies.	8.2%

Source: Intercollegiate Studies Institute, National Civic Literacy Board, *Failing Our Students, Failing America: Holding Colleges Accountable for Teaching America's History and Institutions*, September 18, 2007. Margin of sampling error is ±1 percentage point overall and ±4–5 percentage points for individual schools.

* Correct answers are set in italic. The actual percentage that each answer received from student respondents follows the text of the item.

the schools had average scores reaching 70 percent, even Harvard, although selective colleges scored better than less selective ones. Surprisingly—and distressingly—college seniors only got marginally better average scores than college freshmen and in some colleges did worse.

Newspapers reporting on the survey expressed surprise that seniors had not gotten higher marks than freshmen. The inference most people drew from the generally poor results of college students on this survey of their civic knowledge was that colleges were doing a poor educational job. Not everyone drew this conclusion.

The chairman of the history department at Princeton University, Jeremy Adelman, said that providing students with a foundation in American history and governance should not be the sole mission of

Table 5.2
Political and Historical Literacy of American College Students

	Freshman Average	Senior Average
Harvard	63.59%	69.56%
Yale	68.94%	65.85%
St. Thomas Univ. (Fla.)	29.75%	32.50%
Eastern Conn. State	31.34%	40.99%
Cornell	61.90%	56.95%
State non-flagship universities	41.5%	47.4%
Private, secular non–Ivy League universities	56.2%	60.1%
State flagship universities	50.7%	54.4%
Catholic universities	45.2%	48.3%
Protestant universities	53.8%	56.6%
Ivy League universities	64.0%	64.1%

Source: Intercollegiate Studies Institute, National Civic Literacy Board, *Failing Our Students, Failing America: Holding Colleges Accountable for Teaching America's History and Institutions*, September 18, 2007. Margin of sampling error is ±1 percentage point overall and ±4–5 percentage points for individual schools.
Note: The civic literacy test covered American history, government, and political thought as well as international affairs and the market economy. Both freshmen and seniors were tested at fifty individual schools. Percentages given are of questions answered correctly.

any institution of higher education . . . . "You have to ask what is the social function of the university?" Mr. Adelman said. "If you're in chemical engineering, why study history? Should we require students to study history? I don't think if you polled the history department faculty there would be unanimity on the question." Students at Princeton are required to take one history class, he said. The course does not have to be in American history.[4]

Professor Adelman may have put it tactlessly, but he was identifying a real change in expectations. The then President of the University of California, Clark Kerr, explained what was happening: *uni*versities were turning into *multi*versities.[5] So many departments, institutes, centers, and programs were proliferating that it was becoming impossible to know what knowledge students who graduated from them had in common. Even within a traditional department, English, the variety of courses was becoming a cornucopia; students could concentrate on science fiction or male oppression rather than on Chaucer, Shakespeare, or the Romantic poets of the nineteenth century.

These developments may have disappointed traditional scholars who wanted students to emerge from college with a liberal education. From the point of view of students, however, it gave them greater freedom to learn whatever they liked. In any case, most of them were looking less for a liberal education than for an opportunity to achieve a middle-class standard of living. Education was supposed to have an occupational pay-off. Were the occupational benefits being oversold? Rather than being a purely educational matter, for most students college is an economic and occupational opportunity. In 1949 a distinguished professor of economics at Harvard, Seymour Harris, published a book that questioned those alleged occupational payoffs.[6] *The Market for College Graduates* argued that the United States was sending more young people to colleges and universities than there would be professional and business occupations for college graduates in the decades ahead—in short, that for many college graduates there would be no economic payoff. He admitted that his was a purely economic analysis and that the cultural and psychological benefits of a college education may well justify the investment of time and resources. Nevertheless, he pointed out, his analysis of the American economy indicated that colleges were graduating more students than were be likely to be absorbed in the business and professional occupations to which they aspired. Professor Harris's pessimistic assessment of college education as an investment was almost unanimously pooh-poohed at the time.

In 1949–1950, 432,058 bachelor's degrees were awarded, three-quarters of them to men.[7] In 1949, the 17 to 24 population of the U.S. was 18,381,654, with males accounting for 9,153,410 and females accounting for 9,228,244.[8] Veterans of World War II, most of them male, returned to the colleges they had left for military service, thereby swelling postwar college enrollments, as did veterans who had not been to college before their military service. (Some veterans who enrolled in college after being mustered out could not have afforded a college education without the federal student subsidies contained in the G.I. Bill of Rights.) The college graduates of the late 1940s and early 1950s were, in point of fact, easily absorbed by the expanding American economy—contrary to the fears of some college administrators. Not all college presidents favored expanded college enrollments at the end of WWII. Harvard president James Bryant Conant opposed even the G.I. Bill because he did not believe that the United States needed more college graduates. And President Robert Hutchins of the University of Chicago predicted in 1944 that if the G.I. Bill were passed "colleges and universities will find themselves converted into educational hobo jungles."[9] Professor Harris turned out to have underestimated greatly the economy's potential for growth and therefore its ability to absorb college graduates following the end of World War II.

Professor Harris's warning was not taken seriously, especially after the number of college graduates began to decline as veterans passed through the system of higher education. By 1959–1960, only 392,440 bachelor's degrees were awarded; the proportion awarded to males dropped to 65 percent. However, by 1969–1970 the number of bachelor's degrees awarded rose again—to 792,656, while the proportion earned by males dropped to 57 percent. The main reason for the increase in numbers was the post–World War II baby boom, which began in 1946 and continued until 1964, but another factor was a cultural change: an increasing tendency of female high school graduates to wish to attend college.[10] Demographers interpreted the baby boom as partly due to the economic expansion that Professor Harris had underestimated. By 1979–1980 bachelor's degrees had climbed to 929,417, and women received 49 percent of them. Professor Harris's gloomy prediction was largely forgotten. College administrators feared a *decline* in college enrollments, not an excess of graduates. Demographers predicted that with the ebbing of the baby boom, the number of high school graduates would peak at about three million in 1976–1977 and would probably decline thereafter.[11] Had this predicted decline in high school graduates occurred, resulting in a decrease in college enrollments, a scarcity rather than a glut of college graduates would have soon shown Professor Harris's assessment of the poor market for college graduates to have been a spectacularly bad forecast.

However, demographic predictions of declining college enrollments proved to be as mistaken as Professor Harris's assessment of the American economy's inability to absorb increasing numbers of college graduates. Higher proportions of high school graduates enrolled in college in the 1980s than had enrolled in past decades. Not only did *that* happen, fueled partly by the increasing propensity of female high school graduates to attend college. In addition, sizable numbers of older persons in the workforce, who had missed out on college when they were teenagers, decided to enroll even if it meant continuing to work full-time and becoming part-time students taking evening classes. By 1989–1990 bachelor's degrees exceeded a million and have continued to climb. By 2006–2007, 1,524,092 bachelor's degrees were awarded.[12] Table 5.3 shows the explosion of bachelor's degrees in the United States.

Professor Harris's prediction was not illogical. He based it on extrapolation of the future needs of the American economy for professional, technical, and managerial employees, as well as on his assumption that education is subject to the law of diminishing returns, just as land is subject to the law of diminishing returns. (Economists like to point out that if the law of diminishing returns did not exist, the world's food supply could be grown in a flowerpot.) At certain stages of economic development, the skills of highly educated people are scarce and are therefore rewarded in the job market. At those early stages, investment in higher education pays

Table 5.3
Number of Degrees Awarded in the United States, 1869–2007, by Type and Year

	Associate's	Bachelor's	Master's	First-Professional	Doctor's
1869–1870	–	9,371	0	*	1
1879–1880	–	12,896	879	*	54
1889–1890	–	15,539	1,015	*	149
1899–1900	–	27,410	1,583	*	382
1909–1910	–	37,199	2,113	*	443
1919–1920	–	48,622	4,279	*	615
1929–1930	–	122,484	14,969	*	2,299
1939–1940	–	186,500	26,731	*	3,290
1949–1950	–	432,058	58,183	*	6,420
1959–1960	–	392,440	74,435	*	9,829
1969–1970	206,023	792,316	208,291	34,918	29,866
1974–1975	360,171	922,933	292,450	55,916	34,083
1979–1980	400,910	929,417	298,081	70,131	32,615
1984–1985	454,712	979,477	286,251	75,063	32,943
1989–1990	455,102	1,051,344	324,301	70,988	38,371
1994–1995	539,691	1,160,134	397,629	75,800	44,446
1999–2000	564,933	1,237,875	457,056	80,057	44,808
2000–2001	578,865	1,244,171	468,476	79,707	44,904
2001–2002	595,133	1,291,900	482,118	80,698	44,160
2002–2003	632,912	1,348,503	512,645	80,810	46,024
2003–2004	665,301	1,399,542	558,940	83,041	48,378
2004–2005	696,660	1,439,264	574,618	87,289	52,631
2005–2006	713,066	1,485,242	594,065	87,655	52,631
2006–2007	728,114	1,524,092	604,607	90,064	60,616

Source: U.S. Department of Education, National Center for Education Statistics, *Digest of Education Statistics 2008*, March 2009. Table 268, p. 395. "Degrees Conferred by Degree Granting Institutions, Selected Years, 1869–1870 through 2006-2007." http://nces.ed.gov/pubs2009/2009020_3b.pdf.
* First-professional degrees are included with bachelor's degrees.

both for the individual and for the society. Once the point of diminishing returns is reached, however, the allocation of additional resources to higher education may not be needed for the American economy, although it may still be a worthwhile investment for individual students. Has American society reached that point in the first decade of the twenty-first century? Some evidence suggests that it has, which means that Professor Harris was essentially correct, albeit a half-century too early.

Part of the evidence is statistical. Despite the fact that the earnings of college graduates are, on the average, twice the earnings of the average high school graduate, there have always been some college graduates who worked, at least temporarily, at jobs that did not require a college education and who earned less than the average high school graduate. Statistical studies conducted by labor economists at the Bureau of Labor Statistics, Daniel Hecker and Kristina Shelley, documented this phenomenon.[13] In the late 1960s one in ten college graduates worked at jobs not requiring a college education: typists, file clerks, sales clerks, phone answerers; in the 1980s one in five college graduates held jobs usually performed by those with only a high school education.[14] Furthermore a decade ago the Bureau of Labor Statistics projected that the mismatch would get worse because the number of college graduates entering the labor force would grow to about 1,380,000 per year between 1996 and 2006 but the annual number of college-level jobs available during that period would be only 1,130,000.[15] These statistics notwithstanding, going to college could pay off handsomely for the majority of college graduates. Whether it pays off for individual high school graduates, however, depends partly on whether they choose to major in fields with substantial market demand and partly on whether students got good enough grades to be attractive to prospective employers. Legal education illustrates this phenomenon. Despite the more than one million lawyers in the United States, law school enrollment is growing and very able students compete to be admitted to law schools; most applicants are attracted by the accurate reports of annual starting salaries as high as $160,000 at large law firms in big cities. But in order to get such jobs, they have to be the top students at prestigious law schools. Middling students graduating from mid-level law schools find jobs hard to come by and the pay low, law school deans and professors say.[16] Here is what the publisher of the New York Law School Law Review said about the notion that many college graduates have about the economic rewards of a legal career:

> The legal profession is really two professions: the elite lawyers and everyone else. Most of the former start out at big law firms. Many of the latter never find gainful legal employment. Instead, they work at jobs that might be characterized as "quasi-legal": paralegals, clerks, administrators, doing work for which they probably never needed a J.D. . . . .
>
> Every year I'm surprised by the number of my students who think a J.D. degree is a ticket to fame, fortune and the envy of one's peers— a sure ticket to the upper middle class. Even for the select few for whom it is, not many last long enough at their law firms to really enjoy it.[17]

Anecdotes illustrate the statistical evidence. Newspapers report that with shifts in governmental and corporate expenditures, even some professionals with college educations—engineers, lawyers, and accountants—are laid off and cannot find the well-paid work that they had been doing. For example, Tom Kingsley, a 29-year-old mechanical engineer employed by General Dynamics at the Groton Naval Base in New London, Connecticut, teaching naval officers to operate nuclear reactors, lost his job in 1993 when the Pentagon reduced its budget for Trident submarines. Facing a glut of engineers in similar circumstances at the time, Mr. Kingsley was forced to take a caddying job at the Ridgewood Country Club in Paramus, New Jersey.[18] In a market for labor services, including the market for the services of college graduates, at the same time there can be a seller's market for plumbers and pharmacists and too many mechanical engineers and sociologists. This is inevitable in a dynamic system in which young people are free to prepare for any career that interests them and in which schools and colleges are free to enroll as many students as they wish regardless of whether or not jobs exist for their graduates. Eventually, the lessons of the labor market are heeded. If too many naval architects are being trained in American engineering schools to get jobs in a field that is declining in the United States, fewer engineering students will specialize in naval architecture. But this lesson takes time to sink in; moreover, for those passionately interested in a field, hope trumps market considerations.

"College graduates" are an extremely heterogeneous group, including liberal arts majors in philosophy, English, and Icelandic literature; prospective social workers, actors, and ministers; career military officers; technically trained chemists, physicists, engineers, and computer scientists; and hundreds of other interests and majors. Long before grade inflation muddied the waters, studies of college graduates showed that those employed in some fields made more money than those employed in others. (Later in the chapter I will report detailed data from one of the earliest such studies, an analysis of the earnings of thousands of American college graduates more than a half century ago.[19]) Some college graduates find it easy to secure entry-level jobs in fields that offer prospects of career development. Others discover that little or no market demand exists for the college curriculum that they have pursued. One alternative is to flounder in the job market, taking dead-end jobs that high school graduates can do, while waiting for the market situation to improve in the fields that interest them. Another possibility is to consider retraining, perhaps in graduate school.

For many students, level of remuneration is not the main reason for selecting one college major over another. Intrinsic interest is important. For other students, the principal motive for going to college is the prospect of substantial economic rewards; hence students are very much interested in the financial payoff of a major. When asked on the "College and Beyond" survey about their goals in life, at least a third responded that it is "very important" or "essential" to "be very well off financially."[20] Majors differ in the intellectual demands made on students. Engineering, pharmacy, computer science, and business administration pay graduates better than sociology or criminal justice. However, the process of becoming a graduate is more difficult in those fields. Consequently what frequently happens is that students begin in pharmacy or engineering or pre-med, realize that they are not doing well enough to compete with academically abler students, and transfer into women's studies, Afro-American studies, or English, where good grades are easier to get. A similar process is at work when students graduate. If students have taken a major in one of the crowded fields that serve as refuges from more demanding curricula, they discover after they graduate that good jobs are not easy to get, in part because lots of other students graduated with the same major. One possibility to avoid unattractive employment prospects is to decide to go to graduate school. They cannot usually get admitted to a law or medical school, but it is a lot easier to get into a school of education and become teachers.

THE EARNINGS PREMIUM FOR COLLEGE GRADUATES

Macro-economic analysis show greater financial rewards for majoring in some fields rather than in others. Macro-economic evidence also shows that the earnings of those who go to college continue to be, on the average, twice as great as the earnings of those who graduated from high school and went no further.[21] For example, in 1992, when median annual earnings of high school graduates who went no further are compared with those of college graduates who had no additional degrees, male *high school* graduates 25 years of age and over earned in a year of full-time work only 66 percent of the money earned by male *college graduates*. Similarly, female high school graduates earned in 1992 only 64 percent of the money earned by female college graduates. Furthermore, since 1979 the percentage that the average income of high school graduates was of the average income of college graduates has been falling (from 81 percent for males in 1979 to 66 percent in 1992).[22] The usual inference made from these well-known data is that higher education makes college graduates better off financially over the long term than they would be if they stopped their educations earlier. I believe that such comparisons overstate the economic value of college degrees, especially in less demanding curricula. Nevertheless, these aggregate data tell high school graduates to heed the advice adults give them to go to college, if they possibly can. Going to college appears to pay off financially.

Despite the wage premium enjoyed by college graduates in the aggregate compared with high school graduates, *proving* that going to college is a worthwhile investment for *individual* students is surprisingly difficult. Those who go to college are not a random selection of high school graduates. They are self-selected for enrollment at college. If the abler high school graduates rather than the less able high school graduates are the ones who select themselves for going to college, enrolling in college may be a *result* of their prior abilities rather than the *cause* of their subsequent financial success. Probably they are abler in regard to academic aptitude, but they may be abler also in qualities that would make for occupational success whether or not they attended college.

Certainly, those high school students who anticipate attending college—and especially those hoping to go to *selective* colleges (where high school records enter into the admissions decision)—are motivated to learn more in high school than those who expect to terminate their educations after high school graduation. Their high school experiences prepare them better intellectually not only for college but for other endeavors that require intellectual proficiency. In short, the differences that eventuated in higher earnings was probably due not only to what they learned at college but also due to superior learning experiences in grade school and high school; on top of this advantage was added whatever was learned at college. A leading expert in the economics of higher education pointed this out twenty-five years ago.[23] This explanation of why employers pay college graduates more than high school graduates gives college education partial credit; it attributes higher earnings to higher levels of knowledge in a knowledge-oriented modern society—and assumes that at least for some students, knowledge increases at college.

High school graduates who do not plan to attend college are also self-selected. High school students who anticipate that high school graduation will mark the end of their formal education have less stake in their teachers' good will. They don't think that grades or teacher recommendations will be very useful to them when they start looking for jobs, usually blue-collar jobs. Academically uninterested students might, with good vocational preparation, obtain well-paid blue-collar jobs, but in the United States they usually don't have the opportunity to acquire workforce skills for skilled blue-collar jobs.[24] Professor James Rosenbaum compared American high schools with secondary schools in Germany and Japan; he concluded that these countries are much better than the United States at preparing youngsters heading for skilled blue-collar work instead of college.[25] American high schools, including those that call themselves "comprehensive," gear their curricular offerings essentially to academic subjects that are either college preparatory or dumbed-down versions of college preparatory courses. Instead, Professor Rosenbaum believes, for youngsters planning to end their formal education with a high school diploma, high schools should give them a chance to prepare for skilled blue-collar work. On some level, teachers and guidance counselors realize that these students are hibernating in their courses, just waiting to graduate and take jobs. Although such students don't drop out formally, they drop out psychologically. Some educators call them "internal dropouts." Instead of training them for skilled blue-collar jobs that pay well—plumbers, electricians, television repairers—educators dangle the hope of college attendance for even very poorly prepared students. Some vocational high schools are exceptions to this generalization—Aviation High School in New York City comes to mind.[26] Similarly, the computerization of automobile engines has made auto mechanics a skilled and well-paid occupation, which Automotive High School in Brooklyn capitalizes on.[27] Aviation High School and Automotive High School are exceptions; most high school students not planning to go to college drift aimlessly through comprehensive high schools. When and if they graduate, they lack most skills useful for white-collar jobs or for skilled trades. They apply for dead-end blue-collar jobs in factories, farms, and mines. That is why their average earnings are so low.

In looking for jobs, high school graduates without good blue-collar skills face two additional disadvantages. They are often deficient in nonacademic as well as academic skills—what some educators term "soft skills."[28] ("Soft skills" refer to such characteristics as showing up every day for work on time, being dependable, solving problems, avoiding rule infractions and conflicts with other workers, putting forth effort, and cooperating with coworkers.) Since employers have found that high school graduates often lack these soft skills even when their grades are reasonably good, perhaps because contemporary American high schools are too tolerant of uncivil behavior like being verbally abusive to teachers, employers believe that college graduates are a better bet. In short, an unconscious factor in employer preference for college graduates may be that college graduates are more likely to possess soft skills, not necessarily the knowledge that they possess, although some gain special knowledge in college. Perhaps high school graduates with these soft skills are more likely to apply to college, or perhaps, when they do opt for college, they learn them from classmates and professors. Either way they are better employees. Consequently employers are willing to pay college graduates a financial premium over what high school graduates are offered even for entry-level jobs that do not really depend on college training. And they are in place when jobs leading to career opportunities open up.

Another disadvantage of high school graduates is that the job market for *unskilled* blue-collar work is shrinking. Fewer factory, farm, and mining jobs are available than used to be, partly because of overseas competition. American companies have closed factories in the United States and opened new ones in countries with much lower labor costs—Mexico, Honduras, China, India, Indonesia. Many of the more than two million manufacturing jobs that the United States lost have been low paying, but some of the lost manufacturing jobs were highly paid jobs in the automobile, shipbuilding, and steel industries. Thus, high school graduates not headed for college frequently face an overcrowded job market—with the result that remuneration in these jobs has stagnated. Globalization has put less downward pressure on managerial, service, and professional jobs. The gap between the hourly earnings of blue-collar and white-collar workers has increased over the past decade and probably earlier also. The decline of manufacturing jobs from 1970 to the present time accounts for much of this gap.[29]

Bear in mind that data on comparative blue-collar and white-collar hourly earnings aggregate the earnings of unskilled and highly skilled blue-collar workers. A good market exists for *skilled* blue-collar jobs, better perhaps than the market for college graduates without special skills, as Charles Murray has pointed out:

> A reality about the job market must eventually begin to affect the valuation of a college education: The spread of wealth at the top of American society has created an explosive increase in the demand for craftsmen. Finding a good lawyer or physician is easy. Finding a good carpenter, painter, electrician, plumber, glazier, mason—the list goes on and on—is difficult, and it is a seller's market. Journeymen craftsmen routinely make incomes in the top half of the income distribution while master craftsmen can make six figures. They have work even in a soft economy. Their jobs cannot be outsourced to India.[30]

Dr. Murray compared the comparative advantages of going to a good high school with going to college in terms of a general principle, "It's what you can do that should count when you apply for a job, not where you learned to do it."[31] He recommends national certification examinations instead of college for high school graduates who find alternative ways to obtain what they are really after in college: the knowledge that will prepare them for good jobs. It is cheaper for them as well as for mediocre college graduates encumbered by loans that the United States Treasury may well end up paying after defaults. Dr. Murray does not imply that college is worthless or that the liberal education that some college can provide to some students is not wonderful to have. Nor is he denying that some professional undergraduate courses that involve laboratory skills—engineering, pharmacy, perhaps computer science—might be learned best in colleges or universities. He is saying only that many youngsters nowadays go to college for the wrong reasons.

In considering the earnings premium enjoyed by college graduates compared with those who haven't graduated from college, it is useful to disaggregate those aspects of a college degree that make employers more interested in college graduates. What are they?

- Specialized knowledge or skills.
- Soft skills, including more self-discipline and more capacity to learn than those who leave the educational pipeline earlier. College graduates come, on the average, from families with more formal education, greater financial resources, and greater ability to transmit soft skills to their children. They are more likely to be polite. Those who enter college from less privileged or minority backgrounds have opportunities to learn soft skills from their college peers. Hence, even when their social origins are modest, they seem more promising to prospective employers than mere high school graduates.
- The status "college graduate" carries symbolic cachet.[32] The other side of this coin is that college students often seek the bachelor's degree as a credential that employers will honor rather than the knowledge that the degree is assumed to reflect.
- Age. College graduates are four to six years older, on the average, than high school graduates and are therefore perceived as more likely to be responsible. They are closer to being "adults" than "kids." Not only do they constitute a better bet for initial hiring; they are in place for more on-the-job training opportunities and for moving up when opportunities arise. Thus, the earnings premium over those youngsters whose educations were limited to primary and secondary schools continues through the life cycle. Some high school graduates—but relatively few—possess enough skills and knowledge to compete successfully with college graduates, especially college graduates who have learned very little at college, but not in the first few years after high school graduation. Differential knowledge was measured in three ways: Grade Point Averages, Reading achievement scores on a common test, and the Armed Services Vocational Aptitude Battery. None showed an advantage in the labor market for the more knowledgeable high school graduates until they reached "economic adulthood"—about 22 years of age, which brings them to the age when many college graduates enter the labor market.[33] Apparently what happens is that employers only begin to take account of the knowledge and ability of high school graduates when they reach "economic adulthood." A possible exception is computer skills, which were mastered by some high school students well enough to open the door to computer programming jobs that paid well; this exception was probably temporary as computer science

became an important college major. That is to say, computer skills learned in high school became less of a path to well-paying jobs in the twenty-first century than they were in the twentieth century.

Apart from any knowledge students may gain from studies that they undertake at college, they make contacts with fellow students that they may later utilize in seeking better-paid work. Furthermore, they also learn computer skills that help in the hunt for jobs in better-paying fields, and they receive the benefit of job-placement and other services that colleges provide for their students, particularly graduating seniors. Thus, it is not a simple matter to tease out the components of a college experience that lead to the earnings premium that college graduates enjoy vis-à-vis high school graduates.

Consequently, a mere comparison of the earnings of high school and college graduates probably overstates the educational advantages obtained from the college degree. In addition, some empirical data exist that suggest that, if high school graduates enter college with knowledge deficits due to deficiencies in their primary and secondary school preparation, they may not reach college graduation at all. Professor James Rosenbaum mined the data contained in the "High School and Beyond" data bank, a longitudinal study of 14,825 youngsters who were high school sophomores in 1980 and were reinterviewed in 1982, 1984, 1986, and 1992.[34] Some attrition occurred in the sample, but the researchers responsible for the original study located and reinterviewed 12,640 members of the cohort in the 1992 follow-up. Professor Rosenbaum dealt with outcomes for individuals who responded in both the 1982 and 1992 surveys. He also utilized two other data sources: detailed interviews with a nonrandom sample of seniors in two high schools and a survey of 2,091 high school seniors from a random sample of classes at twelve high schools in the Chicago metropolitan area from 1992 to 1994. He concluded that high school students are seriously misinformed about the benefits of attending college. They are urged to attend college whether they have been doing well academically or not. Following this advice, 71 percent of the 1980 "High School and Beyond" cohort (interviewed in 1982 during their senior year in high school) planned to enter college and work toward a degree.[35] He found, however, that less than 14 percent of those members of the cohort who were academically poor students—C average or less—actually obtained college degrees by 1992, even from two-year colleges, by ten years after their high school graduation.[36] Given grade inflation, which has been occurring in high schools as well as colleges, it is unlikely that many students had a C average in the 1980 "High School and Beyond" cohort—and even fewer more recently. Consequently it is likely that many academically weak high school graduates enter college now with a B average or better and persist until they graduate. Do they get low grades in college and, if so, do they still enjoy an earnings premium? I turn now to this question.

WHICH COLLEGE GRADUATES HAVE LOW EARNINGS?

In his assessment of the job prospects of future college graduates, Professor Harris mentioned in passing that some college degrees were worth more in the marketplace than others. But the main thrust of his analysis was not on the variability of remuneration among college graduates and certainly not on the possibility that different learning experiences at college could account for this variability. But let us consider a plausible long-run scenario. Suppose that the economic payoff is radically different by curriculum so that degrees in intellectually demanding subjects, such as majors in the physical and biological sciences and in mathematics and economics, turn out to be worth much more to employers than those of majors in the humanities and in most of the social sciences. Suppose also that in addition to the variation in usefulness to employers by field, differential learning occurs in every field and prospective employers are rational enough to prefer employees who know something rather than employees who bring little knowledge to their jobs, that is, college graduates who are graduates in name only, whatever their major fields. If fields and superior learning count in employee recruitment, some college graduates will find to their distress that they cannot get jobs or at any rate cannot get the business and professional jobs that they expected. They have to settle for jobs that high school graduates are competing for, thereby increasing unemployment and depressing wages for high school graduates as well as receiving poor remuneration themselves. They are at the tail end of the earnings distribution for college graduates and earn less than many high school graduates. (The frequency distributions of remuneration for high school graduates and for college graduates overlap even though high school graduates earn on the average much less than college graduates.)

In point of fact, empirical data can identify college graduates who find themselves in this unenviable position (1) by contrasting graduates who majored in intellectually demanding curricula like engineering, mathematics, and the physical and biological sciences from those who majored in less rigorous fields like sociology, English literature, Women's Studies, and Black Studies and (2) by contrasting those graduates in the more demanding fields as well as the less demanding curricula who report having received mostly A grades during their college careers with those who received C grades or worse. This operational procedure for separating students who learned more in college from students who learned less is imperfect. Certainly, there are brilliant and diligent students in sociology and English literature and mediocre ones in physics and microbiology. But it is much more possible to pass—and to graduate—without doing appreciable work in some subjects than in others. Certainly too, a C may represent intellectual accomplishment in some courses and an A simply going through the motions in other courses. Usually, despite rampant grade inflation in some departments, A grades represent intellectual accomplishment, whereas Cs do not.

Some data exist that bear out these common-sense conclusions. More than a half century ago, *Time Magazine* commissioned a large survey of its readership, a large proportion of whom were college graduates. Respondents included 9,064 persons who had attended 1,037 colleges. As part of the study of college graduates from this database, the authors related the earnings of respondents to the grades they reported receiving, as well as the curricula they reported pursuing.[37] The results showed that those graduates who got higher grades earned higher incomes. This finding stood up for various curricula, and graduates who had pursued the harder curricula did better financially than graduates who pursued easier curricula. This was an era before grade inflation had set in; the survey was conducted in 1947, more than sixty years ago, so the differences in grades were more meaningful than they would be today.

There is another more recent study. The National Center for Education Statistics of the United States Department of Education has been sponsoring longitudinal studies of American youngsters for years. What these studies do is take an essentially random sample of American students, interview them early in their educational careers, and then reinterview them at various intervals to find out what happened to them. One of its studies is the "Recent College Graduate Survey," which consisted of about 18,000 individuals who received bachelors or master's degrees between July 1, 1989, and June 30, 1990 from 400 American colleges and universities.[38] With the assistance of a graduate student in economics, I analyzed data on those members of the sample who had graduated from college one year after their graduation; that was when the only follow-up occurred. We looked at their self-reported GPAs in college divided into three groups: (1) A students, who reported receiving a 3.25 GPA or better, (2) B students whose reported GPA was between 2.75 and 3.24, and C students whose reported GPA was 2.75 or less. Their work situations were placed in three categories: employed full-time, employed part-time, and unemployed. For those who were employed full-time—14,405 individuals, constituting the bulk of the sample—we analyzed in considerable detail the relationship between reported grades at college and earnings in the year following graduation.

Their different levels of remuneration in different occupations were analyzed in two different ways, first, by dividing the sample into eleven groups of majors: (1) business and management, (2) education, (3) engineering, (4) health professions, (5) public affairs/social services, (6) biological sciences, (7) mathematics, computer science, physical sciences, (8) social sciences and history, (9) humanities, (10) psychology, and (11) all other fields. (We assumed that the occupations that the graduates pursued were related to their college majors.) Second, in each of these eleven groups of majors we divided the sample into five levels of remuneration ranging from the top 20 percent of annual earnings to the bottom 20 percent of annual earnings. Only then did we attempt to relate the level of grades received by students to the percent of them who were in the top quintile of remuneration. Here is what we found:

In some fields of major, subsequent earnings were strongly related to college grades. For instance:

- In engineering 28 percent of the A students were in the top quintile of remuneration as compared with 20.2 percent of the B students and 11.6 percent of the C students.
- In business and management 31.5 percent of the A students were in the top quintile of remuneration as compared with 20.5 percent of the B students and 11.5 percent of the C students.
- In mathematics, computer science, and physical science 26.9 percent of the A students were in the top quintile of remuneration as compared with 17.9 percent of the B students and 8.7 percent of the C students.

In other fields there did not seem to be any relationship between the grades received at college and subsequent earnings after graduation. For instance: In the humanities 18.3 percent of the A students were in the top quintile of remuneration as compared with 20.9 percent of the B students and 23.7 percent of the C students. In the health professions 20.2 percent of the A students were in the top quintile of remuneration as compared with 20.3 percent of the B students and 20.9 percent of the C students. This finding may reflect the greater grading inflation in the soft disciplines than in more demanding subjects. In engineering high grades means that the individual has learned more and is worth more. In the health professions grades seemed to make no difference for earnings and in the humanities high grades apparently resulted in lower average earnings than low grades.

Overall, there was a relationship between reported grades and subsequent earnings. For the A students 24.5 percent ended up in the top quintile of remuneration for their fields of study compared with 20.7 percent of the B students, and 14.7 percent of the C students. Keep in mind, however, that earnings differed from field to field. The engineering majors averaged

$31,125 in the 1990–1991 year following their graduation, and their variability of remuneration around that mean was relatively small. The standard deviation of the distribution of their earnings was only $8,256, which meant that the majority earned between $23,000 and $39,000 per year. The social science and history majors averaged $22,187 in the 1990–1991 year following their graduation, and their variability of remuneration around that mean was relatively large. The standard deviation of the distribution of their earnings was $10,340, which meant that the majority earned between $12,000 and $32,000 per year. Some did very poorly indeed financially. Thus, the social science and history majors were double losers financially. As a group they earned less on the average than college graduates from harder curricula. But coming as they did from a group that had greater than average variability around the group mean—that is the meaning of the standard deviation—those in the bottom tail of the social science and history distribution earned much less relatively than those in the bottom tail of distributions for the engineering and other difficult disciplines.

These data refer to the first year after graduation from college. If the longitudinal design of the study had been implemented, there would have been an opportunity to learn whether these initial differences in earning power resulting from differential intellectual achievement in college expanded as initial advantages continued to produce cumulative advantages or whether they disappeared over time. Unfortunately, no further interviews with members of this cohort occurred. An invaluable opportunity to assess the economic rewards of a college education was lost.

SHOULD PUBLIC POLICY ATTEMPT TO MAXIMIZE LEARNING IN COLLEGE?

Thomas Jefferson was an elitist in intellectual matters. When he founded the University of Virginia, he wanted to recruit students from all walks of life who possessed "genius," not just undergraduates from the landed aristocracy.[39] He wanted the University to have free tuition so that it could nurture that rare talent for learning. Learning for what purpose? Jefferson certainly valued ideas for their own sake; he was what would be called today a public intellectual. Insofar as he thought that attending a university was socially useful, however, the usefulness had to do with learning how to make civic contributions rather than how to make economic contributions.

Over the past two centuries higher education has assumed functions in society not envisioned by Jefferson. Jefferson would have been sympathetic to what college professors say about the value of a liberal education for living a life richer in understanding and what philosophers and even politicians say about the value of attending college for cultivating civic virtues.

Jefferson notwithstanding, few students come to college for those reasons. They come primarily to gain an advantageous foothold in the occupational system. Ideas have turned out to be useful for a wide range of economic activities. Jefferson might be shocked to learn that some students now attending his University of Virginia come to develop expertise in "information technology" and others go to its law school in order to become specialists in "intellectual property" laws. Benjamin Franklin, an amateur scientist who started out as a printer and never went to college, might have appreciated better than Jefferson the close ties between the economy and the system of higher education as it exists today and, by the same token, the motives of contemporary college students.

That is why contemporary college students may more easily admire Franklin than Jefferson. Yet most of them do not have Franklin's intellectual curiosity. Correct but incomplete statements about the career advantages of graduating from college mislead them. Many students hear the words, "college education," and think the emphasis should be put on *college* rather than on *education.* Most students don't fully appreciate that the advantages in the job marketplace accrue disproportionately to those who enroll in the academically more demanding schools, curricula, and majors. Furthermore, whatever their major, those college graduates who have learned nothing substantial in the four or more years spent in college will not come across in job interviews as good prospects for employment. In short, if college graduates expect to launch careers based on their claim to have a college education, they are expected to know something. That is what *education* implies.

CONCLUSION

To get back to Professor Harris's pessimistic assessment of college education as an investment, he was premature (in 1949) to assert that the market for college graduates was deteriorating, although later evidence about the tight labor market for new college graduates and unemployment among *experienced* lawyers, engineers, accountants, and other professionals suggests that Harris was right to be skeptical of a college degree as a cornucopia.[40] While it is correct that the economic rewards for the average college graduate exceed those for high school graduates, some economists who take into account the foregone earnings during college and the investment income obtained from investing those earnings have concluded that going to college may not pay economically.[41] The purely economic advantages of a college education cannot be calculated from a simple comparison between lifetime earnings of high school and college graduates. What also has to be considered are the investments made by students in not working, by parents in funding college costs, and by government and private scholarships and loans. Economists are doing increasingly sophisticated research on these issues.[42] Has college education reached the point at which the financial returns to many students do not justify the costs? While college graduates as an aggregate are financially much better off than high school graduates as an aggregate, college graduates in the aggregate covers students who have studied hard in demanding curricula and learned a lot as well as students who squandered their four years of opportunity to increase their trained intellectual capacity. They may have spent their time having fun, sometimes self-destructive fun. Students who studied diligently and earned high grades obtain degrees worth more financially—as well as in other ways—than the degrees of students who took their studies less seriously (as reflected in reported mediocre grades).

In short, there may be now too many college graduates relative to the number of professional and business occupations to which most of them aspire—at the same time that those college graduates who have majored in the most demanding curricula and have gotten the best grades will find interesting and well-paid jobs. According to the demographers, the overall ratio of college graduates to college-level job opportunities will continue to increase in future years. As in the game of musical chairs, when the music stops, someone will not find a seat. Of course, there is more to life than occupational success. Some college graduates who did not take higher education seriously may be willing to lower their occupational aspirations, to take less interesting and poorer paying jobs than they hoped for as college students, to obtain life satisfactions from raising a family and engaging in hobbies, and to look back on their years of pleasurable college life with nostalgia.

If, however, they decide early enough in their precollege and college years that higher education is an investment in their occupational futures, not fun and games, and follow through with serious efforts to learn, they may become the college graduates for whom a college education pays off financially. In return for deferred gratification, as the psychologists call it, they will have better opportunities for successful careers. Some students will want to pay this price; others won't. In fairness, they ought to know as early as possible what the choices are.

For the majority of unstudious students, attending college may lead not to interesting and well-paying jobs but to a mountain of burdensome debt, not only federal student loans but private loans, credit card debt, and loans from parents). The average credit card debt that students carry with them along with a diploma is $2,864. [43] For society also, sending unstudious students to college is a road leading to disappointment. Rich as the United States is, the resources that even a superpower can afford to spend are limited. Universal entitlement to higher education is an extremely expensive way to locate and nurture the Albert Einsteins and the Isaac Newtons.

This chapter discussed the economic payoff of higher education for individual students and for American society. What about the intellectual payoff? Does higher education increase the ability of graduates to better understand the complex modern world? Students take such diverse courses to graduate from college that their intellectual gains from the college experience are difficult to compare; besides, nearly all colleges prefer to ignore this question. Out of the 3,700 in the United States, 40 are seeking to find out what students learn from college, including the University of Charleston in West Virginia, which has "incoming students take a standardized test designed to measure reasoning and writing skills and then take the test again after sophomore year and once again as seniors."[44] The University of Charleston claims substantial gains in liberal learning outcomes like critical thinking and creativity. Wonderful, if true. The national survey reported in Table 5.1 suggested that college seniors did not *know* more about American history, government, political thought, international affairs, and the market economy than freshmen students at the same colleges; the survey questions did not attempt to assess their critical thinking and creativity. Nevertheless, a group of colleges in Indiana, Minnesota, and Utah are starting a pilot project, financed by a private foundation, to find consensus about what all students should learn from a college education.[45]

NOTES

1. Lyrics of the song, "Brush Up Your Shakespeare," lyrics and music by Cole Porter for the musical comedy, *Kiss Me, Kate*, book by Sam and Bella Spewack, Broadway production in 1948. Reprinted with the permission of Alfred Publishing. Permission granted on April 29, 2009.

2. Anne D. Neal, "The Vanishing Shakespeare," A Report by the American Council of Trustees and Alumni, Washington, D.C., April, 2007, p. 23.

3. Barry Latzer, "The Hollow Core: Failure of the General Education Curriculum," A Report by the American Council of Trustees and Alumni, Washington, D.C., April, 2004.

4. Annie Karni, "Students Know Less after 4 College Years," *New York Sun*, September 19, 2007.

5. Clark Kerr, *The Uses of the University*, Cambridge, MA: Harvard University Press, 1963.

6. Seymour E. Harris, *The Market for College Graduates*, Cambridge, MA: Harvard University Press, 1949.

7. National Center for Education Statistics, *Digest of Education Statistics: 1994*, Washington, D.C.: Government Printing Office, 1994, p. 175.

8. U.S. Census Bureau, Population Estimates, *National Estimates by Age, Sex, Race: 1900–1979 (PE-11)*. Web site accessed in April 2009: www.census.gov/popest/archives/pre-1980/PE-11.html.

9. Wikipedia, the Free Encyclopedia, "Robert Hutchins." Web site accessed in April 2009: http://en.wikipedia.org/wiki/Robert_Hutchins.

10. Landon Y. Jones, *Great Expectations: America and the Baby Boom Generation.* New York: Coward, McConn & Geohegan, 1980.

11. *Digest of Education Statistics: 1994, op. cit,* p. 108.

12. *Digest of Education Statistics 2008, op. cit,* Chapter 3 Postsecondary Education Degrees, Table 268, p. 295.

13. Daniel E. Hecker, "Reconciling Conflicting Data on Jobs for College Graduates," *Monthly Labor Review,* July 1992, pp. 3–12; Kristina J. Shelley, "More Job Openings—Even More New Entrants: The Outlook for College Graduates 1992–2005," *Occupational Outlook Quarterly,* Summer 1994, pp. 4–9.

14. Sylvia Nasar, "More College Graduates Taking Low-Wage Jobs," *New York Times,* August 7, 1992.

15. Mark Mittelhauser, "The Outlook for College Graduates, 1996–2006: Prepare Yourself—Number of College Graduates Exceeds College-Level Jobs," *Occupational Outlook Quarterly,* Summer, 1998.

16. Amir Efrati, "Hard Case: Job Market Wanes for U.S. Lawyers," *Wall Street Journal,* September 24, 2007.

17. Cameron Stracher, "Law School by Default," *The Wall Street Journal,* June 23, 2006; Nathan Koppel, "Best Defense? Seeking a Haven in Law School," *Wall Street Journal,* March 3, 2009.

18. Robert Handley, "Pros: In the Caddy Shack: Country Club Recession," *New York Times,* July 7, 1993.

19. Ernest Havemann and Patricia Salter West, *They Went to College: the College Graduate in America Today,* New York: Harcourt, Brace, 1952.

20. James L. Shulman and William G. Bowen, *The Game of Life: College Sports and Educational Values,* Princeton University Press, Princeton, NJ: 2001, pp. 56–57.

21. Louis Uchitelle, "College Degree Pays, but It's Leveling Off," *New York Times,* January 13, 2005.

22. *Ibid.*

23. Stephen A. Hoenack, "Pricing and Efficiency in Higher Education," *Journal of Higher Education,* Vol. 53, No. 4, 1982, p. 405.

24. Jeffrey Mirel, "The Traditional High School"; Greene, Jay P., "A 'Comprehensive' Problem"; and Chester E. Finn, Jr., "Things Are Falling Apart" in *Education Next,* Vol. 6, No. 1, Winter 2005, pp. 13–22.

25. James Rosenbaum, *Beyond College for All: Career Paths for the Forgotten Half,* New York: Russell Sage Foundation, 2001.

26. Melanie D. G. Kaplan, "Fly Girl," *New York Times,* January 12, 2003.

27. Norimitzu Onishi, "Teaching the Mechanics of Success," *New York Times,* January 16, 1994; Corey Kilgannon, "A High School under the Hood," *New York Times,* October 24, 2007; C. J. Hughes, "At a High School for Future Mechanics, a Gift of Two Engines," *New York Times,* January 15, 2009.

28. Rosenbaum, *op. cit.,* pp. 174, 269–270.

29. Congressional Budget Office, "What Accounts for the Decline in Manufacturing Employment?" February 18, 2004.

30. Charles Murray, "What's Wrong with Vocational School?" *Wall Street Journal*, January 17, 2007.

31. Charles Murray, "Should the Obama Generation Drop Out?" *New York Times*, December 28, 2008.

32. John W. Meyer, "The Effects of Education as an Institution," *American Journal of Sociology*, Vol. 85: 55–77.

33. Paul Barton, "Learn More, Earn More?" *ETS Policy Notes*, Vol. 9, No. 2, Summer 1999.

34. Rosenbaum, *op. cit.*, p. 59.

35. *Ibid.*, p. 66

36. *Ibid.*, p. 67.

37. Havemann and West, *op. cit.*

38. United States Department of Education, National Center for Education Statistics, Recent College Graduate Survey, 1991. A table from this survey, Table 379 "Employment Status of 1989–90 Bachelor's Degree Recipients 1 Year after Graduation, by Field of Study and Occupational Area," was published in the *Digest of Education Statistics 1995*. Web site accessed in April 2009: http://nces.ed.gov/programs/digest/d95/dtab379.asp

39. B. L. Rayner, *Life of Thomas Jefferson*, Boston: Lilly, Wait, Colman, & Holden, 1834.

40. Richard B. Freeman, "The Decline in the Economic Rewards to College Education," *Review of Economics and Statistics*, Vol. 59, No. 1, 1977, pp. 18–29; Richard, B. Freeman, "Inequality, Trade, Skills and Globalization," Chapter 13 in Brian Nolan, Wiemer Salverda, and Timothy Smeedings (eds.), *Handbook on Economic Inequality*, (Oxford University Press, forthcoming in 2008).

41. Robertson Educational Empowerment Foundation, *The Biggest Gamble of Your Life (Is College Worth It?)*, 2006. Web site accessed in April 2009: www.aboutreef.org/is-college-worth-it.html.

42. See, for example, William E Becker, "The Demand for Higher Education," in Stephen A. Hoenack and Eileen L. Collins (eds.) *The Economics of American Universities.* New York: State University of New York Press, 1990, pp. 155–188.

43. "Undergraduate Students and Credit Cards in 2004: An Analysis of Usage Rates and Trends," a study by Nellie Mae, published May 2005. Web site accessed in April 2009: www.nelliemae.com/library/research_12.html.

44. James Traub, "No Gr_du_te Left Behind," *New York Times Magazine*, September 30, 2007.

45. Tamar Lewin, "Colleges in 3 States to Set Basics for Degrees," New *York Times*, April 9, 2009.

Chapter 6

THE PERILS OF THE FINANCIAL AID LABYRINTH

Before World War II, academically excellent students from families unable to finance college for them could apply for the small number of competitive scholarships that were then available from the colleges to which students sought admission or from private foundations. Although many colleges to which they applied for admission received financial support of various kinds from the federal government, the federal government itself made grants only to the colleges rather than making grants to individual high school students to enable them to attend college or to college students already enrolled. However, the federal government's role in student aid changed radically after World War II.

OLD-FASHIONED SCHOLARSHIPS AS INCENTIVES TO PREPARE INTELLECTUALLY FOR COLLEGE

Old-fashioned, academic scholarships still exist. Some traditional scholarships—nowadays renamed "merit-based" scholarships—are provided by colleges themselves out of internal resources like endowments and some by corporations, foundations, or state governments. I call them "traditional" to distinguish them from more recent types of financial awards that give less emphasis to previous academic performance than to promoting maximum *access* to higher education, especially access for students from economically disadvantaged families or from racial and ethnic minorities. Thomas Jefferson would have approved of scholarships based on academic merit. Jefferson believed that genius could arise in poor as well as rich families. Consequently he proposed (in 1817) college scholarships for especially able youth regardless of the economic resources of the family. Even before he advocated scholarships for able youngsters at the University of Virginia, Jefferson advocated educating youngsters of "genius," wherever they could be found. "By that part of our plan [of education in Virginia] which prescribes the selection of the youths of genius from among the classes of the poor, we hope to avail the State of those talents which nature has sown as liberally among the poor as the rich, but which perish without use, if not sought for and cultivated."[1]

Although the performances of athletes certainly require training and diligent effort as well as genetic potentialities, they are not *intellectually* meritorious. Consequently Jefferson probably would have been nonplussed by "athletic" scholarships. His proposal sought students who were intellectually outstanding. Athletic scholarships are not merit-based scholarships in the Jeffersonian sense of rewarding intellectual achievements and potentialities. While there are always some minimum academic requirements for an athletic scholarship, they are low; athletic scholarships reward prowess in some sport important to the college community, usually disregarding in the selection process financial need. Professors have long doubted that athletic "scholarships" are properly named. After all, no one pretends that holders of athletic scholarships are academically superb; they are merely expected to improve the competitive performance of intercollegiate sports teams. From the point of view of the majority of professors, athletic scholarships divert resources that should be committed to financing needy students of demonstrated intellectual ability and studiousness. For example, English Professor William C. Dowling has criticized relentlessly over a period of years the diversion of resources from academic to athletic activities at Rutgers University, where he is a tenured distinguished professor.[2] However, athletic scholarships do not break with meritocratic values; applicants for admission receive athletic scholarships on the basis of previous personal achievements in football, basketball, soccer, or other high school sports. A half century ago faculty and students at most colleges and universities knew that athletic scholarships existed, but athletic scholarships appeared to be minor deviations from general practice; and some elite universities like Harvard, Yale, and Princeton didn't have them at all. Winning a *scholarship* was understood to mean substantial previous *academic* achievement.

States also gave scholarships to academically excellent students. For example, long before World War II, New Jersey had a major program of State scholarships based on academic performance to help five percent of the graduating high school seniors every year to attend college; in 1977, 13,000 academically able New Jersey high school graduates were State Scholars.[3] Rutgers, by then the State University of New Jersey, enrolled 2,400 of them. State Scholars were selected on the basis of student rank in high school and on Scholastic Aptitude Test scores. When future Nobel Laureate Milton Friedman attended Rutgers College from 1928 to 1932, he received one of these State scholarships based on the screening criterion then in place: high grades on a competitive examination for high school applicants needing financial help.[4] While at Rutgers, at that time still a small private college proud of having been founded in 1766, Friedman also worked in a local restaurant for his meals. Indigent students like Friedman often described themselves as "working their way through college," which meant not merely that they valued education enough to have studied diligently in primary and secondary school but that they also worked at part-time menial jobs during their college careers if scholarships did not cover all of their expenses. Winners of traditional scholarships like Friedman were expected to raise the academic quality of the colleges they attended, as Friedman did at Rutgers; he received an A grade in almost every course he took.

New Jersey students were proud to be designated State Scholars as evidence of their achievements even when they received no cash (because they could not satisfy the financial need test that the State Legislature required for monetary awards, namely, the inability of the student's family to contribute much to college expenses). They felt proud because they had demonstrated some degree of mastery of a body of knowledge; our society values knowledge as worthwhile in itself as well as being useful for economic applications, such as information technology. Getting a scholarship is a tribute to this mastery.

Moreover, knowledge has become increasingly useful to modern societies. Political and economic decision-makers need information to inform their decisions; so do voters in a democracy. For instance, sophisticated mathematics was necessary to develop the computer chips basic to the age of information technology. The usefulness of knowledge is not the sole reason that universities value the pursuit of knowledge, as an apocryphal story suggests. A toast given by distinguished mathematician Godfrey H. Hardy at University of Cambridge dinner parties was alleged to have been, "To pure mathematics! May it never be of use to anyone."[5] What this means to most scholars at universities is that there must be room for basic research that extends the boundaries of knowledge in a field whether or not practical applications exist, not that practical applications are disdained. A popular television program of a few decades ago was entitled, "It Pays to Be Ignorant." This title was meant as a joke. Neither the producers of the show or the viewers really believed that being ignorant was better than possessing knowledge.

Giving scholarships also reflects the high value that modern societies place on acquiring knowledge. Colleges, corporations, and governments award academic scholarships; academic scholarships at colleges and universities are part of the institutionalization of the pursuit of knowledge. According to an analysis of the values of American higher education published by the Harvard University Press in 1973, "cognitive rationality" is the central value of the university, trumping less salient values that are embodied in professional training, ideological or religious indoctrination, and the occupational socialization of the young.[6] The pursuit of knowledge is widely valued throughout American society, not just in universities themselves. State legislators, the citizenry of the state, and local corporations take pride that their colleges and universities attract brilliant students and often fund scholarships that help recruit such students. (They also fund the research that attracts award-winning faculty.) In this spirit, colleges and universities compete for prestige with traditional academic scholarships as well as with winning athletic teams. "Merit" scholarships help them to maintain a college's competitive ranking, which is useful for recruiting good students and faculty. The ratings in *U.S. News and World Report* and other magazines, accurate or not, are extensively reported in the media, including student newspapers. When a college's rating goes up, the story is reported with some jubilation in its student newspaper. When its rating goes down, it is reported in its student newspaper along with interviews with professors and administrators who express skepticism about the validity of the methods used in compiling the ratings.

Competition among colleges reinforces their devotion to the principle of promoting knowledge for its own sake, as does competition among large corporations for professional employees; corporations send recruiters to college campuses to recruit employees among university graduates. Awarding academic scholarships helps to create good will in potential professional employees. Corporations like Intel need high-level engineers and computer scientists that will keep them on the cutting edge of the knowledge explosion. It is not surprising, therefore, that the Intel Corporation supports a Science Talent Search Program that rewards the scientific achievements of high school students.

In short, traditional academic scholarships still have considerable symbolic importance, although they are rare compared with new programs of "financial aid." The National Merit Scholarship Program, begun in 1955, awards each year about 8,200 scholarships of $2,500 each to finalists based on their test scores on the Preliminary SAT/National Merit Scholarship Qualifying Test and other purely academic criteria in the fifty states; the National Achievement Scholarship Program, begun in 1964, awards each year about 800 scholarships of $2,500 each to *African American* finalists based on their test scores on the Preliminary SAT/National Merit Scholarship Qualifying Test and other purely academic criteria but compared only with the scores of other *black* students in their state. Since African American students can compete for National Merit Scholarships as well as National Achievement Scholarships, black students are not limited to the 800 scholarship slots reserved for high achieving black students. Apparently the National Merit Corporation was not satisfied with the yield of African American National Merit Scholars from the purely meritocratic main program, so it established the National Achievement Scholarship Program to guarantee that a substantial number of African Americans would receive Merit Scholarships. It could be criticized as a "separate but equal" program for one minority but not for others.

The National Merit Scholarship and National Achievement Programs are the largest, most prestigious, and most visible programs that attempt to encourage general academic excellence. The National Achievement Scholarship program, which is also sponsored by the National Merit Scholarship Corporation, is designed to "honor academically promising high school students who are black Americans and to encourage them to pursue higher education." It is a blend of merit scholarships and a diversity promotion effort. Only black students are eligible—not whites, not Asians, not Hispanics, not American Indians. Within that pool, test scores determine who gets the scholarship, but those who receive such scholarships may have lower scores than those who did not win in the broader national Merit Scholarship competition.

In the science field the prestigious Intel Science Talent Search rewards scientific achievement in high school students handsomely. In 2007, 1,705 students from 487 schools in 44 states entered the Intel Science Talent Search; their research usually began years earlier. Each of the 300 students named a semifinalist in the Intel Science Talent Search receives a $1,000 award for his or her outstanding science research. The top prize is a $100,000 four-year scholarship. The second-place finalist receives a $75,000 scholarship, and the third-prize winner gets a $50,000 scholarship. Fourth-through sixth-place finalists each receive a $25,000 scholarship; seventh-through tenth-prize winners each receive a $20,000 scholarship.[7]

In addition to these merit-based scholarships offered by nongovernmental organizations independent of colleges and universities, nearly every college awards a limited number of scholarships that depend on academic achievement alone or on some mix of academic achievement and financial need. Rutgers, for example, has about two hundred such scholarship winners out of a freshman class of more than 2,500 on its three campuses (New Brunswick, Newark, and Camden). The majority of them, however, are like the National Achievement Program of the National Merit Scholarship Corporation; they search for academic excellence in a pool of minority candidates. A white non-Hispanic applicant for admission to Rutgers cannot be considered for these scholarships.

The financial support that parents give to their children in order to attend college is not usually considered merit-based "scholarships"; it may be an expression of parental love and a misperception of aptitude. In most cases, however, the perception of aptitude is based on the student's previous academic accomplishments, a similar justification to the one used by traditional academic scholarships. A few parents are willing to finance a college education without expecting or requiring their children to treat college attendance as a learning opportunity or as an investment in a future career. For such generous parents college attendance is a pleasant way for their children to spend late adolescence. But even when college attendance was less expensive than it is today, this was an unusual attitude, because most parents had to make financial sacrifices to enable their children to attend college. The explicit or implicit condition for their financial subsidy was that a college education was an investment in the future, as reflected in good grades. Consequently, parents—as well as college committees— monitored their children's work at college by discussing their progress with them and, in days when colleges defined their role as acting *in loco parentis*, by reading grade reports sent directly to them as well as to the students themselves.[8] Parents who received bad enough grade reports about their children might recommend that the student should leave college and get a job because the family's investment in the student's education could not be justified. Unfortunately perhaps, the Family Educational Rights and Privacy Act of 1974 (FERPA), is interpreted by almost all colleges as preventing them from reporting grades to parents (without written permission from the students themselves) of any student over 18 years of age, including students whose attendance at college is being paid for entirely by their parents.[9] According to lawyers, FERPA allows some exceptions to the rule forbidding disclosure of grades and problematic behavior to the parents of *dependent* college students, but most colleges, including my own university, Rutgers, forbid any disclosure without written student consent.[10]

According to Kenneth E. Redd, former director of research and policy analysis at the National Association of Student Financial Aid Administrators, grant money given for merit-based scholarships in 2004 was $7.3 billion compared with $39.1 billion granted for need-based "financial aid."[11] *Federal* financial aid programs, both grants and loans, are unlike traditional scholarships because they generally subsidize good students and bad students alike. In short, traditional scholarships for superior students still exist. But they have shrunk quantitatively relative to "financial aid" that is essentially promiscuous with regard to academic merit or even athletic merit or musical merit. I propose to explain how this happened and what the consequences turned out to be.

THE SHIFT FROM PRIVATE SCHOLARSHIPS
TO FEDERAL FINANCIAL AID

The federal government initiated the shift from "scholarships" to "financial aid" during World War II. On June 22, 1944, President Franklin D. Roosevelt signed The Servicemen's Readjustment Act of 1944—commonly known as the G.I. Bill of Rights—one provision of which gave veterans financial resources to attend college. This provision was an expression of public gratitude, not a Congressional attempt to change the basis for admitting students to college. Although the bill as a whole was controversial, the educational benefits were not; World War II was ongoing both in Europe and in the Pacific, with the outcome still uncertain. Meanwhile American troops were dying in combat—ultimately more than 400,000 died, and many more were wounded.[12] Providing educational opportunities for servicemen and women who served and survived seemed only right.

However, few if any officials anticipated how many veterans would take advantage of these educational benefits. By the time the original G.I. Bill ended on July 25, 1956, 7.8 million of the 16 million World War II veterans had participated in an education or training program.[13] In the peak year of 1947, veterans accounted for 49 percent of college admissions.[14] Virtually alone, the president of Harvard, James Conant, and the president of the University of Chicago, Robert Hutchins, worried about the educational consequences of admitting large numbers of students based on military service to the country rather than on substantial academic criteria.[15] Their fears proved groundless. Reports from colleges suggested that World War II veterans tended to be more serious students than students admitted directly from high school and actually improved the educational atmosphere of the colleges they attended. Since colleges could not expand facilities and staff quickly to accommodate all of the veterans who wished to enroll shortly after demobilization, the influx of veterans probably selected the academically best qualified veterans, at least at first. But an important precedent was set for nonacademic criteria for financing attendance at college. The transformation of "scholarships" into "financial aid" had begun.

Once financial aid was no longer moored to academic excellence, as it was with the traditional basis for "scholarships," other justifications for awarding them presented themselves. The most obvious is financial need, usually phrased in terms of "access." Most traditional scholarships also required financial need before monetary awards were given, as the New Jersey Scholarship program did. But scholarships awarded to academically excellent students who are also needy differ from scholarships to needy students, whatever their academic accomplishments or deficiencies.

Financial aid still was an incentive, but it was an incentive to get *admitted* to college, not to prepare academically for college. Few academic strings were attached. Students who wanted to attend a highly selective college like Princeton or Yale had a strong incentive to prepare academically; financial aid may have been necessary but it was not their main incentive for diligent preparation.

Another basis for awarding financial aid is community service. For instance, President Clinton gave a speech on March 1, 1993, at Rutgers University to an enthusiastic New Jersey audience, including 9,000 students, in which he returned to the theme of "investment" in education. In return for tuition loans to make college attendance more affordable, a theme he had sounded when he ran for election in 1992, "we'll ask you to . . . help control pollution and recycle waste, to paint darkened buildings and clean up neighborhoods, to work with senior citizens and combat homelessness and help children in trouble." The students cheered. Students at the University of New Orleans also cheered on April 30 when he offered a more concrete version of a national service plan.[16] The national service plan turned out to be a relatively small program: only 25,000 community service jobs in 1994, rising to 150,000 in 1997. Still, it was ironic that President Clinton, a former Rhodes Scholar, should propose a basis for college attendance that ignored academic criteria.

Testimonials to the personal and economic obstacles that the student has overcome, cited by applicants themselves or by letters of recommendation, constitute another basis for awarding financial aid.[17] One way of looking at these testimonials is to regard them as a measure of "effort." Instead of assessing achievements directly, the evaluator assesses how hard the student has tried.

As traditional scholarship programs gradually were dwarfed by programs of financial aid, eligibility for which did not include academic excellence, the incentive structure for students changed concomitantly. Most students had to worry less about how much they had learned or were learning and more about these other criteria, including whether their presence in the student body would contribute to the institution's "diversity."

The incentive underlying traditional scholarships is clear: if you put in effort to learn enough before applying to college to get a high grade point average in secondary school and high SAT scores, you have a good chance at scholarships to help with college expenses—along with the symbolic reward of having been demonstrably excellent academically. The incentive underlying financial aid for nonacademic, nonathletic achievements is murkier, involving as it does performing different kinds of community service and overcoming different types of personal problems. (Providing financial aid to students whose presence contributes to "diversity" can't be considered an incentive because one's ethnic or racial contribution is fixed by the happenstance of birth.) Shifting from scholarships based on previously demonstrated academic performance to "financial aid" also dilutes the intellectual qualities that students who enroll in college ought to have. That is why President Conant of Harvard and President Hutchins of the University of Chicago had reservations about the G.I. Bill of Rights.

WHY COLLEGES NEED FINANCIAL AID OFFICES: PROCESSING GRANTS AND LOANS

The Federal government has been a major force in the transition from traditional scholarships to "financial aid." Federal financial aid to students is a mixture of two kinds of subsidies: grants and loans. Be warned. This is a complicated subject. A reasonably complete explanation is necessarily tedious.

Consider grants first. They are gifts from American taxpayers that students do not have to repay. In 1972 Congress established Basic Educational Opportunity Grants, later renamed Pell Grants, which awarded money to college students who demonstrated financial need.[18] The Pell program started relatively modestly. In 1973–1974 Pell grants expended about $224,000,000 (in 2007 inflation-adjusted dollars) to subsidize 176,000 students; the minimum award in constant dollars to a student recipient was $235, the maximum was $2,125.[19] By 2005–2006 the Pell grant program expended $13,531,998,000 to subsidize 5,168,000 students.[20] Some 5,428,000 low-income college students received Pell Grants in 2007–2008 ranging from $400 to $4,310 each, at a cost to taxpayers of more than $14 billion, but 600,000 more applicants asked for grants the following year, requiring an additional $6 billion. The politically popular idea of helping *needy* students have the chance to go to college produced other grant programs that supplement Pell grants for various categories of students: the Federal Supplemental Educational Opportunity Grant (FSEOG) program for undergraduates who are especially needy, the cost of which was $772 million in 2007; the Academic Competitiveness Grant program for first-year college students who have completed a rigorous secondary school program of study; the National Science & Mathematics Access to Retain Talent Grant (National SMART Grant) Program for students whose college major is physical, life, or computer science, engineering, mathematics, technology, or a critical foreign language, and have at least a cumulative 3.0 grade point average on a 4.0 scale; the Federal Work-Study (FWS) program that provides part-time jobs for undergraduate and graduate students helping professors and college staff, which cost the Department of Education $985 million in 2007; and the Teacher Education Assistance for

College and Higher Education (TEACH) Grant Program to students who intend to teach in a public or private elementary or secondary school that serves students from low-income families.[21] Congress assigned the task of determining which of millions of student applicants to these various programs have low enough incomes to justify grants to the Department of Education. This is not a simple task.

The Department of Education was the conduit for grant funds, but it devised a short-cut by delegating part of the task of screening students eligible for federal aid to the colleges in which students were enrolled—and all of the task of counseling them. However, the Department did not want 3,700 different criteria for federal student grants depending on which of the 3,700 colleges a student was in. So the Department developed a form that students in every institution must fill out *every* year: The Free Application for Federal Student Aid (FAFSA). The Commission on Higher Education set up by Secretary of Education Spellings described the FAFSA form as "longer and more complicated than the federal tax return."[22] Once students and their parents have filled it out, students must mail it to a federal processing center where an experienced staff person evaluates it according to uniform standards. Then it is sent back to the college attended—or to be attended—by the student, indicating the extent of parental financial responsibility, how much the student is expected to earn during the summer, and how much the student is eligible for in grants and loans. The college is entrusted with the task of verifying the information that the student submitted on the FAFSA form by means of documents, such as the income tax returns of parents and placing copies of these documents in its files. In most cases this verification process can be accomplished by mail and the student does not have to visit the financial aid office personally. When there are problems, the student may have to make multiple visits to the financial aid offices to straighten them out. The New Brunswick campus of Rutgers University, for example, has about 20,000 students applying for some type of student financial aid annually and only 15 financial aid counselors. It would be impossible to deal with all applications personally.[23]

Some of the information that the student must obtain to fill out the FAFSA form for 2008–2009, taken from the official worksheet of the Department of Education, are

- Your Social Security Number and your parents' Social Security Numbers if you are providing parent information;
- Your driver's license number if you have one;
- Your Alien Registration Number if you are not a U.S. citizen;
- 2007 federal tax information or tax returns (including IRS W-2 information) for yourself (and spouse if you are married) and for your

parents if you are providing parent information. If you have not yet filed a 2007 income tax return, you can still submit your FAFSA but you must provide income and tax information.

- Records of untaxed income, such as Social Security benefits, welfare benefits (e.g., TANF), and veterans benefits, for yourself, and your parents if you are providing parent information; and
- Information on savings, investments, and business and farm assets for yourself, and your parents if you are providing parent information.[24]

The FAFSA worksheet requires parental information "if you are providing parent information." This sounds as though the student can choose whether to provide parent information or not. Not so. All "dependent" students *must* provide parent information because parents are required by the Department of Education to provide financial help toward the education of their dependent children. This requirement led in turn to the department's establishing uniform rules to decide (1) the financial resources of parents and (2) whether students enrolled in college and applying for financial aid are "dependent" on their parents for support or are "independent." The starting presumption was that all students under 24 are "dependent." That presumption works for most cases and requires that most college students asking for financial aid must provide considerable financial information about their parents, which many parents may not want to share with their children. Some students under 24 are nevertheless considered "independent"; students under 24 who are married or have dependent children are automatically considered independent, and students estranged from their biological parents may be considered independent if they can provide good documentation of estrangement. (The reason the question of independence or dependence is important is because federal largesse is greater for independent than for dependent students since parental income and assets do not count for independent students.) In some cases, who the parents are is also problematic. Students whose parents have divorced and remarried may have several step-parents who may or may not be willing to take financial responsibility or to provide financial information.

The FAFSA form requires detailed financial information about both students and their parents because verified neediness is required for most types of federal subsidy. Measuring "neediness" might at first seem uncomplicated, but it is less easy than one might initially think. Financial eligibility of *dependent* students is based partly on parental income substantiated on tax returns, partly on students' incomes and assets—again substantiated by documents, partly on the size of the family, partly on parental assets such as stocks, bonds, real estate, bank accounts—but not the value of the primary residence of parents, partly on an expected financial contributions from the students themselves from summer or part-time employment, and partly on documented special circumstances like serious illness in the family. The deliberate exclusion of the primary residence of the family—whether the home is a castle or a hovel—is an effort to be fair; real estate prices vary greatly in different regions and in suburbs and central cities. Yet the children of families that spend their resources on lavish homes are treated as equally deserving of federal assistance as families that live more frugally in order to help their children attend college. The basic problem is that nonfinancial assets, whether a home, vehicles, boats, home furnishings, or a farm, have ambiguous valuations depending on market considerations, and consequently they are subject to misleading reports on the FAFSA form. Although parental income is easier to check on than parental assets, misrepresentation of parental income occurs. About $365 million went to students who misrepresented their families' incomes on financial aid forms in 2004, John P. Higgins Jr., inspector general for the Department of Education, reported in testimony before the House Government Reform Committee.[25] The Education Department wants Congress to change the Internal Revenue Code to enable it to check student claims of low family income against Internal Revenue Records and thereby to reduce this type of student fraud. The likelihood that parental assets rather than income were underreported is greater because checking on assets is more difficult, if not impossible. Financial eligibility of *independent* students is based only on the student's income and assets except in the case of married students who must document marital status and dependents, if any. A student may not claim a pet as a dependent, although some students have tried to do so. (Students can claim to be "independent" regardless of their age if they are veterans of the U.S. Armed Forces or orphans, but these circumstances must be documented.)

The second form of federal aid is *loans*. In point of fact, the bulk of federal financial aid—about 70 percent in 2007–2008—consists of loans rather than grants.[26] The reason financial aid to college students includes loans as well as grants is that Congress considered the total financial aid needed by college students too expensive to justify as gifts; hence subsidized loans of various kinds were authorized to make up the shortfall. The FAFSA form must be filled out by students to determine their eligibility for federally subsidized loans as well as their eligibility for grants. Unlike grants, *loans are expected to be repaid*—with interest, presumably out of the higher earnings students receive after graduating from college with skills enhanced by their education. The only collateral for student loans is the prospect of the student's future earnings from employment after college—unless parents are cosigners. Therefore, student loans are inherently riskier than mortgage loans because, in the event that students do not repay them, there is nothing to foreclose on. In order to make it possible for students to obtain loans, Congress subsidized Federal Family Education Loan Program (FFEL) loans made by banks, credit unions, and other financial institutions like Sallie Mae, a hybrid private-public company specializing in student loans. Later Congress also established Direct Loans to students made by the Department of Education through the financial aid offices of the colleges where the students were enrolled. All of these loans carry lower interest rates than personal loans that student borrowers could obtain from banks. For FFEL loans from financial institutions, the financial aid office refers the student to Sallie Mae or to another suggested loan organization, and that organization makes the loan, although the Department of Education guarantees its repayment. For Direct Loans, the financial aid office transmits the student's application for a loan directly to the Department of Education, which makes the loan. In addition, the Department of Education pays the interest on loans to low-income students while they are in college and for 270 days thereafter on both Direct and FFEL Loans; the department also reimburses financial institutions for 97 percent of the principal of the loans made to students if students default—as well as the accrued interest.

Unfortunately, tuition and other college expenses have risen more rapidly than the cost of living and more rapidly than family income. As a result of the explosion of the cost of attending college, the proportion of loans to total financial aid has risen. (In academic year 2007–2008 college aid through federal grant programs was about $18 billion whereas college aid through federal loan programs was about $44 billion.[27]) As with grants, different loan programs exist and were established to do a variety of things for a variety of reasons: the Federal Perkins Loan program, a low-interest (5 percent) loan for both undergraduate and graduate students with exceptional financial need, made through a college's financial aid office; the Federal Family Education Loan Program; the William D. Ford Federal Direct Loan (Direct Loan) Program (FFEL); and PLUS Loans (Parent Loans). Perkins loans are made with Department of Education money by the financial aid office of the college itself. All of these loan programs place limits on the amount that students can borrow under their auspices. Perkins loans are limited to $5,500 for each year of undergraduate study (the total an undergraduate can borrow while in college is $27,500). For both FFEL bank loans and Direct Loans, dependent undergraduate first-year students enrolled in a program of study that is at least a full academic year can borrow each year up to $5,500 (for loans first disbursed on or after July 1, 2008). However, no more than $3,500 of this amount can be in "subsidized" loans. ("Subsidized" loans differ from "unsubsidized" loans in the treatment of the interest on the loans; "subsidized" loans are available to students with greater financial need and the interest on the loans is paid by the Department of Education while the student is attending college and for nine months after graduation. The interest on "unsubsidized" loans accrues while students are in college and adds to the total debt that they owe; both types of loans are actually subsidized but to a different extent.) The loan limits are different for independent students and increase for each year of study completed.

What happens when students need more money for college expenses than they can obtain from these federal programs? They can take jobs, and many do. They can try to get private loans from banks—not federally guaranteed subsidized loans—carrying higher interest rates because they are riskier. Students take out these private loans (if they can persuade a financial institution to make them, sometimes with the help of their parents as cosigners), usually when they reach the maximum levels of loan eligibility for various programs of federally guaranteed loans and still need money for tuition and other college expenses. Sallie Mae and bank lenders originate both federally subsidized loans and unsubsidized private loans. Students also use credit cards as high-cost loans. In 2004 the average graduating senior not only had a diploma and payments due on federally guaranteed loans but also credit card debt of $2,864.[28] It is surely higher today. If their parents are willing to help them, parents can obtain loans, including home equity loans and depending on their credit ratings, PLUS Loans from the Department of Education. PLUS Loans are limited yearly to the cost of attendance minus any other financial aid received by the student.

These tiresome details about grants and loans are the reality underlying the seemingly simple idea of providing government money so that needy students can afford college. Federal subsidy of student loans enables many students to obtain loans to pay college costs who might otherwise not obtain them, but choosing the right loan from the available options is perplexing, as are other financial planning decisions faced by undergraduates whose parents cannot simply write checks that cover all the expenses.

Consequently virtually all colleges whose students apply for federal financial aid establish financial aid offices to guide students through the labyrinth of financial aid—as well as making realistic plans for loan repayment. The Department of Education recognizes this reality and pays some of the cost of operating financial aid offices at individual colleges based on the number of grants and loans that students receive at that institution; this partial reimbursement is called the "Administrative Cost Allowance." Because the Administrative Cost Allowance ordinarily covers only partially the cost of operating financial aid offices, the additional cost must be borne by college budgets and, indirectly, raises tuition. One reason that the Administrative Cost Allowance does not cover the full cost of financial aid offices is that they provide additional financial aid services besides dealing with *federal* grants and loans. Although federal grants and loans are the single most important source of financial aid now, there are usually state programs of financial aid as well as scholarships and loans given by colleges themselves or by private foundations. Financial aid personnel call these to the attention of students and help them to apply for scholarships and loans for which they might be eligible.

One subject that offices of financial aid do *not* discuss with students is their academic performance, except tangentially. Aside from a few relatively small grant programs, federal financial aid—grants and loans—does not depend on academic performance in high school or college, not even on average academic performance. True, most federal financial aid is available only to students making "satisfactory academic progress," which means two things: (1) they must maintain a C average or better and (2) they must demonstrate progressing toward graduation—in a four-year program taking no more than six years. But in an era of grade inflation, maintaining a C average is not difficult. And giving students two extra years beyond what was once the expected length of time for college matriculation seems generous. Congress was concerned in the enabling legislation that federal financial aid should be given to needy students so as to make higher education accessible for them, but, aside from saying that students receiving taxpayer aid should make "satisfactory progress," Congress did not address the subject of the ability of students to do college-level work.[29]

Scholarships, on the other hand, used to be designed to promote academic excellence; most federal financial aid ignores academic excellence and seeks merely to promote access. Even more objectionable from the viewpoint of encouraging academic excellence are those financial aid programs that have reversed the basic idea behind traditional scholarships and that target financial aid to students whose past academic records have been deficient. Academic deficiency was renamed "educational disadvantage" so that financial aid could be given to underprepared students without stigmatizing them. Chapter 2 mentioned one such state program, and Chapter 7 will analyze its provisions at length.

UNINTENDED CONSEQUENCES: DIPLOMAS TO NOWHERE AND DEFAULTED LOANS

The purpose of both grants and loans is to increase educational opportunity. The underlying intention behind federal guarantees of student loans is that this "investment" in higher education will not only benefit students who receive such assistance, enabling them to enjoy higher lifetime earnings, but also benefit American society in the form of a more productive economy. But programs usually have unintended consequences as well as the intended ones, and financial aid to college students is no exception. Most federal student grants and federal student loans do not require strong academic credentials, and these flabby requirements enable underprepared students to attend college. Since marginal students know while they are still in high school that they will be able to be admitted and get financial aid at some college, they lack an incentive to try to learn as much as they could in high school, as I pointed out in Chapter 1. Consequently the first unintended consequence of federal financial aid programs is to contribute to poor high school preparation of students who will later attend college.

The second and third unintended consequences apply only to one form of federal financial aid to students: loans. Loans have worse consequences than grants because loans incur an obligation for repayment. *Even for students who graduate from college with good enough résumés to qualify for well-paying jobs,* loans are burdens at a time of life when they want to marry, have children, and buy homes. For subsidized loans made between July 1, 2008, and July 1, 2009 to undergraduates the interest rate on the unpaid balance is 6 percent, and for unsubsidized loans, it is 6.8 percent.[30] Although subsidized loans are less burdensome than unsubsidized loans because the Department of Education pays the interest while the student is in college, students eligible for subsidized loans may nevertheless also take out unsubsidized loans when they need more money for college than the maximum amount allowed for subsidized loans for that academic year. Thus, freshmen are permitted to borrow $5,500 for their first academic year but only $3,500 of that amount can be subsidized loans. Similarly, sophomores are permitted to borrow $6,500 for that academic year but only $4,500 can be subsidized loans. The disadvantage of unsubsidized federal loans is that the interest accrues immediately upon getting the loan. If the student chooses to defer payment until graduation, which seems like the rational strategy for an impecunious student, the interest accumulates and adds to the size of the debt. Conceivably then, a graduating senior can end up at graduation with four subsidized loans and four unsubsidized loans with accrued interest, each with different terms, plus several Perkins loans, one for each year in college, plus credit card debt. Parents may also take out PLUS loans or home equity loans not part of the federal loan program, and students may feel obliged to take responsibility for at least some of this parental debt. Federal student loans sound complicated because they *are* very, very complicated—despite the fact that when students graduate with an array of loans having different interest rates and different payment requirements, the Department of Education permits them to take out one consolidation loan to amalgamate all of these federal loans into one loan with one schedule of interest and principal payments. Consolidation loans, however, cannot include credit card debt or personal loans from banks. Apart from the complexity of a multi-plicity of loans, the burden of timely repayment hangs over the graduate. True, there is a grace period of nine months after graduation before pay-ments must begin, but the transition to work may take longer, especially in an economic recession. In short, one unintended consequence of federal loans is that they impose for many years after graduation a heavy burden on students who take them out in order to afford the expenses of higher education.

How much does the average college graduate owe in loans? The average federally guaranteed debt of graduating college seniors was about $21,000 in 2007, but the debt level varied by state from a high of $26,208 in Iowa to a low of $11,709 in Utah.[31] These data include only debt incurred through Department of Education loan programs. They do not include private loans or credit card debt or home equity loans to parents.

In addition to regional variations reflected in these state averages, the average federally guaranteed debts of students who attended public col-leges and universities are lower, on the average, than the debts of students who attended private ones, which are much more expensive. Moreover, besides the differences in debt levels between public and private institu-tions, the debts of students who attended two-year institutions are smaller, on the average, than the debts of students who attended four-year colleges and universities, partly because they had fewer years in which to incur debts and partly because many students attending two-year colleges lived at home with their parents and commuted to school. In short, the average size of student debt does not reflect the tremendous variation that actually exists. Some students graduated without any debt at all, and some have very large debts to pay off. The average debt of graduates of four-year *pri-vate* colleges in 2006–2007 was almost $24,000 for those students who bor-rowed and about two-thirds of graduates in that academic year borrowed.[32] Since that amount was almost twice the average debt incurred by graduates of four-year private colleges in 1992–1993, student debt obli-gations of graduates are apparently growing.[33] The average debt of gradu-ates of *public* colleges in 2006–2007 for those students who borrowed was less, about $19,000, and only 55 percent of the graduates of public four-year colleges borrowed.[34] More important perhaps than the size of the debt is the ability of graduates to obtain good jobs and to pay off the loan. For students whose college educations did not prepare them well for the job market, the burden of college loans is heavier than for students who, for example, studied engineering or pharmacy as undergraduates and obtained well-paying positions immediately after graduating. Some grad-uates find that they cannot keep up the payments they promised to pay. They may be compelled to "default," sometimes temporarily, sometimes permanently. Defaulting on student loans has serious consequences. What "default" means, according to the part of a Web site on student loans dealing with defaults, is this:

> You are responsible for repaying your student loans even if you do not graduate, have trouble finding a job after graduation, or just didn't like your school. If you do not make any payments on your student loans for 270 days and do not make special arrangements with your lender to get a deferment or forbearance, your loans will be in default. Defaulting on your student loans has serious consequences.
>
> Note that student loans are now generally not dischargeable through bankruptcy. It is fairly difficult to satisfy the requirements for an undue hardship petition, which generally requires demonstrating that you made a good faith effort to repay the debt, that you will not be able to maintain a minimal standard of living and still repay the debt (usually using the lowest monthly payment under any of the repayment plans, typically income-contingent or income-based repayment), and that the conditions that prevent you from repaying the debt will likely persist for most of the full term of the loan. Even if you satisfy the requirements of an undue hardship discharge, often this will result in just a partial discharge of the debt.
>
> If you default on your student loan:
> - Your loans may be turned over to a collection agency.
> - You'll be liable for the costs associated with collecting your loan, including court costs and attorney fees.
> - You can be sued for the entire amount of your loan.
> - Your wages may be garnished. (Federal law limits the amount that may be garnished to 15 percent of the borrower's take-home pay.)
> - Your federal and state income tax refunds may be intercepted.
> - The federal government may withhold part of your Social Security benefit payments. (The U.S. Supreme Court upheld the government's ability to collect defaulted student loans in this manner without a statute of limitations in *Lockhart v. U.S.* (04-881, December 2005).)
> - Your defaulted loans will appear on your credit record, making it difficult for you to obtain an auto loan, mortgage, or even credit cards. A bad credit record can also harm your ability to find a job.
> - You won't receive any more federal financial aid until you repay the loan in full or make arrangements to repay what you already owe and make at least six consecutive, on-time, monthly payments. (You will also be ineligible for assistance under most federal benefit programs.)

- You'll be ineligible for deferments.
- Subsidized interest benefits will be denied.
- You may not be able to renew a professional license you hold.

And of course, you will still owe the full amount of your loan.[35]

Consider some of the consequences for a former student who, as a result of defaulting on student loans to the Department of Education, can no longer obtain a credit card without much difficulty, cannot get a mortgage on a house he might wish to buy, cannot buy a car or other consumer durables on credit because of his bad credit rating and, if he gets a job, is subject to garnishment of his wages. These consequences are in addition to being harassed by collection agencies and, possibly, sued. This may mean that a former student in such a predicament may be worse off by going to college than if he or she had not gone to college at all. If one of the main goals of attending college is to help achieve middle-class status, defaulting on student loans defeats that goal, at least for the time being.

The Department of Education tries to help students avoid this catastrophe, as do financial aid counselors. Students are warned not to take on too much debt. The rule of thumb is that the total debt assumed by a student should not be more than twice the expected annual employment earnings after graduation. That is probably the objective of the limits imposed on how much students are permitted to borrow each year through federal programs. In addition, the Department of Education has two processes designed to avoid default: *deferments* and *forbearances*. Deferments, which may be granted to borrowers who explain on their applications for deferments that they have become unemployed or are experiencing other economic hardship, allow borrowers to postpone repaying the principal of the loan. If it is a subsidized loan, the Department of Education pays the interest while the loan is in deferment. If it is an unsubsidized loan, however, the borrower must either pay the interest on the loan as it accrues or add it to the principal to be paid—as well as the additional interest—when the deferment period ends. Students who took out loans as undergraduates and are in danger of defaulting can also defer repayment automatically by enrolling in a graduate or professional degree program. This is a perverse incentive to enroll in a graduate program. It postpones default but increases the student's ultimate debt as the student adds graduate school loans and accumulated interest. Forbearances, which may be granted to borrowers not eligible for deferments, are less generous than deferments; they require payments of interest as it accrues and is limited to three one-year periods.[36] Finally, it is possible to get *out* of default—with difficulty— by working out a repayment plan with the lending agency. The Department of Education has established a Default Resolution Group and provides a toll-free telephone number for borrowers in default to discuss their problems. The danger of default is real. It is possible for students to graduate with $100,000 in student loans and owing payments of interest and principal of $1,000 a month to keep from defaulting.[37]

Some students are more burdened by the responsibility of dealing with their debts than others. The biggest single factor contributing to the extent of the financial burden is the type of jobs that students obtain after graduating; the higher the remuneration from employment and the less vulnerable the former student is to the possibility of being laid off, the easier it is for graduates to gradually pay back their loans. However, other factors affect the probability of default. The National Center for Education Statistics conducted a ten-year follow up study of 1992–1993 graduates from four-year colleges in order to discover which students are more likely to default.[38] The larger the total debt, the greater the chances of default; 20 percent of students who owed $15,000 or more were in default within ten years. Not surprisingly, graduates with the lowest salaries defaulted within ten years at four times the rate of graduates with high salaries. Ethnicity mattered also. Black graduates defaulted at five times the rate of white non-Hispanic students and nine times the rate of Asian students. Here is how one expert on student loans, Erin Dillon, described the results of the study:

> For black and Hispanic students, students who enter low paying, often public service, careers, or students who take on extremely high amounts of debt, defaulting is a very real possibility. And defaulting on student loans can be a crushing financial blow to a student, particularly if that student does not have outside support, such as family or friends, to rely on. At each default, collection costs of up to 40 percent of the loan balance are added to the loan plus any unpaid interest. If a borrower defaults multiple times, his or her balance can quickly balloon, making the total debt to be repaid even more daunting.[39]

Apart from this catastrophic unintended consequence for individual student borrowers, the unintended consequence for American society is that the ballooning impact of these defaults is getting to be a serious burden to the federal budget. As the late Senator Dirksen is supposed to have said apropos of federal expenditures generally, "A billion here and a billion there, and pretty soon you're talking real money."[40] The problem is that the fairly low rate of *cohort* defaults—about 5 percent overall—is only for the first two years after students graduate, not a good indication of what the cumulative default rate over ten or twenty years will be. The cohort default rate is used appropriately to calculate which institutions have more than

25 percent defaults, too high a rate to continue to be eligible for the federal loan program. The cohort default rate tracks all borrowers who are scheduled to begin repaying their student loans in a given year and calculates the rate of defaults in the next two years. The ten-year longitudinal study—which calculates the *cumulative* default rate—showed that defaults, on the average, occur four years after graduation.[41]

Overall, the NCES sample had a ten-year default rate of 9.7 percent. This means that the costs of defaults to the federal budget are substantial and will inevitably rise in the years ahead. Why? Because more college and professional school students are taking out loans from year to year as postsecondary school enrollment grows, and the loans are getting larger due to increase in tuition and other college expenses. Defaults will also increase if a faltering economy fails to generate enough good jobs to provide employment to college graduates. Defaults increase as the unemployment rate rises, as it has been doing in 2007, 2008, and 2009. Already at 9.5 percent for June 2009, the highest level in twenty-six years, economists believe the unemployment rate will continue to rise throughout 2009.[42]

According to college placement offices that schedule recruiting appointments for graduating seniors, the employment prospects for the 1,585,000 students who will receive bachelor's degrees in 2008–2009 from American colleges and universities are worse than the experiences of the 1,544,000 students who received such degrees in 2007–2008 academic year might suggest.[43] This does not bode well for the repayment of their student loans. In short, the student loan program not only has repayment problems for students who take out student loans and cannot repay them. It also incurs taxpayer problems as the United State Treasury has to make good on these defaulted loans, as promised in the original legislation "guaranteeing" them.

American society learned from the subprime mortgage crisis that all loans are not created equal. Some were more risky than others. Labeled "subprime," such mortgages were provided to borrowers with little or no equity in the property, bad credit ratings, or poorly documented annual incomes, partly because successive Congresses and successive presidents wanted the semi-public lending giants, Fannie Mae and Freddie Mac, to encourage home ownership, not because the risks of subprime mortgages went unrecognized. Home ownership set records. A similar problem exists with student loans. All student loans are not created equal. While the future economic prospects of high school graduates or even of college students are always difficult to predict, the student loan program did not utilize available information on the basis of which fairly good predictions were possible about prospects for loan repayment: good high school academic records, high scores on tests of academic aptitude like the SAT or ACT tests, good credit ratings, and college grades. The default rate on private student loans is half the default rate on federally guaranteed student loans; the most likely explanation for this difference is that private lenders use credit ratings and other assessments of the likelihood of repayment that the Department of Education does not use for making federal loans. In effect, successive Congresses and successive presidents authorized subprime student loans.

The ongoing subprime mortgage crises and the impending subprime student loan crisis arose for essentially the same reason: the desire of Congress and of presidents to promote social policies that everyone believed were good for the country: in one case, increasing rates of home ownership and in the other increasing access to higher education. The present economic downturn has exacerbated the default problem on student loans because some college graduates from earlier years who had obtained good jobs and had been repaying their loans were let go when the subprime mortgage crisis developed. If they had no savings, they could no longer keep up payments. The longer the recession continues and the more difficult the job prospects are for college graduates with student loans—and for everyone else, the greater the likelihood is of a higher rate of defaults. At present more than half a trillion dollars of student loans are either guaranteed by the U.S. Department of Education or, in the case of Direct Loans, are loans from the Department of Education itself; defaults on some of these student loans are very likely to increase in the years ahead.[44] Defaulting student loans will not pose problems to the financial system as serious as those caused by the subprime mortgage crisis because most student loans are in programs where the federal government is responsible for repayment of the principal. However, some private loans were securitized as were subprime mortgages, and these toxic securitized loans drag down the asset value of bank portfolios. Toxic private student loans is one reason why Sallie Mae's stock has fallen so much—but Sallie Mae and the banks that made private student loans have more federally guaranteed loans than private loans.

CONCLUSION

Until the recent widespread usage of the term, "financial aid," the term, "scholarships," referred to traditional academic scholarships. The G.I. Bill of Rights, which financed college for discharged veterans, foreshadowed broader programs of *federal* grants and loans—twenty at present: seventeen from the Department of Education and three more from other federal agencies—that essentially universalized "financial aid." Few of them require better than mediocre previous or current academic achievement. Pell grants and other federal grant programs for college students such as work-study programs for enrolled needy college students are gifts that do not have to be repaid. However, the various federal grant programs, though supplemented by state and private grant programs, were not enough to cover the financial needs of the millions of college students whose families could not afford the rising costs of attending college. So Congress established several loan programs, some indirect loans with subsidies that made them attractive to banks, credit unions, and other financial institutions and some financed directly by the Department of Education.

Once the federal camel got its nose under the tent of financial aid to individual students, complex rules and regulations were required to organize the process of packaging them. Financial aid offices were established at colleges and universities to provide help in filing application forms, explaining how the various pieces of the financial aid package fitted together to provide enough money to cover college costs, and for counseling students about the choices they have to make regarding, for example, the type of loans they must take out. Thus, financial aid offices have become one of the most important offices of colleges whose students apply for financial aid, as the majority of students do at most colleges.

The student financial aid system was created by Congress not as an integrated system but in pieces: to do a variety of things for a variety of reasons. One of its major objectives is to help youngsters from low-income families have access to colleges and universities. In a democratic society with egalitarian ideals, it seems immoral to limit the educational escalator to good careers to children fortunate enough to have educated and affluent parents. Another reason for promoting college access for youngsters from low-income families is that, as Jefferson argued, persons of extraordinary talent may be born in humble circumstances. This Jeffersonian notion lies behind another reason Congress devised its financial aid program to promote college attendance: to enable the American economy to be more productive. The knowledge explosion during the twentieth century demonstrated that ideas are extremely important to the "creative destruction" that a market system needs in order for the economy to grow. Institutions of higher education are where many new ideas are developed by adults through research and transmitted to youngsters through teaching. Politicians are referring to this economic growth function when they speak euphorically about student grants and loans as "investments." Only a few federal grant programs—and none of the loan programs—seek out top-notch students who will presumably contribute to the productivity of the American economy; others aim only to make accessible the college experience for children of the poor. A third objective is to find a fair way to allocate scarce taxpayer resources to accomplish the first two objectives. The existing system is an uneasy compromise among these objectives.

It is an uneasy compromise partly because promoting access for youngsters from low-income families sometimes conflicts with the meritocratic ideal of educating youngsters most capable of making great intellectual contributions to knowledge. Perhaps a better compromise could have been made to realize these two objectives by targeting the grants and loans devised by the federal financial aid program to needy students *preparing to go to college by studying diligently.* Instead they were set up mainly as incentives simply to *go* to college, prepared or not. Perhaps Congress assumed that the colleges would screen admissions appropriately or perhaps Congress was afraid to appear elitist by imposing meritocratic conditions. Federal aid to college students removed financial barriers. Applications increased as the message was heard that college attendance led to well-paid interesting careers and was now affordable. Many colleges expanded enrollments and lowered academic standards for admission so that virtually any high school graduate could get into some college. The result is that access is approaching universality. Students might have had an incentive to work harder in high school if they had *had* to in order to gain admission to college and to obtain financial aid to cover expenses while enrolled. The consequence of this poorly designed incentive are students graduating from college or dropping out without learning enough to get the well-paying jobs that they expected. Many of them default on their loans.

Among the measures being taken to deal with the credit freeze-up triggered by subprime mortgage loans is tightening lending standards, for example by requiring larger down payments and better evidence of employment. A similar remedy could be adopted to prevent the financial hemorrhaging from defaulted student loans if a standard were adopted that made student loans contingent on the best available evidence of the student's prospects for repaying them, such as credit ratings and indications of good job prospects. There would still be defaults. Predicting the earning potential of college students is chancy. However, almost certainly there would be *fewer* defaulted loans.

NOTES

1. *Notes on Virginia,* 1782. *The Jeffersonian Cyclopedia,* Electronic Text Center, University of Virginia Library.

2. William C. Dowling, *Confessions of a Spoilsport: My Life and Hard Times Fighting Sports Corruption at an Old Eastern University,* University Park: Pennsylvania State University Press, 2007. On the other hand, thirty-eight university teachers and administrators from South Africa concluded after visiting colleges in Tennessee that athletic programs raise academic standards by contributing to institutional loyalty. Richard Rothstein, "Athletics' valuable place on the American campus," *New York Times,* July 17, 2002.

3. Exactly when New Jersey State Scholarships were phased out is not clear, according to Rutgers officials dealing with financial aid.

4. Milton Friedman, "Autobiography," Web site accessed in April 2009: http://nobelprize.org/economics/laureates/1976/friedman-autobio.html.

5. E. R. Love, "Godfrey Harold Hardy, 1877–1947," *Australian Mathematical Society Web Site—the Gazette*, Vol. 25 Part 1 (1998).

6. Talcott Parsons and Gerald M. Platt, *The American University*, Cambridge, MA: Harvard University Press, 1973, Chapter 3.

7. Joseph Berger, "Intel Competition Is Where Science Rules and Research Is the Key," *New York Times*, March 7, 2007.

8. Jackson Toby, "A Vote for *In Loco Parentis*," *Rutgers Alumni Monthly*, Vol. 58, No.3, February, 1979, p. 32.

9. "*In Loco Parentis* Goes Loco," *Wall Street Journal*, September 23, 2005.

10. Here is how Mark Kantrowitz, the publisher of FinAid.org and FastWeb.com, summarized the issue: "The regulations at 34 CFR 99.31(a)(8) allow disclosure without consent if 'The disclosure is to parents, as defined in §99.3, of a dependent student, as defined in section 152 of the Internal Revenue Code of 1986.'" [Personal email communication.]

11. Allan Finder, "Aid Lets Small Colleges Ask, 'Why Pay Ivy Retail?'" *New York Times*, January 1, 2006.

12. Congressional Research Report—American War and Military Operations Casualties. Updated June 29, 2007.

13. Source: U.S. Department of Veterans Affairs: "Born of Controversy: The G. I. Bill of Rights." Web site accessed in April 2009: www.gibill.va.gov/GI_Bill_Info/ history.htm.

14. *Ibid.*

15. Keith Olson, *The G. I. Bill, The Veterans, and The Colleges,* Lexington: University Press of Kentucky, 1974.

16. "President Clinton Unveils His National Service Program," Archives of National Public Radio, "All Things Considered," April 30, 1993.

17. Clyde Haberman, "20 Triumphant Spirits Win *New York Times* Scholarships," *New York Times*, March 8, 2003.

18. Thomas R. Wolanin, *Reauthorizing the Higher Education Act: Issues and Options*, Washington, D.C.: Institute for Higher Education Policy, March, 2003, ch. 3; Michael S. McPherson and Morton. O. Schapiro, *The Student Aid Game.* Princeton: Princeton University Press, 1998.

19. The College Board, *Trends in Student Aid 2008.* Washington: College Entrance Examination Board, 2008, Table 8, "Federal Pell Grant Awards in Current and Constant (2007) Dollars, 1973–74 to 2007–08" (Table 8 prepared in October 2008). Web site accessed in April 2009: www.collegeboard.com/html/costs/aid/3_2_pell_grants .html?CollapsiblePanel5#table8.

20. *Ibid.*

21. U.S. Department of Education, *Federal Student Aid, 2008,* p. 356. Web site accessed in April 2009: www.whitehouse.gov/omb/budget/fy2009/pdf/appendix/ edu.pdf.

22. U.S. Department of Education, *A Test of Leadership: Charting the Future of U.S. Higher Education,* A Report of the Commission Appointed by Secretary of

Education Margaret Spellings, September 2006, p. 18. Web site accessed April 2009: www.ed.gov/about/bdscomm/list/hiedfuture/index.html.

23. Source: Telephone conversation with Jean Rash, Director of the Office of Financial Aid, Rutgers University.

24. U.S. Department of Education, *Free Application for Federal Student Aid (FAFSA)*, Web site: www.fafsa.ed.gov/

25. Kristen A. Lee, "Identity Thief Teaches Colleges about Fraud," *New York Times*, May 30, 2005.

26. College Board, *Trends in Student Aid, 2008, op cit.*

27. *Ibid.*

28. Nellie Mae, "Undergraduate Students and Credit Cards in 2004: An Analysis of Usage Rates and Trends." A study by Nellie Mae, published May 2005. Web site accessed in April 2009: www.nelliemae.com/library/research_12.html

29. "Satisfactory progress" was defined in Section 484(c) of the Higher Education Act of 1965 as follows:

"(c) SATISFACTORY PROGRESS—

For the purpose of subsection (a)(2), a student is maintaining satisfactory progress if—

(A) the institution at which the student is in attendance, reviews the progress of the student at the end of each academic year, or its equivalent, as determined by the institution, and

(B) the student has a cumulative C average, or its equivalent or academic standing consistent with the requirements for graduation, as determined by the institution, at the end of the second such academic year.

(2) Whenever a student fails to meet the eligibility requirements of subsection (a)(2) as a result of the application of this subsection and subsequent to that failure the student has academic standing consistent with the requirements for graduation, as determined by the institution, for any grading period, the student may, subject to this subsection, again be eligible under subsection (a)(2) for a grant, loan, or work assistance under this title.

(3) Any institution of higher education at which the student is in attendance may waive the provisions of paragraph (1) or paragraph (2) of this subsection for undue hardship based on—

(A) the death of a relative of the student,

(B) the personal injury or illness of the student, or

(C) special circumstances as determined by the institution.

Congress apparently provided considerable leeway for marginal academic performance.

30. Perkins loans do not charge an origination fee but Direct and FFEL charge as much as 2 percent of the principal amount to reimburse the Department of Education or the financial institution in the case of FFEL loans for part of the cost of processing the loan.

31. Institute for College Access & Success, The Project on Student Debt, "Student Debt and the Class of 2007," October, 2008; Beth Kobliner, "Learn Now, Pay Back (Somewhat Less) Later," *New York Times*, June 30, 2002.

32. College Board, *Trends in Student Aid, 2008, op cit.*, Student debt, Figure 8, p. 11.

33. *Ibid.*

34. *Ibid.*

35. FinAid, The Smart Student Guide to Financial Aid, "Defaulting on Student Loans," Web site accessed in April 2009: www.finaid.org/loans/default.phtml.

36. *Ibid.*

37. "Student Debt Levels Portend Rising Loan Default Rates," *Wall Street Journal*, December 1, 2008.

38. Susan P. Choy and C. Dennis Carroll, "Dealing with Debt: 1992–1993 Bachelor's Degree Recipients Ten Years Later," United States Office of Education, National Center for Education Statistics, June, 2006.

39. Erin Dillon, "Hidden Details: A Closer Look at Student Default Rates," *Education Sector,* October 23, 2007, p. 6, Web site accessed in July 2009: http:// ednews.org/articles/hidden-details-a-closer-look-at-student-loan-default-rates .html; Kathy Kristof, "The Great College Hoax," *Forbes*, February 2, 2009.

40. According to the Dirksen Center, he never said exactly that, but it conveys the sense of many things he did say. Web site accessed in April 2009: www.dirksen-center.org.

41. Erin Dillon, *op. cit,* p. 5.

42. Louis Uchitelle, "Unemployment Rate Hits 7.2%, a Sixteen-Year High," *New York Times*, January 9, 2009: Kelly Evans, "Unemployment Rate of 8% Is Highest in 26 Years," *Wall Street Journal*, March 9, 2009; Sudeep Reddy, "Jobless Rate Hits 8.5%," *Wall Street Journal*, April 15, 2009; Associated Press, "U.S. Jobless Claims Rise More Than Expected," *New York Times,* April 23, 2009; Andrea Coombes, "Men Suffer Brunt of Job Losses in Recession," *Wall Street Journal*, July 16, 2009.

43. Cari Tuna, "For '09 Grads, Job Prospects Take a Dive," *Wall Street Journal*, October 22, 2008.

44. Mark Kantrowitz, the publisher of FinAid.org and FastWeb.com, calculated the data from the Office of Management and Budget Web site and concluded that the total amount of student debt guaranteed by the Department of Education has been rising. He explained what he did in an e-mail to me dated May 8, 2009. He added the amount of FFEL and Direct Loans covering outstanding student debt, which was actually $530,610,000 in Fiscal Year 2008. The Web site provided estimates of $597,528,000 for Fiscal Year 2009 and $679,645,000 for Fiscal Year 2010. It grows because new loans are taken out faster than old loans are paid off or defaulted on. In order to calculate these numbers, Mr. Kantrowitz had to add loans from various cohorts of student borrowers because neither the Department of Education nor the Office of Management and Budget makes and publishes these calculations. The latest Management and Budget Web site—made available in May 2009 is: www.whitehouse.gov/omb/budget/fy2010/assets/edu.pdf

Chapter 7

How a Change in Public Policy Can Improve American College Education

As was pointed out in the first chapter, the late President of the American Federation of Teachers, Albert Shanker, condemned the failure of all but the most selective American colleges to insist on strong high school records from applicants to college. He expressed regret that most American colleges are not selective academically. Less than 10 percent of undergraduate colleges of the 3,700 American postsecondary colleges and universities whose students are eligible to receive federal financial aid reject more than half of applicants for freshman admission.[1] Shanker pointed to the likelihood that *rewards* for diligence in high school would increase the number of high school students who prepare themselves to profit intellectually from *higher* education. But Mr. Shanker limited his argument to only one incentive: the decision of colleges to admit or to reject applicants for admission. Conceivably, if American college admissions offices had tougher admissions policies, Shanker's approach would have led to better high school preparation for college. However, as previous chapters showed, the clamor for admission to college led to colleges to expand facilities and faculties to fulfill the demand for higher education. This created overcapacity, which prevented all but the most prestigious American colleges requiring high levels of student academic preparation. Hence the admission offices of most colleges *could not* be tough gatekeepers while keeping their colleges solvent.

This reality does not invalidate Shanker's notion that high school students could be motivated to take their high school educations more seriously if the right incentives were offered. What about financial incentives?

In the money economies of modern societies, money is a powerful incentive. It is especially worth considering in an era of exploding college tuition.

> Tuition and fees at public and private universities have risen this year at more than double the rate of inflation, with prices increasing faster at public institutions, the College Board said in reports released yesterday.
> These increases in the cost of higher education continue to drive up the amount that students and families borrow, with the fastest growth in private loans, the reports found.[2]

Rising tuition costs mean that unless applicants come from wealthy homes and have parents who will pay tuition and college living expenses, whatever they may be, students need and want financial aid. The political process, being responsive to public sentiment in a democracy, has made sure that students receive federal grants and loans. As intended, grants and loans *are* an incentive to attend college. Unfortunately, they are a promiscuous incentive because of the way politicians drafted the legislation authorizing them. They are not completely promiscuous. Despite some difficulties in assessing the resources of families that could be used to help finance college for their children and some fraudulent claims of poverty, the federal program of financial aid to students helps students from low-income families obtain greater financial aid than students from higher-income families. However, except for a few small grant programs that give money to students with good preparation in special subject areas, grants and loans awarded to students admitted to American colleges are given without considering whether students are well prepared for college or not.

Should all financial aid be contingent on student performance in high school and college? It would probably not be possible politically to insert a merit component into such a large and popular grant program as Pell Grants. Politics in a democracy is the art of the possible. Even if it were phased in gradually so that students enrolled in high school before the merit requirement was added could still obtain Pell Grants without considering their academic performance, it would be difficult to change the entitlement expectations surrounding Pell Grants. Like the Head Start Program, it is doubtful that elected senators and representatives would dare to touch the Pell Grant program, the Work-Study program, or the Federal Supplemental Educational Opportunity Grant (FSEOG) program for undergraduates who are especially needy. A few small federal grant programs are already based on academic considerations: the Academic Competitiveness Grant program for first-year college students who have completed a rigorous secondary school program of study and the National Science & Mathematics Access to Retain Talent Grant (National SMART Grant) Program for students whose college major is physical, life, or computer science, engineering, mathematics, technology, or a critical foreign language, and have at least a cumulative 3.0 grade point average on a 4.0 scale. It could be argued that the Teacher Education Assistance for College and Higher Education (TEACH) Grant Program to students who intend to teach in a public or private elementary or secondary school that serves students from low-income families ought to be based on student performance in order to provide good teachers for disadvantaged students. But it would seem discriminatory to single out this grant program for imposing academic standards and leave the others alone.

On their face, Pell Grants and the work-study program seem poorly devised from an incentive point of view. But even worse as an incentive to learn as much as possible in primary and secondary schools are grant programs that provide greater rewards for *substandard* educational performance. Are there such grant programs? As far as I know, the United States Department of Education does not support such programs. But several states do. For example, forty years ago the State of New Jersey began using a criterion for financial aid that was the mirror image of traditional scholarships. In the wake of black riots in several New Jersey cities in the summer of 1968, a leading Democrat, Assemblyman Robert Wilentz, later the Chief Justice of the New Jersey Supreme Court, and a leading Republican, Assemblyman Thomas Kean, later to become Governor of New Jersey and then the President of Drew University, sponsored the New Jersey Educational Opportunity Act of 1968.[3] The Act provided grants for low-income high school graduates to help them attend college in New Jersey. Few anticipated the effect of a provision in the bill establishing an Educational Opportunity Board in the New Jersey Department of Higher Education to implement the Act. Almost immediately, the racially diverse Board added a criterion for grants nowhere mentioned in the Act itself: "*educational disadvantage.*"

What "educational disadvantage" was interpreted to mean in the eligibility guidelines issued by the Educational Opportunity Board is that the students given grants must be academically *underprepared* for the New Jersey college of their choice—in addition to being economically needy. In order to be eligible for an Educational Opportunity Fund grant—$500 for residential students and $350 for commuters at that time—the guidelines require that a student:

i. [has] not demonstrated a sufficient academic preparation to gain admission to an approved institution of higher education under its regular standards of admission . . . ; and

ii. [has] standard test scores . . . below the institutional norms; and

iii. [has an] educational background [that] indicates a need for improvement of basic skills.[4]

The EOF program, which is still in operation, gives relatively small grants, but it has a large impact on public colleges in New Jersey because the State bureaucracy requires *public* colleges to include in their freshman classes a substantial proportion of EOF grantees (10 percent). In order to meet this requirement, admission offices try to attract the best applicants they can find who are economically and educationally disadvantaged enough to satisfy the EOF guidelines. For example, one out of ten New Jersey residents admitted to the Rutgers College of Engineering—as in all public colleges—is expected to be an EOF special-admit student. Yet the College of Engineering has difficulty finding needy students who want to become engineers, who meet the EOF "educationally disadvantaged" criterion, and who also seem likely to succeed in an engineering curriculum. Consequently the College of Engineering has a much higher dropout/flunkout rate for EOF students than for non-EOF students—despite a great deal of remedial work. Other public colleges have lowered their grading standards in the face of bitter complaints from EOF students that the colleges were hypocritical to admit them and then to impose academic standards that they could not meet. Students enrolling at *private* colleges in New Jersey are also eligible for EOF grants, but these grants have much less impact on private colleges and universities, partly because the State does not mandate any minimum proportion of freshmen at its private colleges who must receive EOF grants and partly because the tuition at private colleges is so large compared to the size of EOF grants that the tail cannot wag the dog.

Bitter EOF students have a point, although not the colleges but the EOF guidelines program them for failure. "Educational disadvantage" is defined relative to the freshman class at the college to which the student applies. A student who would qualify as educationally disadvantaged at Rutgers College and therefore eligible for an EOF grant at that college might have too high a high school rank in class or too high an SAT score for Montclair State or for a community college to be eligible for an EOF grant. Thus, the EOF guidelines tempt a high school graduate to apply to a college where, relative to other students at *that* college, he or she must work extraordinarily hard to succeed academically. The public colleges face a complementary temptation: to recruit EOF students who, by definition, are not as likely to succeed academically as regular-admit students. In short, the EOF program makes attrition more likely because it places poorly prepared students in colleges where they are over their heads—competing with better prepared students who observe them at the bottom of the grade distribution.[5] Understandably, despite heroic efforts on the part of EOF administrators to build the self-esteem of their clients as well as remedial services specially tailored to the needs of EOF students, calling EOF students "educationally disadvantaged" stigmatizes them.

One consequence of the EOF selection requirements is that New Jersey public colleges have the burden of providing remedial work for many students with poor prospects of succeeding academically *in those colleges*. An equally perverse consequence is that New Jersey high school students from low-income backgrounds who hope to obtain financial aid to attend colleges may infer from the criteria of selection for EOF grants that academic achievement does not matter. Doing well in high school might even be disadvantageous. New York State and other states follow the New Jersey pattern and assume that students who perform inadequately on measures of academic achievement are victims of bad schools, poor teachers, racial prejudice, or all three—and therefore deserve college scholarships based on criteria other than traditional academic accomplishment. In some cases this explanation of poor performance is correct; in other cases it is due to student rejection of studying at school as reflected in tardiness, truancy, and inattention in class. Whatever the explanation, however, providing a college scholarship does not appear to be a remedy fair to colleges, to other applicants, or even to the deficient students themselves. From the point of view of incentives to excel academically, scholarships for "educationally disadvantaged" students appear to be a *disincentive*.

State and county governments subsidize community colleges more heavily than they do senior public colleges in their states, thus making possible very low tuition or no tuition at all at community colleges. Their admissions policies are essentially open enrollment. An ungenerous way to interpret this combination of features is as a scholarship program for underprepared students, a program similar to special-admit programs at senior colleges like the EOF program. Not all students who elect to attend community colleges are underprepared. For some well-prepared students who cannot afford to go away to college or who prefer to live at home and commute to college, community colleges are an opportunity to gain access to the first two years of college at minimum cost. Students who do well academically at community colleges gain admission with junior standing in the senior public colleges of their states after obtaining their two-year degrees, sometimes automatically, sometimes after an evaluation of the academic records they established at the community colleges. In effect, then, junior college students are admitted through the back doors of public senior colleges in their states; the senior colleges must count on the quality of the two years of study leading to the degrees of the transfer students being comparable to the quality of freshman and sophomore instruction in the senior colleges themselves. Still more access to four-year-college degrees is emerging. The community colleges have begun offering four-year degrees in selected fields.[6] Miami-Dade Community College, which began doing this for degrees in teaching two years ago, dropped "Community" from its name to reflect its expanded educational scope. Others of the 980 public community colleges and 148 private ones—enrolling 6.6 million students in for-credit courses and five million in noncredit courses—have begun offering four-year degrees in criminal justice and nursing as well as in education.[7] At the least, this portends a considerable expansion of the number of four-year college graduates in the years ahead. Whether those graduates will be of comparable academic quality to the better graduates of the past is an open question.

Unlike the Educational Opportunity Grants in New Jersey, Pell grants were established without rewarding either superior or inferior academic aptitude. Why did Congress enact them in this form? Politicians probably expected merit-neutral grants to please low-income voters whose children don't perform as well in school, on the average, as the children of middle-class parents living in suburbia or attending private schools. Or perhaps they sincerely believed the conventional wisdom, namely, that promoting greater *access* to college by making grants and loans available to attend college is sufficient to increase the number of highly educated Americans. Politicians, like all of us, make mistakes. Underprepared students can be tempted by governmental grants and loans to consider attending college when otherwise they are not strongly motivated to do so—motivated, that is, for educational reasons. Access to college is not sufficient, let alone a guarantee, that admitted students are prepared to profit intellectually from the educational opportunities they are offered. Nevertheless, it is probably too late to reverse course on grants. Strong expectations have been built up over the years that federal grants for low-income students will be there for them. That said, what about loans?

A stronger case can be made for incorporating merit criteria into federal student loan programs than into grant programs like Pell or work-study. Loans offer a politically more acceptable way to introduce student performance into federal financial aid for two reasons. For one, loans are more dangerous than grants to underprepared students because of the repayment problem discussed in the previous chapter. For another, loans are also more dangerous to the economic system itself because defaults on student loans, like defaults on subprime mortgages, threaten the solvency of lending institutions and increase the national debt. Unlike grants, which show up in the budget in the years that they are made, it is difficult to know what federal loans ultimately will cost the United States Treasury.

The ultimate cost depends on what proportion is repaid and what proportion is defaulted on, so the cost can only be estimated at any given time. Conceivably the cost could be small or it could be enormous. Loans are not "transparent," as the experts on mortgage debt lament about *their* loans. What Congress could do is continue to allow Pell *Grants* to be available to all needy students admitted to any degree-granting college but reserve federally guaranteed *loans* for students who can demonstrate good prospects for repaying them.

THE CASE AGAINST MAKING ALL FEDERAL AID TO COLLEGE STUDENTS AN ENTITLEMENT

This different treatment of federal *grants* to students and federal *loans* obviously collides with the notion that all federal aid to college students should be an entitlement. On the other hand, such a distinction has the advantage of dispelling a myth subscribed to by many students. They mistakenly believe that college is a free lunch: a fun-filled four years that is cost-free. Despite generous financial aid from the federal government, from the states, from the colleges themselves, and from private foundations and corporations, attending college has costs. Not only do students forego the opportunity to earn wages or salaries at full-time jobs during those years; because college tuition and living arrangements are expensive, most students take out loans that all of them will find burdensome and some of them will not be able to repay.[8]

The burden of repaying college loans surely accounts for some of the personal bankruptcies among college graduates, despite loan programs with forgiveness provisions for graduates who work in low-paid fields that are socially useful like teaching.[9] It may account also for a return to protracted adolescence for some college graduates who move back into the homes of their parents to economize on rent.[10] A 2001 report found that "56 percent of current college students plan to live with their parents for some period of time after they graduate."[11] This 2001 report antedated the current downturn in the economy in the wake of the collapse of the housing market in 2007–2008, which increased unemployment and thereby the ability of recent college graduates to repay their loans. Surely a higher proportion of college students anticipate returning "home" nowadays. This extends adolescence for them. Plans to marry and raise a family have to be put on hold. They may think of themselves as forced by poverty to return to dependency on their parents. Most college graduates in these situations are experiencing only *temporary* poverty. Eventually those who obtained a good education at college will find occupational niches. For other college graduates, however, the disadvantages are more permanent. Such graduates may have enjoyed their hedonistic years at college. However, if they find that their college degrees do not help them obtain the kinds of jobs they expected, they may come to believe with some bitterness that their degrees are empty credentials.[12] Have they wasted several years of their lives? Some illiterate high school graduates have already sued their high schools for educational malpractice; disappointed college graduates may follow suit.[13] To put it another way, subprime student loans are analogous to the subprime mortgages that led to the credit crunch of 2007; some diplomas are "tickets to nowhere." The Department of Education should encourage loans that a reasonable scrutiny of the potential borrowers would suggest will be repaid.

What changes are necessary so that the federal loan program becomes more realistic? The first and most important change is a change in educational philosophy. American voters and their elected representatives would have to examine the drawbacks as well as the advantages of educational entitlements. For one, entitlements tend to trivialize the level of undergraduate instruction because students admitted to a college without meeting its intellectual standards for course work tempt professors to expect less reading and writing from students than they otherwise would. For another, entitlements promote a fun culture instead of a learning culture. Third, entitlements drive up the cost of tuition because they impose the resource burden of attempting to remediate the deficiencies of students who seek the benefits of having attended college. Finally, entitlements swell total enrollments beyond what American society really needs for the growth of its economy.

Doesn't the contention that higher education should not be an entitlement, only an opportunity, apply with equal force to student *grants* as well as to student *loans*? On a strictly logical level, perhaps it does. However, for two reasons student grants are more appealing than student loans as an approach to subsidizing higher education for low-income students. First, grants do not present the same dangers either to students or to the economy as do loans; they do not burden students with debts that they may not be able to repay and they do not burden the economy with complex financial instruments that can produce a credit crisis. Second, student grants that ignore academic merit are an expression of society's interest in making higher education available even to students who have not done comparatively well in high school. Giving Pell Grants is a societal bet that mediocre students can do better scholastically in the future, not that mediocrity is valuable in itself. Maybe they *are* late bloomers. Students who receive grants and are also scholastically excellent are not receiving a pure welfare benefit; they are exactly the kinds of people Congress had in mind when authorizing financial aid to students. The problem is students who are needy economically and want to go to college but are academically subpar. What the Department of Education now does is simply give them loans as well as grants. What the Department of Education probably ought to do is to accompany the grants for such students with (1) a warning that in the light of their records, success in college is problematical and (2) an offer to provide programs to improve their chances of doing well at the college they wish to attend. They are free to reject this offer of what is in fact remediation, although it should not be called that, and no doubt many will reject such an offer. The symbolic point of the offer is to call attention to the fact that a grant does not ignore lack of preparedness; it offers a second chance to succeed academically. Getting the grant should not be grounds for complacency. Congress would have to appropriate funds to the Department of Education for establishing these remedial programs for underprepared grant students on more than three thousand college campuses. Given the unfortunate facts (1) that the United States and indeed the world is currently in a recession and (2) President Obama is urging a stimulus for the economy, such remedial programs might be as useful an investment as infrastructure repair.

Why should the Department of Education establish remedial programs for grant recipients with academic deficiencies when colleges already have remedial programs aimed at all of their students with academic deficiencies? For several reasons. First, giving grants to academically underprepared students to attend college and not helping them survive academically is callous; it is programming some Pell grant recipients for failure and dropping out before completing college, which certainly is not what Congress intended in establishing education grants for needy students. Second, a voluntary program has a self-selected clientele. Unlike college-mandated remedial programs, these programs would be designed for students whose previous academic records do not justify a federal education loan. They are on warning that getting a Pell grant does not mean that they are fully prepared to succeed. Students who accept the offer of help are much more likely to succeed. Third, as was pointed out in a previous chapter, the financial burden of remediation is beyond the resources of many colleges. As a result, their efforts to repair deficiencies of student preparation are genuflections toward remediation but not demonstrably effective. Setting up separate programs for federal grant recipients with academic deficiencies would relieve colleges of part of their immediate remedial burdens and help them financially to deal with their other students with remediation problems more effectively. Finally, the emphasis of these federally supported programs, tied as they would be to grants to needy students, is success in college, not merely the repair of past deficiencies. Although the money will come from the Department of Education, the program itself will be designed individually at each college under contract with the Department, thus providing an opportunity for comparing programs that work better with programs that are not so effective.

What about underprepared students who receive need-based grants to attend and refuse the offer to participate in special courses? Denial of deficiencies is common. The Department of Education has a trump card. Grants for needy students are usually not sufficient to finance college without additional sources of funds. They also need loans, and the Department offers subsidized loans. Federal loans can be allocated quite differently from grants. A condition for receiving these loans might be to participate in programs that address academic deficiencies or to show by improved grades that those deficiencies have been addressed. Students who cannot receive loans but who do receive grants surely receive the message that they have to do better academically to receive federally guaranteed loans. This line of reasoning suggests that grants can ignore academic merit without necessarily undermining the incentives for stronger student performance.

To utilize student loans as an incentive to improve academic performance, the Department of Education would have to redesign the system of untargeted student loans for higher education now in place. Before suggesting how a system of targeted student loans might be designed, I shall discuss a targeted scholarship program in the State of Georgia, the HOPE Scholarship program, which may provide lessons relevant to redesigning the federal student loan program. Other states were impressed with the HOPE Scholarship program and have copied it with some variations.

THE HOPE SCHOLARSHIP EXPERIMENT

The State of Georgia has conducted what amounts to an experiment in institutionalizing academic merit as a basis for awarding financial aid in the form of grants. Examining the effects of this program might seem like an unlikely source of insights into what might happen if the federal student *loan* program were similarly geared to academic merit. However, it does throw light on two issues that might offer some parallels: public support for a merit-based program and student response to a merit-based program.

HOPE Scholarships, as they are called in Georgia, was the result of legislation passed in 1993, one goal of which was to diminish the outflow of excellent students to colleges in other states.[14] This legislation provided that high school students who enrolled in degree-granting colleges in the state—either public or private—would receive scholarship money for tuition and other mandatory expenses *if they had maintained at least a B average in their high school courses.* In addition to reducing the outflow of superior Georgia high school graduates to colleges in other states, the legislation was intended to improve the preparation of high school students for Georgia colleges. The program was fully funded by the Georgia Lottery for Education. At its inception HOPE Scholarships fully covered tuition and fees plus $300 for books at *public* degree-granting institutions. At its beginning, however, the monetary value of the HOPE Scholarship awards for individual students was fairly modest, even at the flagship university, the University of Georgia. Later, for example during the 2005–2006 academic year, the total value of the HOPE award had risen to about $4600 in the top public universities.[15] (A cap is now set at $3,000 for private colleges and universities, although there is no cap on the amount of the HOPE Scholarship award at Georgia's public colleges and universities.)

Initially students could receive both Federal Pell grants and HOPE Scholarships only if they were especially needy. *Now* the full HOPE Scholarship award is available regardless of Pell grant eligibility. HOPE is not a small program. Since 1993 students who have received HOPE Scholarships received more than $3,610,000,000.[16] In the 1998–1999 school year, for example, twice as much money was distributed in Georgia for HOPE Scholarships as was distributed for federal Pell grants. The HOPE Scholarship Program does not base its awards on SAT scores or on letters of recommendation, just on high school grades. Nevertheless, SAT scores rose at Georgia colleges and universities after high school students became aware of the financial benefits they could obtain from utilizing the HOPE Scholarship Program to attend colleges or universities in Georgia. At the University of Georgia, for example, the average SAT score for incoming freshmen was 1086 in 1993; it rose to 1203 in 2001 when the national average of incoming freshmen was 1019; by 2005 the average SAT score at the University of Georgia had risen to 1270.[17] The increase was smaller in academically less selective schools. Apparently a financial incentive resulted either in Georgia high schools producing students better prepared for college or in more of the better prepared students staying in Georgia for college as a result of the financial incentive.[18] It is difficult to disentangle these two effects. Economists who have studied the impact of the program believe that the retention effect is clear but the academic improvement of high school graduates is less clear.[19] This result must have pleased the legislators who authorized the program because one of their reasons for supporting it was to retain in the State able students who might subsequently take positions in Georgia industry and government.

Economists found some evidence of improved academic achievement of Georgia high school students after students learned that if they performed well in high school, HOPE provided substantial financial benefits for college attendance within the State.[20] Since the quality-enhancement effect was considerably greater for African American male and female students than for white male and female students, this finding suggests that incentive programs like HOPE can potentially reduce some of the gap in college attendance between white and African American students.[21] In the HOPE Scholarship Program, the financial incentive continues in college. In order to keep their scholarships, students must maintain a B average every year, which is computed after the spring grades are in. The HOPE Scholarship Program has been widely imitated. At least sixteen other states now have merit-based scholarships, some of them explicitly inspired by the Georgia model.[22]

Various criticisms can be leveled at HOPE Scholarships. Although HOPE is an acronym for Helping Outstanding Pupils Educationally, its academic requirements are modest. More than two-thirds of the graduating seniors in Georgia high schools in 2000 obtained the B average needed to be eligible for HOPE Scholarships for their freshman year at college. "Outstanding" seems to be interpreted as approximately average performance. Furthermore, since high schools vary in quality over Georgia as they do in every state, depending on socioeconomic and ethnic composition of their students, a B average may mean above average only in a mediocre educational environment. Socioeconomic variability *within* high schools may explain why more than 70 percent of the white students met the standard compared to 55 percent of black students.[23] While the HOPE Scholarship Program is not perfect, it nevertheless communicates quite clearly its intended meaning: that getting good grades in high school and college are necessary for public scholarship support from the State of Georgia. Getting good grades does not necessarily mean that the student does homework conscientiously and pays attention in class. It could mean only that students put increased pressure on teachers to award high grades, thus feeding grade inflation. More likely though, most students try to do what their teachers require for high grades after becoming aware of the greater power of teachers over their prospects for college scholarships.

To get back to the issue of the criterion of merit used by the HOPE Scholarship Program, why is it so low that 70 percent of the white high school graduates and 55 percent of the black high school graduates are considered *outstanding*? Shouldn't "outstanding" include a much smaller percentage of the graduating seniors? Strictly speaking, the HOPE Scholarship Program would constitute a better test of the incentive for studying if greater effort were necessary for achieving "outstanding" grades. On the other hand, political support for a meritocratic scholarship program was necessary. And the fact that such a large proportion of students became eligible for the grants provided—and continues to provide—political support for a program that might otherwise be rejected by voters as elitist.

With revenues of most states falling, Georgia and other states that have adopted versions of the HOPE Scholarship Program may have to reduce college scholarships. Possibly at least some of them will do so by raising the criterion for "outstanding" students. At that point researchers could assess more conclusively the effect of a monetary incentive on student effort over the substantial period of time that would be needed.

Even if all 50 states adopted merit programs like HOPE, the existence of Pell grants and federal loans with a negligible merit component would undercut to some extent the financial incentive to study diligently in high school and college. What is probably needed is greater emphasis on academic performance in *federal* grants and loans in order to assess the effect of a financial incentive on high school students to take their studies more seriously. To some extent this is already happening. An entering wedge for increasing the merit component of the Pell grant program existed in the State Scholars Program operating in 2004 in fourteen states (Arkansas, Connecticut, Indiana, Kentucky, Maryland, Mississippi, New Jersey, New Mexico, Oklahoma, Rhode Island, Tennessee, Texas, Washington, and Virginia). The State Scholars Program began when the Eastman Chemical Company, located in Longview, Texas, found that graduates of the local public-school system were poorly prepared for jobs with their company. It established partnerships with schools (1) to develop a curriculum that includes challenging courses, like physics and foreign languages, in order to prepare students for college and the workplace and (2) to send company volunteers to visit eighth-grade classrooms and explain to students that they can improve their career opportunities if they take State Scholars courses in high school. If the State Scholars students went to college, they received ordinary Pell grants just like other students. There were no special financial awards to students who enrolled in the State Scholars Program or when they got to college. Nevertheless appreciable numbers of students enrolled in them. The Department of Education wanted to expand the State Scholars program from the fourteen states in which it operated to the entire country and in every school district. Even in those fourteen states, only Arkansas and Texas had it in nearly every school district. The Bush administration had planned to spend $12 million to expand the program to all 50 states within five years, a trivial expenditure compared with the Pell Grant program to which it might have become attached. In his 2004 State of the Union address to Congress, President Bush suggested a small expansion of the State Scholars Program. He recommended that Congress provide an extra $1,000 to Pell Grant recipients who had been part of a State Scholars Program. This financial incentive—$1,000 on top of the then $4,050 top Pell award for the most needy students—was designed to make becoming a State Scholar more attractive and thereby to improve the preparation of high school students, especially students from low-income families.[24] The financial Pell add-on would be given only to 36,000 low-income students, a tiny fraction of the millions of students receiving Pell grants without a merit component. The legislative process modified the President's proposal somewhat. In early 2006, Republican senators proposed a new program that would award $750 to low-income college freshmen and sophomores for pursuing "a rigorous secondary school program of study." It would similarly award larger sums to juniors and seniors majoring in math and science and rank American high schools according to their academic rigor. The bill was backed by President Bush's administration and was presented to the House for vote in March 2006.[25] Apparently a version of this approach made it into the bill overhauling financial aid to college students signed by President Bush in September 2007, which gradually raised the maximum Pell grant over the next four years from $4,310 to $5,400.[26] As a result, the Academic Competitiveness Grant was made available for the first time for the 2006–2007 school year for first-year college students who graduated from high school after January 1, 2006 and for second-year college students who graduated from high school after January 1, 2005. This grant program gives Pell grant recipients in their freshman year $750 extra money and Pell grant recipients in their sophomore years $1,300 extra money *if they completed a rigorous secondary school program of study*. Despite the Academic Competitiveness Grant program and the National SMART Grant, which also is an add-on to the Pell grant program, the bulk of Pell grants overwhelmingly ignores academic accomplishment in its awards. Congress authorized $13 billion in 2006 for the overall Pell grant program and $790 million for the Academic Competitiveness Grant program.[27]

THE CASE FOR ACADEMIC REQUIREMENTS FOR STUDENT LOANS: AN INCENTIVE FOR BETTER PERFORMANCE

Unlike the debt incurred by mortgaging a house or buying a car, student debt does not have tangible assets in the background that can be repossessed by the lender. Student debt is based on the expectation that students will get good jobs and earn enough when they graduate to pay their debts off. In the case of the student borrowing from private lenders, the lender assesses the likelihood of this happening. In the case of students who borrow directly from the Department of Education or have bank debt guaranteed by a federal agency, no attempt occurs at the present time to assess the risk-worthiness of the borrower. Thus, an unknown but substantial amount of this debt may not be repaid by student borrowers. Ultimately, taxpayers will have to pay for these defaulted loans. Exacerbating the cost of student debt is the growing practice of students of staying in college five, six, or more years before graduating or quitting. Since students are not required to pay interest charges on their federal debts until after they leave college, this increases the cost of federal loan programs.[28]

All loans are not created equal. The debt burden incurred by the graduates of two-year public colleges is less than the debt burden of those attending four-year colleges. The median debt for students graduating from private colleges attached to universities is higher—$28,000—and for students graduating from public colleges not attached to universities lower—$15,000. For those who manage to land high-paying jobs, these debts are manageable. But for those who work in low-paying jobs in restaurants, hotels, or retail stores after graduating or dropping out before graduating, while trying to launch careers in the arts or in writing, their debts from college often follow them around for many years and for many constitute a serious burden. Furthermore, for those who choose out of humanitarian ideals to work in the nonprofit sector of the economy, salaries as ministers, guidance counselors, or social workers are usually too low to enable them to repay large student loans without great difficulty.

The precariousness of the huge portfolio of federally guaranteed student loans has not received much attention, certainly not as much attention as subprime mortgages. Yet almost all student loans resemble subprime mortgages in that they do not have any collateral behind them. Furthermore, federally subsidized loans to college students are an administrative mess. Too many different student loan programs exist with different criteria of eligibility and different interest rates. Here is how one issue paper prepared for The Secretary of Education's Commission on the Future of Higher Education in 2006 put it:

> The current labyrinth of federal higher education financial aid was developed over the years as the cumulative product of individual programs enacted one at a time by Congress, often lacking a defined purpose or even the efficiency of a well-coordinated uniform application process. Federal policymakers have never attempted to integrate and restructure that system into a cohesive policy-driven program, despite the obvious benefits and cost savings. The resulting tangle of bureaucracy yields results that are difficult to measure while generating confusion in the marketplace of higher education consumers.[29]

This paper went on to illustrate the multiplicity of programs—including grant programs as well as loans—either administered by the Department of Education or directly benefiting students attending colleges or universities:

1. Pell Grant;
2. Supplemental Educational Opportunity Grant (SEOG);

3. Federal work study;
4. Perkins loan;
5. Leveraging Educational Assistance Partnership (LEAP);
6. Military aid;
7. Federal Family Educational Loan Program (FFELP)
8. The Direct Loan Program;
9. HOPE Scholarship Credit;
10. Lifetime Learning Credit;
11. Federal PLUS Loans;
12. Coverdell Education Savings Account (Education IRAs);
13. Above-the-line tuition deduction;
14. Tax-free, employer-provided education benefit;
15. Student loan interest deduction;
16. Section 529 savings plan;
17. Penalty-free IRA withdrawal

Adding more complexity, other federal agencies administer other educational benefit programs. The Defense Department has G.I. Bill programs; the Department of Health and Human Services has Health Professional Student Loans, Nursing Student Loans, Primary Care Loans, National Health Service Corps Scholarships, and loans and grants to disadvantaged students; and the Bureau of Indian Affairs administers grants and loans for Native Americans.

Here is what the Commission itself said in its final report, criticizing the financial aid programs of the federal government for college students and recommending integrating and simplifying them:

> We found that our financial aid system is confusing, complex, ineffi-
> cient, duplicative, and frequently does not direct aid to students who
> truly need it. There are at least 20 separate federal programs provid-
> ing direct financial aid or tax benefits to individuals pursuing post-
> secondary education . . . . We propose replacing the current maze of
> financial aid programs, rules, and regulations with a system more in
> line with student needs and national priorities. That effort would
> require a significant increase in need-based financial aid and a com-
> plete restructuring of the current federal financial aid system. Our
> recommendations call for consolidating programs, streamlining
> processes, and replacing the FAFSA with a much shorter and simpler
> application.[30]

Nothing happened to implement the recommendations of this Commission, possibly because one of the most nationally prominent members

of the Commission, David Ward, president of the American Council on Education, the largest association of colleges and universities, refused to sign it. The recommendations that the commission made were reasonable and sensible but except for the support of then Secretary of Education Margaret Spellings, it received very little political or media attention when it was delivered in 2006.

The federal government provided almost $96 billion in financial aid to post-secondary students in 2007–2008, up from $52 billion in 1997–1998; of those $96 billion, $14 billion was for Pell grants, and nearly $67 billion went toward various kinds of subsidized loans.[31] States, the colleges and universities themselves, employer grants, and a variety of nonfederal loans provided the rest of the $163 billion used by students in 2007–2008 to finance their higher education, up from the $81 billion that students used in 1997–1998.[32] In short, the federal government provided the majority of the financial aid for college that students received in 2007–2008, and the bulk of what the federal government provided was in the form of loans. The proportion in the form of loans is increasing from year to year as tuition and other college expenses rise. One issue is whether American society can afford the increasing billions of dollars of expenditures devoted to educational loans to college students that are potentially defaulted. A separate issue is whether the aid is distributed in a manner most helpful to students and to the system of higher education. One possibility that could address both of these issues is to introduce a merit component into the loan program.

How might this be done? The elaborate procedure for assessing student need required both for the various federal college grant programs and for federal college loan programs as well might serve as the prototype for an analogous programs to assess eligibility for federal loans. What happens now is that students fill out a complex Free Application for Federal Student Aid (FAFSA) form that they send to a Department of Education processing center for evaluation. The results are sent to the financial student aid department at the college to which students are enrolled or are applying for admission, and students learn their eligibility for various grant and loan programs based on an assessment of financial need. What might be possible is to separate the eligibility for grants and loans at the processing centers and have them done by different people with different skills and to add a section to the form concerning academic performance and credit worthiness. Once the decision is made to provide grants at various levels or not to provide grants at all, the FAFSA form might be passed along to the loan eligibility group, which would assess the academic accomplishments of each applicant under consideration for loans compared with the academic performance and creditworthiness of other applicants to the specific college to which the applicant is enrolled or applying. The applicant would receive a rating above or below the mean academic performance rating of other students from that college. The higher above the mean the applicant's performance score is, the greater the size of the loan and the lower the interest rate for it. For scores at or below the mean performance score, the allowable size of the loan is smaller and the interest rate is higher than private loans would be, and possibly not made available at all. In effect, when interest rates exceed the interest rates that borrowers could receive for private loans, the federal program would be denying loan eligibility. Just as the eligibility for grants depend on the extent of neediness, the eligibility for loans would depend on the student performance profile in relationship to the performance profile of the students at the particular college. The system of grants and loans as it currently works requires annual applications. This would not change except that the students' performance profile would be affected by the grades they receive over the academic year compared with the college profile of student performance for that year. This system would have several practical implications:

1. It would work towards raising the performance profile of every college because granting subsidized loans increases the likelihood of students who receive them of enrolling and, conversely, decreases the attractiveness of enrollment for students who are not offered loans or only loans at high interest rates.
2. It would provide an incentive for students to work harder at their studies both in high school and in college in order to compete for loans.
3. It could be a flexible system. The level against which students compete for loans does not have to be the mean of the performance scores of all applicants for loans for that college in that year. In a highly selective college or in difficult curricula like engineering, pharmacy, or physics, the level could be above the lowest quartile. It could be also be flexible in the extent to which neediness is a prerequisite for loans. At the present time neediness is a prerequisite for Perkins loans, lower levels of neediness for other loans, and no neediness necessary for most federal education loans. If Congress followed the recommendations of the Spellings Commission on the Future of Higher Education to simplify the awarding of student financial aid, it would be simpler to keep the awarding of grants based on financial need entirely separate from the awarding of loans based on academic merit. The political question would be how much to put in the grant pot and how much to put in the loan pot. Congress and the president would have to make that decision. Federal

financial aid would be a lot more transparent. Some students would receive both grants and loans; some would receive neither; and some would receive one but not the other.

4. High school and college teachers would wield more influence over student academic behavior than they have at present. Since loan eligibility would depend at least partly on grades, grades would become more important. Possibly students would pressure teachers to give them high grades without evidence of scholastic improvement, thereby increasing grade inflation rather than raising student performance. The HOPE Scholarship Program did not find that grade inflation increased noticeably after the program was established. Nevertheless grade inflation is a possibility and should be investigated.

5. The total amount of federal money committed to student loans need not decrease. The crucial point is that as a result of instituting this effort to control the quality of loans, defaults on large loans will probably decline because control on student quality will keep subprime loans small and expensive. Since the default rate on private loans that screen for quality has half the default rate of Department of Education loans, this is a fairly safe prediction.

6. If federal student loans became targeted to students likely to repay them, this would dramatize the point that borrowing taxpayer money is not an entitlement but rather an opportunity available to students whose performance earns that opportunity, American colleges and universities might well develop a more studious atmosphere than prevails today.

WILL THE FINANCIAL INCENTIVE WORK?

Providing financial incentives to students to take learning more seriously at all levels of the educational system assumes, first, that ways can be found to measure taking learning seriously and, second, that a sizable proportion of students will respond positively to those incentives. How sizable? No one knows. We know that incentives motivate people, and the free markets of modern societies show that money is a powerful incentive. However, the case for introducing academic merit as a basis for federal loans to college students would be greatly strengthened if it were demonstrated that two-thirds of high school and college students sought to learn more—and actually did learn more—in response to the greater availability of merit loans to college. If only 5 percent of high school and college students responded to the financial incentive by modifying their behavior, opponents of merit loans could argue that such small gains are outweighed by a disadvantage of the program, excluding from it mediocre students who might eventually blossom.

But how can we *know* whether, in response to a financial incentive, students learn more than they did before? One possibility is through standardized tests administered over some years. This presents less difficulty in one respect than the measuring procedure embodied in the "No Child Left Behind" program that seeks to find out whether students in primary schools are learning as much as they need to know. "No Child Left Behind" permits each state to develop its own measurement program. This effectively prevents interstate comparisons of learning success. Measuring readiness for college is already being done on a national basis by two widely used existing testing programs. The admissions offices of colleges in the United States use these national tests (SAT or ACT scores) to measure what students have learned or have the potential for learning, thus providing national data available on what students who take the tests have learned and/or have aptitude for learning.

What about the validity of these standardized tests—the ACT tests and the SATs—as measures of student aptitude for college work? The main criticisms of them boil down to the argument that there are abilities that these tests do not capture. Probably so; no test is perfect, although more than a half-century of research has demonstrated a correlation between scores on the tests and freshman grades in college.[33] Although research studies of the correlation between SAT scores and freshman grades have been consistently positive over the years, they are modest. Several reasons exist for this. The SAT measures aptitude, not attitude. If a freshman with the ability to do excellent academic work spends more time partying than studying, his resulting poor academic record works against a strong correlation. Second, the dependent variable, grades, tends to be inflated. If a professor gives all the students in his freshman class A grades, this also reduces the correlation between SAT scores and freshman grades. Third and finally, colleges recruit from a narrow range of SAT scores. While it is true that even the most selective colleges sometimes accept outstanding athletes, talented musicians, or the offspring of alumni or alumnae who are not in the range of their normal admits, not enough of these admissions occur to generate much variability in the independent variable, SAT scores. Lack of such variability necessarily compresses the correlation. Nevertheless, the admissions offices at most colleges are convinced that these scores tell them something meaningful about the academic potentiality of applicants for admission. That is why admissions offices urge applicants to submit these scores. Some admissions offices attempt to adjust these quantitative measures by requiring personal essays, lists of achievements, accounts of overcoming adversity, and even face-to-face interviews. Admissions personnel tend to believe that these qualitative materials have improved the validity of the selection process. However, no studies demonstrate that these qualitative measures add much predictability of freshman performance to the more impersonal quantitative measures.

It is true that the proportion of high school seniors taking the SAT or ACT tests has risen over time, and some psychometricians point out that the observed drop in scores in some years, particularly verbal scores, may be due to the self-selected population taking them, including increased proportions of minority students. While this may be a reason to avoid basing generalizations about high school education over time on SAT or ACT scores, it should not invalidate the use of SAT and ACT scores for measuring the effectiveness of financial incentives on high school academic performance. The high school seniors who could reasonably be expected to respond to this incentive are only those for whom college is a goal. Consequently the phenomenon of self-selection for taking SAT and ACT tests identifies the population exposed to the incentive. If SAT and ACT scores gradually rose, after a lag of some years for students to accept the idea that in order to obtain federal subsidized loans for college they need good grades, this would be evidence for the impact of targeted loans on student performance. As for those not planning to go to college, they would not take the SAT or the ACT tests, so they could not serve as a control group; whether their academic achievement increased or stayed the same after merit incentives were put in place could not be determined. However, if half of the students in a high school are motivated to take education more seriously because of the incentive of merit-based college loans, students not planning to attend college might well be influenced by the example of peers to take education more seriously also.

Unlike the United States, Japan uses a different approach: rigorous examinations for applicants devised and administered separately by each university.[34] This is not a perfect system either. Since each university uses its own examinations, the results cannot be compared from one university to another. Furthermore, Japanese universities make no attempt to utilize for admission anything but grades on these entrance exams to select undergraduates best prepared for higher education. No qualitative materials. No transcripts of grades. No reports of extracurricular activities. No personal interviews.

Are there downsides to changing the financial incentives for studying in the precollege years? The main one is that students from disadvantaged backgrounds might, through no fault of their own, have less opportunity to attend college. Taxpayers would not loan them money unless they could demonstrate past academic achievement and other indications of creditworthiness, which serves to predict the likelihood of loan repayment—or at least willingness to attempt to redress their deficiencies. This may sound cruel, but the current system is worse; the current system gives some underprepared students access to college without the likelihood of graduating with an occupationally useful degree.

CONCLUSION

The Broadway musical *Oklahoma* contains a song with the refrain, "Everything's up to date in Kansas City. They've gone about as far as they can go." Like Kansas City, American colleges and universities have gone about as far as they can go to promote *access*. The United States spends an enormous amount of money so that more than half of our high school graduates are admitted to college. Total expenditures by postsecondary degree granting institutions were $250 billion for public colleges and universities and $136 billion for private ones in 2007–2008.[35] However, many students enter college unprepared for college-level study, require remedial courses in writing and mathematics, and drop out without receiving any degree at all. Of students who started their postsecondary education in 1995–1996 at two-year institutions, only 38.4 percent had a degree or certificate by 2001. Of students who started at four-year institutions, it was 65.1 percent.[36] Some of the dropouts may have borrowed a large amount of money to pay for tuition and living expenses. The default rate of dropouts is higher than the default rate of graduates, as might be expected.

Furthermore, it is not clear that a majority of American college graduates have learned much, judging by quantitative evidence and by the reported experiences of their current employers and of professors who have evaluated their performance. As philosopher Steven M. Cahn put it, "Never have so many spent so long learning so little."[37] The problem of delayed graduation has become so serious that, while in office, former New York State Governor Pataki proposed giving public four-year colleges in his state $500 for each student who graduated in four years and $250 for each student who graduated in two years from two-year colleges.[38]

A point of leverage for the improvement of American undergraduate education is making student loans conditional on student performance, both in high school and in college. That change is necessary if voters take seriously the notion of "investing" in the *higher* education of high school graduates. An incentive (in the form of greater merit-based loans) should be provided to better students—on the reasonable assumption that better students are more likely than mediocre students to make economic and even civic contributions to American society in the twenty-first century— as well as better prospects for repaying taxpayers.

Determining which college students offer the best prospects of making economic and civic contributions is difficult but probably no more difficult than determining who is truly needy. A reasonable approach is to reward with loans high school students who have taken rigorous courses as preparation for college and gotten high grades in them—in addition to more promiscuous grants to all needy students. However, since high schools differ so much in their level of instruction and in their extent of grading inflation, for comparative purposes scores on standardized national tests of students' knowledge and abilities should supplement high school records as a criterion of a credit-worthy borrower.

Superior academic performance should be a qualification not only for student loans on admission to college but also as a condition for keeping the aid as students proceed through their academic careers. What about youngsters with dyslexia or other problems beyond their control who try hard but lose out in competition with luckier kids? What about youngsters who don't listen to their parents or teachers to give priority to studying when they should be laying the basis for the academic performance necessary for financial aid later? What about youngsters whose parents don't know enough or care enough to encourage academic effort when their kids are too young to appreciate fully the consequences on *not* setting this priority? Such youngsters wouldn't get federal loans for college, at least to begin with, although at least some of them may be able to get other financial help from their parents or by working for a year or two before applying to college or from nonfederal sources of financial aid. Although merit aid is not a panacea, not utilizing it lowers higher education.

Denying federally subsidized loans to youngsters who want to go to college and can persuade a college to admit them sounds callous. But competition for college loans subsidized by taxpayers will not be any tougher than the competition for jobs that graduates will face after college. The question is whether this imperfect way of allocating *federal* college loans is fairer to a greater portion of their recipients than other allocation systems—such as promiscuous aid or idiosyncratic scholarships given by private persons or organizations. Private scholarships set up by wills written in the nineteenth or early twentieth centuries have quaint provisions; Loyola University in Chicago still awards scholarships for Catholics with the last name of Zolp, and Juniata College in Pennsylvania has $1,000 scholarships for left-handed students.[39] Less capricious are student loans reserved for those who can make best use of them, based on their previous performance.

Emphasizing academic merit to a greater extent in subsidizing loans for college will not solve all the problems of American higher education. Keep in mind, however, that the stagnant rate of college completion over the past 30 years and the weak performance of many American college graduates threaten to undermine our competitiveness in the globalized world economy. Education is no longer fueling the economy as it once did.[40] The rising cost of attending college may not be an unadulterated catastrophe.

It may drive us to allocate taxpayer subsidized loans for college to those more likely to contribute to the continuation of the American miracle.

A case can be made—and has been made—for the value of a college education as an intellectually elevating experience quite apart from whatever it contributes to individual careers or to economic growth.[41] That may be, but it must be remembered that federal grants and loans for needy students to attend college are justified mainly in two ways: as the promotion of a more egalitarian society and as a means of making the economy more productive. Those goals are usually assumed to be compatible with one another. A case can be made for their incompatibility. The reason for establishing college prep courses and advanced placement courses in high schools and for establishing honors colleges within colleges is the hard and stubborn fact is that top students learn more—and enjoy school more—when they are challenged in the company of other high-ability students than when they are taught with less able or less motivated students. Students with less intellectual ability or less intellectual curiosity do not enjoy such courses or do well in college; they degrade the atmosphere in which better students can thrive. Ideology to the contrary notwithstanding, if college is not useful for everybody seeking well-paid jobs, not every high school graduate should be encouraged to attend college.

NOTES

1. Thomas R. Wolanin, Ed., *Reauthorizing the Higher Education Act: Issues and Options.* Washington, D.C.: Institute for Higher Education Policy, March 2003, pp. 7–8.

2. Jonathan D. Glater, "College Costs Outpace Inflation Rate," *New York Times*, October 23, 2007.

3. Jackson Toby, "Ill-Advised Guidelines Put Students at Disadvantage," *Sunday Star-Ledger*, October 10, 1993, p. 71.

4. New Jersey Commission on Higher Education, *Educational Opportunity Fund.* Web site last accessed in April 2009: www.nj.gov/highereducation/EOF/.

5. Thomas Sowell, *Inside American Education: The Decline, the Deception, the Dogmas.* New York: Free Press, 1993.

6. Elizabeth Olson, "Something New: A 4-Year Degree at a 2-Year College," *New York Times*, December 14, 2005.

7. *Ibid.*

8. Diana Jean Schemo, "Private Loans Deepen a Crisis in Student Debt," *New York Times*, June 10, 2007.

9. Amy Manzetti, "Highly Educated and Deep in Debt," Washington, D.C.: Credit Union National Association, April 21, 2003. Web site accessed in April 2009: http://hffo.cuna.org/33330/article/339/html.

10. Haya El Nasser, "Why Grown Kids Come Home," *USA Today*, January 10, 2005.

11. "Echo Boomerang—Number of Adult Children Moving Back Home—Statistical Data Included," *American Demographics*, June 1, 2001. Web site accessed

in April 2009: http://findarticles.com/p/articles/mi_m4021/is_2001_June_1/ai_76579415.

12. Mark Mittelhauser, "The Outlook for College Graduates, 1996–2006: Prepare Yourself—Number of College Graduates Exceeds College-Level Jobs," *Occupational Outlook Quarterly*, Summer, 1998.

13. Casey Lartigue, "Why Not Sue 'Big Schooling'?" Washington: Cato Institute, November 23, 2002.

14. University System of Georgia, Office of Planning and Policy Analysis, *Financial Aid Report*, Atlanta, GA: Summer 2000; Christopher Cornwell, David B. Mustard, and Deepa Sridhar, "The Enrollment Effects of Merit-Based Financial Aid: Evidence from Georgia's HOPE Scholarship," Department of Economics, University of Georgia, June 22, 2004. HOPE grants, also funded by the lottery, were dedicated to nonmerit financial aid to students taking nondegree postsecondary programs in Georgia vocational institutions; they are not directly relevant to the HOPE Scholarship experiment.

15. Christopher M. Cornwell and David B. Mustard, "Assessing Public Education in Georgia at the Start of the 21st Century," from a chapter in a forthcoming book; Christopher M. Cornwell and David B. Mustard, "Evaluating HOPE-Style Merit Scholarships," in *Innovation in Education*. Federal Reserve Bank of Cleveland Conference Proceedings, 2006.

16. Terry College of Business, University of Georgia, Cornwell-Mustard HOPE Scholarship Page, Web page accessed in April 2009: www.terry.uga.edu/hope/.

17. David Firestone, "Free-Tuition Program Transforms the University of Georgia," *New York Times*, February 4, 2001. David Mustard, the economist whose work the news article drew upon, supplied the 2005 figure in an e-mail dated October 20, 2005.

18. Christopher Cornwell, K. Lee, and David B Mustard, "Student Responses to Merit Scholarship Rules," *Journal of Human Resources*, forthcoming, p. 9 of manuscript.

19. *Ibid.*

20. Gary T. Henry and Ross Rubinstein, "Paying for Grades: Impact of Merit-Based Financial Aid on Educational Quality," *Journal of Policy Analysis and Management*, Vol. 21, No. 1, 2002, pp. 93–209.

21. *Ibid.*, p. 106.

22. *Ibid*, p. 2.

23. Christopher M. Cornwell, and David B. Mustard. 2004. "Georgia's HOPE Scholarship and Minority and Low-Income Students: Program Effects and Proposed Reforms." *In State Merit Programs and Racial Inequality*. Edited by Donald E. Heller and Patricia Marin, Cambridge, MA: The Civil Rights Project, Harvard University, p. 93; Christopher M. Cornwell, and David B. Mustard, 2002. "Race and the effects of Georgia's HOPE Scholarship." In *Who Should We Help? The Negative Social Consequences of Merit Scholarships*. Edited by Donald E. Heller and Patricia Marin, Cambridge, MA: The Civil Rights Project, Harvard University, pp. 64–65; Greg Winter, "B's, Not Need, Are Enough for Some State Scholarships," *New York Times*, October 31, 2002.

24. Alyson Klein, "Bush Proposes Larger Pell Grants, but with a Catch: Plan Would Focus $1,000 Increase on Students in Little-Known State Scholars Program," *Chronicle of Higher Education*, March 26, 2004.

25. Sam Dillon, "College Aid Plan Widens U.S. Role in High Schools," *New York Times*, January 22, 2006.

26. Jonathan D. Glater, "President Signs Overhaul of Student Aid," *New York Times*, September 27, 2007.

27. Sam Dillon, "Eligibility Criteria Announced for New College Aid Program," *New York Times*, May 3, 2006.

28. As I pointed out in the previous chapter, the interest on federal loans is treated differently if they are on subsidized loans or on unsubsidized loans. If the student qualifies for *unsubsidized* loans because of coming from a low-income family, the interest being paid on the loans either to the Department of Education or to a financial institution is paid for in its entirety during the student's years in college and for nine months thereafter. If the student is not needy enough to qualify for *subsidized* loans, the interest starts to accrue immediately after the unsubsidized loan is issued. The student has the option of not paying the accrued interest while in college and for nine months thereafter, but the interest is not forgiven or forgotten; it is added to the principal of the loans. Since most students take advantage of this option, this drives up the ultimate cost of *unsubsidized* federal loans and increases the likelihood of default. Unsubsidized loans are not fully unsubsidized; they are subsidized by the willingness of the Department of Education to guarantee ultimate repayment and to repay them in the case of defaults.

29. Barry D. Burgdorf and Kent Kostka, "Eliminating Complexity and Inconsistency in Federal Financial Aid Programs for Higher Education Students: Towards a More Strategic Approach," p. 7, Commission Document, 2006.

30. U.S. Department of Education, *A Test of Leadership: Charting the Future of U.S. Higher Education, op. cit.*, p. 19.

31. College Entrance Examination Board, *Trends in Student Aid, 2008*, Washington: www.collegeboard.com, p. 6. Web site accessed in April 2009: http://professionals.collegeboard.com/profdownload/trends-in-student-aid-2008.pdf.

32. *Ibid.*

33. See Figure 3.2 Average SAT Scores of College-bound High School Students, 1967–2008 in Chapter 3.

34. Thomas P. Rohlen, *Japan's High Schools*, Berkeley, CA: 1983, Chapter 3.

35. U.S. Department of Education, National Center for Education Statistics, *Digest of Education Statistics 2008*, March 2007. Table 26. Expenditures of educational institutions, by level and control of institution: Selected years, 1899–1900 through 2007–08. Web site accessed in April 2009: http://nces.ed.gov/pubs2009/2009020_1.pdf.

36. *Ibid.*, Table 317 "Percentage Distribution of Enrollment and Completion Status of First-Time Postsecondary Students Starting during the 1995–96 Academic Year, by Type of Institution and Other Student Characteristics: 2001." Web site accessed in April 2009: http://nces.ed.gov/programs/digest/d06/tables/dt06_317.asp.

37. Steven M. Cahn, *The Eclipse of Excellence*, Washington, D.C.: Public Affairs Press, 1973, p. 1.

38. Karen W. Arenson, "Pataki Proposes Bonus to Colleges Whose Students Graduate on Time," *New York Times*, January 26, 2005.

39. Michelle York, "What's in a Name? Some Obscure Scholarships Often Go Begging," *New York Times*, January 3, 2006.

40. David Brooks, "Fresh Start Conservatism," *New York Times*, February 15, 2008.

41. John Henry Cardinal Newman, *The Idea of a University, Defined and Illustrated in Nine Discourses Delivered to the Catholics of Dublin in Occasional Lectures and Essays Addressed to the Members of the Catholic University*, Notre Dame, IN: University of Notre Dame Press, 1982.

INDEX

Note: Page numbers followed by n and a number indicate that the reference is to a designated note on the indicated page. For example, 34n50 indicates that the reference is to note 50 on page 34. When multiple notes on a single page are referenced, a nn is used.

About the Author

JACKSON TOBY, Professor of Sociology Emeritus at Rutgers University, was awarded a Ph.D. in sociology at Harvard University in 1950. He was director of the Institute for Criminological Research at Rutgers from 1968 to 1994. In addition to numerous professional publications he also has written several dozen op-ed pieces (directed at the general public) concerning criminological topics including his major research interest, the causes of and remedies for school violence, in such newspapers as the *Wall Street Journal*, the *New York Times*, the *Washington Post*, the *Chicago Tribune*, and the *Los Angeles Times*. His most recent popular article, "Let Them Drop Out: A Response to Killings in Suburban High Schools" appeared in the *Weekly Standard* on April 9, 2001. His most recent scholarly article—about streaking—appeared in the November 2005 issue of the *Journal of Classical Sociology*. He has been listed in *Who's Who in America* for forty years.